BARBAROSSA THE PIRATES

Historical Novel
by George Leonardos.

TITLE: BARBAROSSA THE PIRATES
GENRE: HISTORICAL NOVEL
AUTHOR: George Leonardos
LANGUAGE: English
PAGES: 310
WORDS: 83,290

Copyright © George Leonardos 2013

The right of George Leonardos to be identified as the Author of the Work has been asserted by him in accordance with the Copyright, Designs and Patents Act 1988. All rights reserved. No part of this publication may be reproduced, stored in a retrieval system, or transmitted, in any form or by any means without the prior written permission of the author and publisher, nor be otherwise circulated in any form of binding or cover other than that in which it is published and without a similar condition being imposed on die subsequent purchaser.

All characters in this publication are fictitious and any resemblance to real persons, living or dead is purely coincidental.

Web: www.leonardos.gr

Also by George Leonardos

- GRANDMA'S RED SOFA *1992*
- THE HOUSE OVER THE CATACOMBS *1993*
- EVA *1994*
- THE MAGNET'S POLES *1995*
- EARTH'S LOVERS *1996*
- A SONG FROM THE SOUL *1997*
- BARBAROSSA THE PIRATE *1998*
- MARA, THE CHRISTIAN SULTANA *1999*
- MARIA MAGDALENE *2001*
- SLEEPING BEAUTY *2003*
- MICHAEL VIII PALEOLOGOS *2004*
- THE PALEOLOGUES *2006*
- THE LAST PALEOLOGUE *2007*
- SOPHIA PALEOLOGINA *2008*
- MAGELLAN *2009*
- SEEKING THE ULTIMA THULE *2010*
- THE ALEXANDRIA RHAPSODY 2011
- ISLANDS FORGOTTEN IN TIME, 2914

- JUSTINIAN II, the slit-nosed emperor. 2016
- EUSEBIA, the sorrowful empress. 2017
- EMPRESS IRENE. The overthrown Saint.

ESSAYS
- <u>THE NOVEL'S STRUCTURE, *2000*</u>
- <u>ENGLISH-GREEK DICTIONARY OF SCIENTIFIC AND MILITARY TERMS, *1980*</u>

Preface

Although the English words 'pirate' and 'piracy' are adopted by many other languages, they are originally derived from the ancient Greek verb pirao, or piro, which means endeavourer, attempt and try my luck in a combative expedition. And further means attack, assault, assail and violate.

Based on this fact, we may deduce that piracy in the Greek water territories has spread since the ancient times.

According to the English historian Philip Gosse, piracy, like murder, is one of the expressions of human nature that we meet in earlier history on the coasts of the African and Asiatic continents.

Piracy passed through three significant phases. In the beginning, a group of very poor people from the deprived areas of the world who lived in coastal areas, started to unite and attack weak merchant vessels at sea. Later, in the so-called 'period of organization', the strongest of these groups 'absorbed' the weaker ones and became autonomous organizations. Finally came the phase when pirates assumed greater power achieved in establishing self-governing or independent nations that could sign treaties and agreements with stronger nations and jointly wage wars against others for religious or economic reasons. Consequently, what was once considered an act of pillaging and marauding developed into a 'legitimate' act of war.

The periods in which piracy reached its highest point were the years before, during and after the fall of Constantinople in 1453. The

Western forces of Venice, Genoa and Spain employed pirates for their personal benefits. The sultans of the Ottoman Empire did the same, every time their urge for domination in the Aegean Sea was kindled.

Piracy prevailed in Greece for the four centuries during the Turkish domination of its mainland. The Greek inhabitants of the Ionian and Aegean islands after Barbarossa and especially after the naval battle in Nafpactos began to act more methodically. They started to construct bigger ships and undertook missions of escort and protection of merchant ships in exchange for handsome rewards, without wasting opportunities to engage in forays on their way.

Later, they began to construct even bigger and more powerful ships and progressively they took over the transportation of merchandise on the seas. Thus, the groundwork for the development in shipping as well as their victorious naval battle of 1821 was established in Greece.

After the independence and the creation of the new Greek nation, a decree was issued on 27 March 1835, in which piracy was considered a criminal act and was prosecuted. A few years later, in 1845, a new law was introduced for even harsher punishments for pirates.

The piracy on the northern coasts of Africa was eliminated altogether after the occupation of Algiers by the French in 1830 and the expansion of French domination on the whole Northern African coast.

Piracy was a flourishing business at that time; a business that involved protectors, financiers and all the elements of a successful business. But except for the 'businessmen' who invested in it, there were also kings, sultans and local tyrants who asked for its services.

The sultan recruited pirates to wage his naval wars against Venice and did not hesitate to appoint former pirates to high posts of office in the navy. The same was done much later on with Queen Elizabeth of England and Sir Francis Drake, but". This is a different issue.

To write an historical novel, such as Barbarossa the Pirate, the author must follow one of the three 'accepted' types of writing.

The first is what we call romantic and dramatic, the second, the philosophical and scientific and the third, realistic or modern, where the myth is combined with fiction to shed light on the characters and the circumstances of a historical era without violating the element of history itself...

I have used the third type of writing for my book, so that in my attempt to create fiction, historical truth has not been violated, however bitter or repulsive it might be. This was not easy to achieve, because in such a case the reader could not easily sympathy with the heroes in the novel or identify with them.

At the end is an alphabetical list of foreign and Greek books from which I derived my information, which could be useful to the reader who would like to know more about a specific era or piracy in general.

The language I have used in my book is simple and direct in my attempt to make it more accessible to the reader.

George Leonardos

June 1999

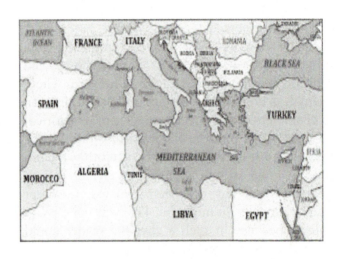

One

Simoon was blowing hard, raising clouds of dust in the air. I was kneeling outside the Mosque of Algiers holding a bulky piece of log steadily to the ground, when the condemned convict, a young man of noble origin, placed his head carefully on the log as if he was afraid to scratch his face on its abrasive surface. He was staring at me, whilst I with overflowing awe was trying to avoid his beseeching eyes. He persistently continued to gaze at me though with an expression that was filled with wonder and supplication. His obstinate look captured my senses so much that I was unable to take my eyes from his...

At that particular moment, the sword of Arouz Barbarossa fell heavily on his nape, his blood gushed fiercely from the cut arteries of his neck and I was soaked in it. My face, my hands, even my clothes were dripping with his thick, sticky, red liquid. His body was cruelly separated from his head, and, as it was released from its reason, it started to shake and quiver like a snake and then fell listless to the ground. For a few moments, the head was left alone on the log as if it was still connected to the body, the eyes still gazing at me, full of wonder and supplication. Then it fell off and rolled down the road.

I jumped from my bed agitated and sweating and I looked around me. In the dim light of my cell I could not see anything except for the flickering light of the candle placed below the icon of Saint George and two pairs of eyes staring at me in confusion.

'Holy Father...' I heard a child's voice calling me. 'We came to receive your blessing...'

I turned towards the voice whilst trying to regain consciousness but I still could not understand what was happening. I could only discern two short shadows standing in front of me.

'Forgive us, Father, for disturbing your sleep...' the child's voice apologised. 'But we came early at dawn to bring you some bread and a jug of fresh milk... Your blessing, Father...'

I approached the shadows and, unaware of giving my blessings using my three fingers, while at the same time I scrutinised my hands for any signs of blood.

When the children had received my blessing, they placed their supplies on the ground and left the cell hurriedly as if they were afraid of me...

Progressively I began to recover from my nightmarish sleep... I left my cell and walked outside. I threw water on my head from an ewer I had placed outside the entrance of the church, and looked around me; everything was so serene and peaceful. The two seas, overlooked aloofly by the small chapel of Saint George, in Avlemonas, in the island of Kythira, were not yet wrinkled by the waves and the waves would not wrinkle them before sunrise.

I was all alone on the peak of the mountain where the small chapel of Saint George invariably observed the two seas the Mirtoan Sea on the side of Diakofto and Cape Malea and the Cretan Sea, on the side of Antikythira and ancient Scandia...

I took a deep breath to relieve myself of the appalling nightmare that had haunted me almost every night since the very first day my soul had taken refuge in this chapel. But today I was even more confused and flustered, as the Erinyes again brought to my mind the beheading of the young boy in Algiers.

I had witnessed so many gruesome acts in my life executions, savage killings and rapes. Why then did this particular decapitation kept pestering my mind and spirit? Maybe, it was injustice itself that pestered me; the injustice of one man to another...

I could not bear my own thoughts any more. I went into the church, fell on my knees in front of the holy altar and prayed.

'Dear Lord, You Sacred and Omnipotent Father, You, who are the radiant and glowing light in our bodies and souls, why are You still torturing me?... Why are You still sending me those Erinyes to torment my mind and soul? In your religion there are no such creatures so where do they come from to pester my mind, then? You know well that I have repented and have already asked for Your absolution and forgiveness... If I had a priest I would confess, but there is no priest or confessor in this world who can tolerate listening to my sins those which were committed intentionally and those I was forced to commit without cursing me. Only You merciful, immaculate God, only You, can hear me out and grant me the pardon that is desperately sought by my soul...'

As I had stooped in front of the holy shrine, I felt feeble and weary and I spread my hand to get hold of the holy table. At that moment I touched a pen, the pen I had brought from Constantinople, which I do not really recall why I had kept with me all these years. As my fingers fondled it clumsily, it fell on the ground in front of my knees. Only then did I realise what I had to do...

Yes, Lord...' I cried, full of alleviation and relief. 'I received Your message. I have to direct my confession straight to You, to You, merciful and compassionate Father...'

All was quiet and peaceful in my cell, next to the chapel of Saint George. The flickering candle shed faint light on the icons of the saints that hung on the four walls of my cell and they were all scowling at me...

I took my pen and started to write my story, or rather my confession, to God. Everything I wrote, I wrote to Him and I buried it there, beneath the altar of the holy chapel of Saint George, so that all my sins would remain recorded...

And you, my present or future reader, if you ever happen to lay hands on my manuscripts, read them carefully and bestow on me your forgiveness for the fate I was doomed to have, and I, in my turn, will forgive you from up there where I will soon be for the sins that you have committed... Because no one is infallible or sinless.

If my father, Vretos, from the island of Kythira, had not fallen in love with my Venetian mother and had not kidnapped her to escape later from his birthplace having been chased by the schismatic Franks maybe, I say maybe, my fate would not have driven me to where it did; to the piratical galleys.

The Greek saying admits, and very wisely indeed, 'Parents' sins harass children for the rest of their lives', and in my case, the situation gets even worse because a common person like my father falls in love with someone of gentlefolk descent such as Isabelle, my mother not to mention the fact that she faithfully followed him to the orthodox doctrine and changed her name to Chrissa, after my paternal grandmother of course.

Chased by the Franks, the couple eloped from Kythira at that time my father lived in Saint Dimitrios and my mother in Chora and took refuge on the island of Lesvos, which had just fallen into the hands of Mehmed the Conqueror. They ended up at the Bay of Gera, near Plakado, in a village which was at that time named Paleokipos, and which was renowned for its orange orchards and lush gardens but also for the tough Genovese, Venetian, Kalabrian, Katalanian, Greek and Berber pirates who also took refuge there...

Our village lay in the Bay of Gera, formerly named Palaios Kipos, which was changed to Paleokipos. It is also said that the same village was the native village of Kipion, the famous guitar singer. Its haven was Evriaki, which, in the Greek language, originates from Evria Akti, 'the wide coast'... All sorts of seamen gathered there as well as many Jewish tradesmen, as commerce was flourishing in that area. Many used to call the area Hebrewki, probably due to the fact that many Hebrews lived there.

Our village produced earthenware pottery the renowned pottery of Gera and there were many ceramic workshops in Kirchana, on the east side of the village, in the area that leads to Evriaki. Yakub, the father of Arouz, also had a workshop there, where he worked with his wife, the widow of the village priest.

Our compatriot Pirros the pirate who renounced his religion and named himself Pirri describes the Bay of Gera, where Evriaki, along with our village Paleokipos and many others, was situated. Before captain Pirri or Pirri reis1 became a mapmaker in the service of the sultan, we used to have him with us, for, with Barbarossa that is, he was one of our most competent skippers.

Captain Pirri or Pirri reis say about the Bay of Gera: 'It is a distance of twenty miles from the entrance to the Bay of Kalannia (Kalloni) to the bay of Kelemie (Gera). The evidence of this bay, when one sails from the sea, is the following: There is a big mountain, which is called Orogiano, and opposite the mountain there are hilly little islands (right across the bay of Mirsina). You must follow those islands on the west side and sail near the coast of Mintilou (Mytilene). When one sails near the coast for about three miles, the entrance of Kelemie (Gera) is reached. It is a narrow passage and the space in between is as long as the length of two ship's head ropes. At the entrance to the bay there is a rock which juts out from the surface of the water. A ship can pass through on both its sides, however, its west side is more accessible. If one needs to drink water, there is a river that is called Zire near the entrance, on its west side. The distance between the entrance to the bay and its outer edge or coast, is twelve miles. At the end of the same bay there are settlements, adjacent to each other, which are known by the name of Kelemie...

(the surrounding... villages of Gera). When one departs from that bay and sails to Eski, a port in Mitilini, every inch of it is suitable for mooring, as the water is easy'

Pirri mapped the area and marked the rivers to help the pirates, to whom water was, at times, more precious than gold. I refer to his description to indicate what pirates thought of the area at that time and what advantages this particular refuge offered them.

It was not agriculture that attracted my father to Paleokipos. His business and the persecution by the Franks brought him there. My father was a ship's mender and the Bay of Gera the notorious hideout of the pirates back then was the appropriate place for him to make a living.

There were always things to do for the pirates, including the repairing of their black, battered galleys, therefore, he always had work and at times money to support his beautiful, gentle wife and myself, his only son. I would also say that those pirates, who knew no limits to their pay, the patches on their worn out ships, or even their barbaric and savage actions every time they laid hands upon a commercial galley, rewarded him handsomely: very often my father would return home with a face swollen or bruised by the punches they gave him, instead of money; those cantankerous and greedy pirates.

In that piratical bay, I was born nine months after the elopement and matrimony of my parents, which was carried out in a small chapel somewhere in Gera, as my sweet and humble mother used to tell me when I was a grownup boy. Every time she happened to recollect that glorious and joyful day her face would blush and her eyes would beam... God rest her soul amongst all angels. As to all of us a mother has a place only in heaven when she departs from this miserable world...

I was christened Ermolaos, after the protector saint of Paleokipos, Saint Ermolaos. Tradition says that Saint Ermolaos substituted all his predecessor saints. Consequently, the church of

Agioi Anargiri the doctors who cured people without charging them a fee was changed to Saint Ermolaos who, along with his fellow saints, Ermipos and Ermokratis, and also his bosom friend Maximianos, suffered martyrdom, during the reign of Dioklitianos.

In front of the two idolater tyrants, Saint Panteleimon another doctor was tortured to death after his attempt to reveal Christianity to his posterior executioners... All this happened in the first years of the fourth century after the birth of our Saviour, Jesus Christ. Therefore the chapel was dedicated to Agioi Anargiri, Saint Ermolaos and Saint Panteleimon, so that no saint is dissatisfied or disgruntled.

It was not until later that I earned my sobriquet Aigiopelagitis[1], as I could never settle on any island of the Archipelagos[2],3 except now in Tsirigo, at this advanced age.

I realized the world around me when I was seven years old. I was coming home from school one day it was a Catholic school affiliated to the Roman Catholic Church in the town of Mitilini, some distance away from our village and which my mother had chosen for my education when a boy grabbed me by my neck and forcefully pushed me to the ground. I still do not know for certain why he did so, or if I would have survived the attack if his older brother had not intervened to save me from his ruthless grip.

The boy who assaulted me was Christos, the youngest of seven children from a weird family whom most of the village people avoided. The one who saved me was Aris, the brother of Christos, a

---

[1] One who chooses to live in the islands of the Aegean.
[2] The Aegean Sea.

boy a bit older than me who was short but robust with strong arms and legs. He was known in the neighbourhood because of his heroic deeds and achievements, which everyone looked up to and praised at that time.

Once he had seized a rabid dog by the neck, whirled it over his head several times and had eventually thrown it forcefully against a wall. The dog didn't even bark. Its dead body lay there for many days until the black crows ate it up. This was only one of his memorable or heroic actions when he, Aris, was just a hairless boy. He was such a daredevil that everyone in the village, even the adults, was avoiding him for they were afraid of his strength and his extraordinary powers.

When Aris was still very young, he was a very handsome and sweet boy, but as he grew older he assumed a fearful expression, mainly enhanced by the beard he had grown; his notorious red beard.

Aris who changed his name to Arouz at his adolescence, and so I shall call him from now on grew very fond of me or rather sympathised with my weak and frail body, for I was a very thin and sickly boy at that time. He would protect me, not allowing anyone to annoy of even come near me, including his brother Christos, who had received several blows the day he had attacked me. Christos who changed his name to Hizr, and that is how we shall refer to him from now on did not forgive the fact that his brother liked me and supported me. It was not until much later that he had to compromise and conform to his brother's rules and wishes.

'Didn't I warn you not to go near those boys?' my mother chided me, as she was putting me naked in my bed in the sole room of our house. And then she went on searching my feeble body inch by inch, to check if I had any bruises.

'He was the one who attacked, I did not even go near him,' I explained.

The black spots around my neck agitated my mother and extended her agony. She carried on examining my body with her fingers, her eyes, and even her nose to detect everything.

At this particular moment my father came in. The scene he witnessed alarmed him and my mother had to explain.

'Didn't I warn you to stay away from those bums?' my father shouted angrily at me. 'I had warned you to stay away from that damned family...'

He had raised his hand to direct a blow on my small face, but my sweet mother grabbed it.

'Leave the boy alone,' she said. 'He does not deserve to be punished for what others have done to him.'

Somehow abashed my father lowered his hand. He loved my mother too much to cause her any pain and maybe that was the main reason why he never treated me cruelly. I was spared the slap, then, not because he did not mean to hurt me but because he did not wish to distress her.

My mother dressed me at once. She wrapped my neck with a patch of cloth soaked with raki, so that the bruises would go, and fixed me some soup to soothe my pain.

I was promptly tucked in my bed, mainly to keep the bruises away from my father's still angry eyes. I would have soon fallen asleep if my parents hadn't started this intriguing conversation.

'I do not want any kind of contact with that family,' Vretos said. 'I do not like the lot of them. Besides, we do not even know where they come from or what they do.'

'They are poor people, for God's sake. The father works all day to feed eight mouths along with his and his wife's.'

'He is an illhumoured, unsmiling old fellow. He is grouchy and grumpy all the time and nobody knows anything about his roots.'

'I think he comes from Gianena, or at least somewhere around there. We came to the island at almost the same time.'

'No, he arrived at the island first,' my father corrected her. 'He came with the troops of Mehmed the infidel, when he seized Lesvos. Yakub was his spahi.4 At first he settled down in Molivos, where he had his bastards with the priest's widow. Then he moved here to Paleokipos and became a potter.'

'He has changed now. He has become a peaceful man, don't you think?'

'A peaceful man whom nobody talks to. We do not even know what God he believes in. It is said that he used to be a Greek Orthodox, his name then was Iakov. Then he worked for the Jews and converted to Judaism, renaming himself Jacob. Then he became an Ottoman, as he himself claims, and again changed his name, to Yakub God knows how many other times he will be apostate. I even think he was circumcised to fit in!'

Ottomans get circumcised as well; even Christians would have done if the Apostle had not interfered. You know these matters better than I.'

She mentioned the last phrase to alleviate his temper, but also to array her knowledge against his on this sensitive subject

'He became a Christian after he had converted to Judaism just to be accepted by the Moslems. Don't you know that Moslems force Jews to embrace Christianity first, before Islam?'

My mother did not add another word, as she had already said enough. She knew his nature too well to insist; besides she was aware of her role as a woman. It was not appropriate for a woman to exceed her husband's knowledge, although she knew so much about circumcision and other religious matters. If she had not been a Frank, and if my father had not loved her the way he did, he would have been provoked by her impertinent exposition of knowledge, but instead, he continued to converse with her.

'And the other matter—'

'What other matter?'

'He married the priest's widow!'

'She was still very young when her husband died. The priest was an old man and Katherine just a young girl back then. What do you expect a young and helpless woman to do?'

The conversation fascinated me. I had already forgotten about my pain, and sleep just slipped away from my eyelids. Although I was still covered with the bedclothes and had my eyes shut, my ears were wide open like two ship's sails.

'Young lass, my ass,' my father commented sarcastically. 'She was the wife of a priest for God's sake! No sooner had she married than she had six little devils with him in a row, with Arouz on top of them. But as the saying goes, 'The priest's wife's children are the devil's grandsons.'

'Do not speak like that about the boy. Arouz was the one who saved your son from the hands of his evil brother, Hizr.'

'He is the worst of them all... You look at him and you think he is going to lam into you, once you turn your back on him. His mother is to blame.'

'Don't be so unfeeling. She is a nice, Godfearing woman. It is not her fault that two of her children are untamed. Look at her two daughters. They are modest and religious and they never skip church on Sundays.'

At this point, I raised my head slightly. I could not deny that I was attracted to Katherine's youngest daughter and perhaps that was the reason why her brother, Hizr, had attacked me so violently he may have sensed something.

'Didn't I tell you?' my father went on. 'The two sons, the eldest and the youngest, are rogues. They drift aimlessly around the village creating trouble. And the other one, Elias, he spends all his day outside the medresse6 and has some weird dealings with the oulemads.7 What kind of family is this? The father is of an obscure religion, the mother and the two girls are Christian and the boys go to a Moslem school. God knows what...'

'Do not judge people so harshly,' my mother interrupted. You can never know, you can never tell...'

How wise and prophetic my mother was. Her fears would have been confirmed if God had not taken her away from me so soon. She departed from this world before she could witness what had become of me, unless she was watching me from the sky, but even then i am sure her chaste heart would have forgiven me.

At this point in the conversation I fell asleep. It was a restless sleep, full of nightmares and demons. I dreamt of ferocious spirits and repugnant creatures trying to attack me and tear my feeble body apart, whilst I was helplessly trying to defend myself all the time.

When I woke up the following day the first thing my mother did was to advise me to stay away from Yakub's sons.

You have no business whatsoever with them,' she admonished me.

An hour later, I was searching for Arouz on my way to school. When I found him, he expressed his willingness to keep me company. He asked me about things I had learned at the Catholic school and I told him all I knew. To my surprise, I managed to win both his respect and admiration.

My meetings with Arouz became more frequent. I would meet him at least once a week on my way back from school in Mitilini. My father had warned me never to ever talk to him and I did just the opposite. The fact that this strong, obstreperous boy would sit next to me like a tame tiger and listen to my stories and instructions, gave me an immense satisfaction.

He was condemned to stay illiterate since neither of his parents really cared about his education or bothered to send him to any kind of school, Christian or Moslem. He helped his father in the pottery workshop Yakub knew how to make beautiful and watertight jugs and very often he would accompany his father on his travels to Aivali, in Smyrna, and Constantinople, in a small sailing boat his father owned to sell jugs, when there was little demand for them in our area.

Consequently, Arouz and his brother, Hizr, learned about the art of sailing when they were still very young, but only in practice as they were ignorant of the theory, i.e. how to determine their course or find the position of their boat in the open sea. My father had mended their boat several times without charging them a fee, just because he wanted to avoid any kind of business dealings with Yakub, the illtempered apostate.

At this point, I should refer to the fact that in my village there were no Turks, but a good number of Greeks who had converted to I; lam. This tendency was initiated by the Genovese potentati of Lesvos, Nicholas Gatelousos, who took over the leadership of the island after killing his own brother Dominic, assisted by his cousin Leukines.

When Nicholas became the leader of Lesvos, Mehmed the Conqueror, after his consecutive victories and the seizure of Constantinople, did not tolerate the fact that there were foreign lands in front of his coastline. He sent a few troops to Lesvos and besieged Mitilini. The Turks, however, were always afraid to cross the sea, for they had adopted the Arabic saying, 'Allah granted the land to the Moslems and conceded the sea to the infidels.'

That was the main problem of Mehmed the Conqueror and his successors. They conquered the whole continent of Asia Minor and Greece, the mainland across it, but they could not set foot on the Aegean islands. It was not until the death of Mehmed the Conqueror that the sultans mobilised the Greek pirates who had no faith whatsoever against the Greek islands, and the pirates offered their services willingly, not only to satisfy their insatiable greed for wealth but also to get the protection of the Dovleti.8 the same happened with Hizr and Arouz.

Mehmed himself did not cross the sea to Mitilini. On safe land he awaited the news of the subjugation by his commanderinchief, Vezir Mahmout Pasha. Even when the island was conquered, Mehmed stayed on the opposite coastline waiting for Gatelousos to hand him the keys of the island's fort, a symbolic gesture that indicated the surrender of the island.

Despite the fact that Nicholas Gatelousos could have held a strong and long resistance as the fort of Mitilini had a lot of ammunition and food supplies and the native people were determined to fight he preferred to save himself and betray his compatriots. They were the ones who always ended up paying dearly for the VenetianTurkish wars and the piratical assaults against the islands occupied by the Franks.

Only twentyseven days later, he assented to surrendering the island and in return to receiving another city the same size as Lesvos. That was a deal, the terms of which had been set by his cousin Loukinos on the coast of Asia Minor, near Agiasmaton, where the sultan had camped with the remaining troops.

Nicholas and Loukinos offered to convert to Islam, and after the handing over of the island they both went to Constantinople to receive the ransom of their treason and to proselytise. Nevertheless, before the pangs of circumcision were over, the sultan beheaded Nicholas under the pretext that a young boy from the sultan's harem had found protection under his wings. Loukinos was also beheaded for a different reason.

All these events are not figments of my imagination. Leonard, the Catholic archbishop of Mitilini who survived two captures, described them in his memoirs in detail, when he reached Venice.

The first capture took place in Constantinople on 12 December 1452. He was confirming the affiliation of the two churches in the church of Saint Sofia, whilst people were being killed and massacred outside. All priests ever cared about at that time was their Filioque.9 Lord, forgive me for my saying so, but it is so difficult for me not to mention such incidents.

Well, Leonard was arrested but was soon released after the intervention of the Pope. The capture and its devastating consequences were narrated i \ his report to Nicholas the Fifth, the pope at that time. Leonard also witnessed the second capture that took place in Mitilini. Mehmed the Conqueror arrested Leonard again and sent him to Constantinople. The Turks eventually released him after the intervention of the new Pope, Pius the Second, to whom Leonard submitted a new report in which he listed the particulars of the capture of our island.

The archbishop died in the island of Chios in 1482... God bless his soul.

After the capture of Mitilini, many of our compatriots those who survived the massacre, that is renounced their religion and converted to Islam, only to avoid the misfortunes and calamities harbored by fate and save themselves from the ravaging acts of the Turks. Many of them even took refuge in the new religion, so that they would not be considered citizens of an inferior rank by their conquerors, who tended to attribute derogatory names to them such as giagour10 and others. And strangely enough, those converted compatriots, in their attempt to exhibit their real faith and loyalty to the Turks, became more ruthless and more fervent devotees than the followers of Mehmed themselves.

At this point I have to mention that many of the Turks were converted to Christianity with the help of our priests and that they, unlike the Greek apostates, blissfully stayed waiting to be slaughtered like cattle by their former coreligionists. They were happily dying believing that they were accomplishing a sacred mission and that the church would recognise them as saints. Forgive me, Lord!

Those were the conditions at that disturbing time: confusion, chaos and disorder.

In Paleokipos, our village, Moslems and Turks still lived peacefully and I continued to keep company with Arouz and Hizr, the sons of Yakub. I would talk to Arouz, whilst Hizr would sit on a stone farther away and follow our conversation with eyes and ears wide open. I would steal looks at his face for I must admit I never trusted him after his unreasonable attack and could detect in his eyes both his admiration and envy. Admiration for all the wonderful things I knew and he had never had the chance to learn, and envy because his brother preferred my company to his. In contrast, Arouz harbored pure admiration for me and would always pose questions in case he did not understand something too well. Naturally, Hizr, fearing his brother's anger, never dared to interrupt me.

I gave Arouz answers to his questions. He was mainly interested in the geography of the Mediterranean Sea, its islands, coasts and shores. Whenever I was unable to satisfy his curiosity, I took the questions to my teachers, the Catholic priests, only to return to my friend and protector with the appropriate answers. No one dared to mock or harass me any more, not even Hizr himself, for Arouz was always ready to attack anyone who dared come near me and to blow their brains out with his steel arms.

'What is there beyond the Mediterranean?' he asked me, one day.

'Beyond the Mediterranean? What do you mean?' 'What is there beyond the horizon?' I gravely thought about his question, but I was not knowledgeable enough to answer. I only knew a little about some islands that were discovered by a Genovese sailor called Colon," but that was all.

There is chaos,' I exclaimed. 'Beyond the Mediterranean there is nothing but chaos.'

'This can't be true,' he answered wisely. 'I assume you don't know. Why don't you ask your priest teachers? If there was chaos, man would have found out about it.'

'There is chaos!' I insisted, fearing that he would lose trust and faith in me.

'I refuse to believe that! Whatever exists, it exists here on our earth.'

'And what about the stars?' Hizr intervened, suddenly. 'Do they also exist in chaos?'

I was puzzled, confused and embarrassed because of my lame knowledge. I also got upset because it was obvious that Hizr had taken advantage of my ignorance in this matter to belittle me in his brother's eyes. Therefore, I tried to rescue the admiration that was left.

'Don't you worry,' I said to Arouz. 'I will ask my teachers for the details and I will answer you as soon as I can.'

I defined the questions as trivial, in my attempt to degrade the significance of being unable to answer them.

The following week I was ready to answer his question. I told him about Colombo's achievement and the weird looking natives he had encountered on the islands he had named the West Indies.

In trying to quench my friend's thirst for knowledge, I learned so much about the art of sailing at least in theory from my teachers the priests. I knew about the astrolabe that seamen measured the angle of elevation of the stars with, or their height from the horizon. With a mere instrument, I was told, seamen could determine which coast they would reach after a long journey at sea and know the height of a definite star from the horizon pirates knew those heights for every coastal city, by heart. I was also taught a great deal about geography and got acquainted with the magnetic needle that always indicated the point on the horizon to which the ship sails as well as much other nautical information.

'Do you want to become a seaman?' one of my teachers asked me one day. He was a Catholic monk who had a good command of the art of sailing.

'No!' I answered hurriedly and lowered my face so that he would not extend the conversation.

'So, why do all your questions revolve around this subject, my son?'

'Out of curiosity, Father,' I replied, while my face was getting redder. I knew I was lying to him and that my interest originated from my wish to remain Arouz's trusted friend.

'So, you are just curious?' the monk insisted. Tes, I am just curious.'

The monk stopped posing questions at that point, but my persistent curiosity stimulated his worry and concern. He diverted his conversation to religious and ecclesiastical matters and I followed his instructions with feigned zeal so as not to incite any more of his suspicions, besides, he still knew so much about sailing.

Arouz and Hizr were thrilled with the nautical information I conveyed to them on a weekly basis. They would even wait eagerly for my return from school every Friday, at the end of the village. They never stopped asking me questions and I would always make sure to answer them all. They would absorb and assimilate everything I said and register the information in their minds with 'unfading ink' as they used to say, and they never forgot what I had taught them.

Arouz, on his part, wishing to reward me for the knowledge I gave him, would sit patiently and teach me the principles of practical sailing on his father's boat.

Very soon, my nautical vocabulary was enriched with words such as, bollard, derrick, forecastle, gunwale, stern, fore, rails, headropes, bulkhead, bulwark, stem, windward and leeward, and sonorous phrases such as, 'hoist and rouse', 'lever and strive', 'change the course' or 'the wind's changed', along with all the nautical terms that sailors used when they received orders from their skippers.

When the lesson was over we would run to the village and play war with other children a game that my mother hated for me to play as she was afraid I would get irredeemably hurt. However, following her ingenious apophthegm, 'Man is stronger than the lion as he has a brain', and since I was the smallest one of all in size, I chose to stay behind at the field of battle and give directions or recommend the point of attack against the rival gang.

Arouz and Hizr would always follow my instructions with willingness and enthusiasm as our fights ended victoriously. Arouz ever since that time commanded me to stay behind and give him directions or indicate tactics. All of a sudden, I realized that I had become so important to him at that position, that if I ever moved to the front he would reprove my recklessness and demand that I return to my former position. He had the power and strength to manage for the both of us and I had the brain to lead him to the way.

One afternoon whilst we were sailing in Yakub's boat in the waters of Gera, we saw a buoy proudly floating in the sea. A fisherman had dropped his nets to fish 'prima sera', as Arouz had phrased it, or else, early in the morning. Judging from the rope's level, we presumed that the nets had to be loaded with fish!

It was then that Hizr proposed an idea and Arouz accomplished it at once!

'Why don't we lift it to find out what kind of fish the net has caughi?' Hizr suggested.

'Good idea,' Arouz consented, and with strong hands he started pulling the ropes, raising the net to the boat's level. He heaved it and then threw it back into the water again Arouz could lift a load twice his own weight with his bare hands. However, when the net reached the surface of the water, we saw that the catch was indeed very rich and tempting. Arouz, with no sign of hesitation, emptied the contents into our boat and threw the net back into the water.

When we reached land, we divided the 'prey' equally among ourselves and we proudly returned home. That was the first piratical action that we had ever committed in our lives!

When my mother saw the fish spread on her kitchen counter she was startled and surprised.

'Where did you get this fish?' she demanded to know.

'I fished it, mother!' I replied, whilst my face was turning dangerously red.

'Where did you fish it?'

'The sea. Where else?'

'And how did you manage to fish without your fishing rod?' she cunningly asked.

'Yakub has fishing equipment in his boat,' I explained, whilst my face almost got burnt in the invisible flames of guilt.

'Please, do not lie to me, do not ever lie to your mother. I demand that you tell me the truth, son. Besides, I can easily tell if you are not being honest with me.'

My mother knew how to handle her son and could see his weaknesses. After her persistent urging I had to confess, and when I did, she was utterly disappointed and disturbed at my despicable actions. She did not hit me though although she really wished to do so she just accused me of being thoughtless and blamed the horrible little devils I got involved with.

'What should I do with you?' she asked me, completely alarmed. You have put me in a most embarrassing position.'

At first, I did not quite understand why she was so upset, but then when she threw the fish into the wastebasket, I realized what she had really feared. She could neither cook the fish as it was stolen, nor could she return it to the fisherman, for she would then expose her son and his friends. Thus, the cats devoured the fish, secretly, and away from the eyes of the people in the village.

The next day Arouz asked me, 'Did you enjoy the fish? It was deliciot4sV

'Absolutely delicious,' I had to confirm, whilst my blood froze within my veins.

'It made a fantastic soup,' Arouz insisted.

Yes, it made a wonderful soup,' I repeated.

I did not dare tell him what my mother had done with the fish for I was afraid I would offend him or lose his trust in me. No, I could not bear to lose his confidence for anything in the world, whatever the cost and the cost I paid, later on, was so very dear!

Thus, the first piratical act had already been performed and there still remained many others to be acted in my troubled life.

It was the year 1490. The war between Venice and Turkey had come to an end a decade ago with great losses on the part of the Venetians. Among the losses we should also count the unsuccessful attempt of the Venetians to drive the Turks away from the island of Lesvos, an attempt that cost our island ten thousand captives, who were transported to Chalkida to reinforce their defence line. Not much was achieved though. The only thing that the Venetians managed to accomplish was to capture the island of Limnos from the Turks as well as Thassos, Tenedos and Imvros, which was lost again, a fe w years later.

I was almost sixteen at that time, if my memory does not deceive me, and I was still attending the Catholic school of the Assumption church that was operating with very few students at that time due to the fact that the church was considered the property of the Genovese, ruthless enemies of the Venetians. Despite all these changes, my mother insisted that I should continue my education there during those disturbed years, as she believed that my learning would enable me one day to leave the island that was seething with pirates and be safe somewhere far away. Paleokipos was not a safe place any more.

It was then that Bishop Francis made his appearance at my school and in my life...

Bishop Francis, or Frangiscosm as the Greeks called him, was the Pope's representative in Mitilini; at least that was how the other priests and our teachers introduced him to us. He had come to our island as a mediator, and his task was to settle along with the Turkish governor of the island the pending matters of the Roman Catholic church of Gatelousos, the church of the Assumption which, as I repeatedly mentioned in my confession, I had attended since I was a young boy.

In contrast to my friends in Paleokipos, who considered me petty and incompetent, the priests at school thought very highly of me and harbored their regard and esteem for my promising abilities. They behaved towards me as if I were a responsible, mature person and respected me for both my conduct and my extraordinary aptitude in learning.

Francis had received a formal invitation from our school and he accepted it with enthusiasm. He was a handsome man in his early forties with a fair complexion and a blond, pointed beard that made his 'beluga' chin look even sharper. He received the priests' compliments as if they were a debt for which he had to be paid he never thanked anyone or gave anyone the chance to express an opinion when he did the talking. He kept his 'beluga' chin up all the time, a movement that exposed his arrogance and haughtiness, which he did not even try to conceal.

Our priests and teachers pretended that they did not take any notice of his airs and continued to behave submissively as if they were compelled to do so or as if they had been advised to do so by their superiors.

During the first days of his stay on the premises of the church where we were also accommodated on weekdays Francis called us to attend a Mass at which he officiated. After delivering his longwinded speech on Catholicism and its benefits, he invited each and every one of the students for an interview in the presence of his teachers.

During the Mass, I had noticed that he had paid most of his attention to my person for he kept staring at me most of the time, and when my turn had come to appear in front of him at the interview, he kept me in the room longer than any of the other students. He asked me where I came from; what lessons I was mostly interested in; what kind of knowledge I had acquired all these years and other relative matters...

I gave him answers assisted by my teacher, the priest, who proudly added that I could speak Greek, Turkish and Latin.

'And where did you learn Latin, my son?' he asked.

At this point my teacher hurriedly intervened.

'He also speaks good Italian, Your Eminence. His mother is of Venetian origin, she comes from Tsirigo but she has been living here on this island since her child was born.'

I did not expect my teacher to know so much about my life, since my mother never talked about her. Later on I realized that she was compelled to reveal her origin in order that I could be accepted at the school.

Francis listened to my teacher with great interest and suddenly his eyes sparked, probably because of a thought that had just crossed his mind. His attention was even more intensified and he posed some more questions to me.

'So, you speak four languages?'

'Three. The first one is my mother tongue.'

'Which one are you referring to?'

'I am referring to Greek, my native language,' I demurred, somewhat offended.

'But your mother's origin is Venetian. Your mother tongue must be Italian. Greek is, perhaps, your paternal language.'

I got confused; nevertheless I did not feel like arguing with him. That was the sort of discussion we avoided opening at home.

'Besides the languages he speaks...' My teacher went on to change the critical subject and direct it to another path. 'He has also extensively studied the ancient Greek and Latin writers. He is keen on history but he is more interested in geography, especially the geography of the Aegean Sea.'

'So, you are interested in geography,' Francis remarked, thoughtfully scratching his hairy and pointed chin.

Yes, Sir,' I answered plainly.

A mere yes does not really harm anyone, I thought.

'I assume you would very much wish to travel and witness everything you have read about in the books with your own eyes. Have I guessed correctly?'

Yes, you have, Sir,' I said.

If I had known then how that answer would affect the rest of my life, I wouldn't have uttered it so thoughtlessly.

Answers determine our lives and if we know how decisive some of them could be for our future, we would definitely be more careful when we utter them but unfortunately, I had already given my answer.

'Very well,' Francis said. 'We shall speak again.'

With that phrase and an overbearing nod, that indicated that His Eminence had ended the session, my teacher and I stood up, bowed with courtesy and humbly departed from the room.

*You made a good impression on him, son,' my teacher said the moment we were outside his office.

'I do not really think so,' I objected. *We shall speak again rather means the meeting is over. It is a polite way of saying 'Go now, I have had enough of you'.'

'No, no, I do not share your opinion. I definitely do not agree,' my teacher insisted.

We separated at the entrance to the building, each one of us carrying his own thoughts in his mind, and although I believed I had done with Francis, something inside me, perhaps my instinct, was telling me that I was not yet through with him.

The following day it was Friday, and I was preparing my things to go back to Paleokipos, to my family. With a mind seething with piratical assaults and the other games I would play with Arouz during the weekend, I was called by the head priest to his office.

I had only been to the head priest's office once or perhaps twice to deliver a paper or a document to the headmaster. I remembered then that in the middle of his spacious room there was a huge carved, wooden desk with a comfortable armchair behind it, invariably accommodating the head priest. Around this desk, chairs upholstered with red velvet were arrayed in a semicircular pattern. They were comfortable enough to receive the behinds of the priests during the long meetings that were usually held on Saturday mornings. During those meetings, the priests were supposed to handle the various problems that emerged every now and then due to the pertinacity of the Turkish officials on the island.

Portraits of late archbishops and directors of the school hung on the walls holy people who stared at you with their grave and sedate manner as if they were blaming you for all the wrongdoings of the world. They glared, as if they were ready to impose a punishment for a crime you may have committed unconsciously. In the farthest corner of the room was an armchair that was always vacant. No one ever used it and its upholstery was still new and shiny. I had figured, once, that only the head priest had the privilege of sitting in a comfortable armchair, whilst the rest of the priests would merely accommodate themselves in plain chairs, in this way demonstrating their obedience, their submission and respect for the hierarchy of priesthood.

As soon as I entered the room I was astounded. All the teachers, including the head priest, were gathered there and to my greatest surprise, everyone was sitting in the chairs even the head priest himself except for Francis, who was sitting behind the desk in the armchair that was originally destined to receive the bottom of our director.

Only then did I realise that even our headmaster was inferior in rank to Francis.

'Come child. Ermo... Ermo...' Francis said to me.

'Ermolaos, Sir. My name is Ermolaos,' I corrected him shyly.

Yes, Yes. Ermo... Leo, Ermo... leo. Is that right? Very well, sit down, my child.'

He pointed to the armchair, which for years now had not been used only this time it was placed directly in front of the oak desk and suggested that I should sit in it. I was baffled. I directed my look to the head priest and when I received his sign of consent, I hesitantly obeyed. However, as I was still in urgent need of somebody's support in this overwhelming situation, I desperately sought my teacher's presence. When my eyes finally came upon him, I saw that he had his head lowered and was looking attentively at his shoes, moving his legs restlessly as if he wanted to make sure that there was nothing wrong with them.

'Ermoleo, my child,' Francis said, when I eventually turned my face to him, feeling more uneasy than my teacher. 'We called you for a very delicate matter or rather task that we have all decided to assign to you.'

I looked behind me.

'Are you addressing me, Sir?'

Yes, of course. Your knowledge and performance at school have been highly commended by your teachers and they have even informed me that you speak Turkish fluently.'

Yes, Sir. I can read and write very well in Turkish...' 'For the time being, it is enough that you speak the language, my son,' Francis interrupted me. Yes, Sire,' I muttered, clumsily.

'Well, we shall assign you to a very delicate mission a mission that will make us all very proud of you.'

At this point he paused for a moment. Another thought must have crossed his mind for his eyes sparkled once more.

'But you did not mention which village you come from.' 'I come from Paleokipos.'

'Is that where you learned to speak Turkish? Because, as far as I know, you are not taught this language here.'

Yes, Sir. I learned to speak Turkish in Paleokipos.'

'Do many Turks live in that village?'

Yes, many Turks, as well as Genovese, Catalonians and—'

'And Greeks.'

'And Greeks.'

'Have many of the Greeks converted to Islam?' 'A few of them have.'

He rubbed his hairy chin once more and went on.

'Are you on good terms with the Turks? Is that how you have come to learn their language?'

'No, Sir,' I stammered. You see... daily practice in our village requires the learning of Turkish. How else we can communicate with each other?'

'I see.'

He remained silent for a short while and it was quite obvious that he was contemplating a notion. Then he spoke as if he had just taken a decision.

'We must assign a delicate mission to you. But you mustn't reveal it to anyone.'

'I will not,' I answered, obediently.

'Not even to your parents.'

'I will not.'

'Not even to your mother.'

Agitation and nervousness captured my body and soul, I could keep a secret from my father, but I could never hide anything from my sweet mother, not even my games with Arouz.

'Do not be worried, my boy. We shall talk to your parents in proper time. As for now, we do not wish anyone to know where you come from.'

'And how shall we achieve that, Sir?'

'With the help of God everything becomes possible,' he replied somewhat abruptly. 'I want you to accompany me tomorrow to the Bey12 of Mitilini, to be my interpreter. I will address him in Latin and you will translate everything I say into his language and vice versa. What do you think? Is it feasible?'

I pondered over his words for a few moments. I did not really understand what kind of mission that would be, however, the way he described it made it sound rather an effortless task. I did the same during our games with the boys in my village, when a Greek child wouldn't understand my friend Arouz.

'I will manage, Sir,' I replied, with confidence. 'But don't you think my parents should be informed, first?'

Yes, of course, we have all agreed that your parents are to be informed promptly. Do not worry.'

'But, today, I have to return to the village. It's Friday and if I do not go back, my mother would be immensely alarmed, Sir.'

It was not only Mother I was thinking about for I would also miss the games with Arouz and the rest of the gang.

'We shall send them a message so that they will come tomorrow. Today you shall stay with us here on the premises of the school. Don't you want us?'

The tone of his voice suggested that my reluctant mood had insulted him.

'No, no. On the contrary, I would like to stay...'

'Very well then, everything is settled. Your teacher will inform you about what you have to do when we go to see the Bey, how to behave and what to say about yourself

'What should I tell him about myself?' I asked full of agony, directing my look at my teacher, once more.

At last he had unstuck his eyes from his shoes, and directing them to my face, he nodded reassuringly.

'But his name... It is too much Greek,' the head priest suddenly remembered.

I turned and looked at him. What does he really mean? I wondered.

'I guess that is a very reasonable remark,' Francis said. 'It is too Greek, indeed. What is the name again? Ah! Ermoleo?'

'Ermolaos,' I corrected.

'There is no saint with such a name in our church as far as I know,' said the head priest and director of our school.

Yes, I quite agree... There is not. What should we do with such an obstacle?'

Bishop Francis submerged into deep thought whilst muttering my mispronounced name, over and over again. 'Ermo... leo, Ermoleo... Leo. Leo,' he suddenly exclaimed. 'There b a Saint Leonard of Limoge, the confessor... Well, that is how we shall temporarily call him, Leonar.'

'But my name is Ermola...'

But who was listening to me, I thought, everyone was already giving his consent to Francis about my new name and they even started to congratulate him on his brilliant idea!

'Leonar! And don't complain, my boy. It is only going to last for a day and you are soon going to obtain you named back after our visit to the Turk. It is for your own welfare and safety, I assure you. The Bey must not understand that you live here in Mitilini. Yes, of course, it is for your own welfare... I will introduce you to him as my personal secretary. Do you understand?'

I nodded, but only to grant them my understanding, not my approval. But Francis did not really pay any attention to my feelings, or rather did not really care about how I felt. He stood up and so did everyone else, including myself. At that point he noticed the clothes I was wearing.

'No, no, he is not properly dressed; these are not suitable clothes for a bishop's secretary. You must do something about it. Along with everything else you must please find new clothes for him and you should do that at once!'

No sooner was the meeting adjourned, than the priests in the room dispersed at once and started running in different directions inside the room as if they were looking for the clothes in there. In the afternoon, the storekeeper of the monastery found a black costume that had belonged to a monk before he was ordained. I was still thin and bony and in my new costume I looked even thinner.

In the evening my teacher visited me and lectured me on the mission I had taken over, According to his instructions, I would not mention that I was born in Lesvos, I would instead say that I had nothing to do with the island and this, he repeated, was for my personal safety and the safety of my parents.

'He must not know where you come from...' he said, to reassure me but also to emphasise what he wanted me to do.

I had to say that I came from Constantinople, from Genovese parents who lived in Peran, where I was brought up and educated. He also advised me to be submissive and compliant to the Turk, never raise objections to his sayings, and that my responsibility was to translate everything he and Francis stated to each other. He suggested that I should be careful with the translation and not to make mistakes.

'Keep your head lowered to show respect and have your hands crossed over your chest to show modesty,' he added. He told me so many other things, which I do not quite recall now.

Some time later, a group of priests came to escort me to the church. There, they placed me in front of the altar and asked me to give an oath that I would keep the mission a secret, that I would not reveal it to anyone in my village and that I would be able to speak freely to nobody except my superior, Francis, that is if he asked for my opinion or my personal evaluation of the circumstances.

I repeated the oath with a stabbing pain in my chest. It was the first time in my life that I was forced into entering a maze the end of which I was not sure if I could ever reach, besides, my dear mother was not there to advise me.

During the ritual of the oathtaking, Francis did not take his eyes off me. He kept scrutinising me as if he was trying to penetrate my mind and my soul, and wished to delve into my innermost thoughts and inspect what was going on inside this adolescent head. I felt his piercing looks on me but I did not turn my head towards him so that I would not kindle any of his suspicions.

After the ceremony was over, they invited me to dine with the rest of the priests at the long table, the head of which was occupied by Francis. One of the priests started reading prayers out of a prayer book, while I was thinking that despite everything else, I would enjoy a lush and delicious meal that night, as the table accommodated all sorts of food.

I ate avidly and at night I suffered from both indigestion and nightmares. I dreamt of fiends, devils of the underworld, even the monsters of the Apocalypse. They all wanted to drag me to a devilish dance whilst I, helpless and defenceless, was trying to resist them. I woke up in the middle of the night gasping and terrified, when all these monsters started hurling flames from their mouths at me...

I could not go back to sleep. I lurked patiently in the dark until daybreak. When the first rays of the sun crept into my cell through the small scuttle [I was put up in a monk's cell to sleep] I regained my courage and hope and I repossessed both my physical and spiritual strength once more. Our ancient ancestors, I thought, were so wise to attribute invigoratiori and liferendering qualities to the sun... Forgive me, Lord, for my pagan thoughts!

Now, I was contemplating ways and simulating manners to act more convincingly and look more subservient to the Turkish officer. I even assumed a new expression on my face, such as the one feigned by the Roman Catholic priests when they had to address or report to their superiors.

I put on my black attire, and a priest gave me a calpaki[13] which I placed upon my head, 'so that I would not be recognised', as he said. Then I met with Francis at the gate of the church, and we walked together to the governing house that was not so far from the old and deserted castle of Mitilini.

Francis, with his haughty and arrogant manners, his upright stature and supercilious air, meant to make his presence felt to the people in the island.

I put on the 'face' I had improvised in my cell earlier in the morning of the same day and I followed him with smaller footsteps — or rather smaller skips that contrasted to his wide, steady and confident stride. I had hidden my face in my chest and I could only see the tip of his cassock, which I did not fail to follow. I had my hands crossed over my stomach, as I believed that it was the most appropriate way to display subordination.

We reached the governor's headquarters and after a short delay as the Turks had to make their own ploys to make sure that we meant well we were led to a special chamber where the governor received his guests.

When we first entered, the Bey did not pay any attention to us. He was sitting there with a vacant look in his eyes and with his legs crossed on a huge pillow, which was placed on a raised wooden floor, a position that gave him the advantage of 'looking down' on his guests. He had placed his narghile'4 in front of him and he was smoking, nonchalantly.

When eventually his eyes rested upon us, he offered Francis a narghile without uttering a word. Francis refused his offer with hidden disgust, whilst keeping his pretentious smile all the time.

The whole room smelt of incense and I wondered at that time if Moslems used the same kind of incense as Christians... It was not until much later that I was informed about the difference...

After standing for quite some time it felt like eternity to me the Turkish officer decided to take the hose out of his mouth and nod to us to sit down. Two of his servants dashed from the entrance and brought a very uncomfortable short stool for Francis and an even shorter one for myself.

As soon as Francis sat on his stool, he directed a warm salutation to the Turk and conveyed the cordial greetings and wishes on behalf of the pope. I translated his words simultaneously. He then started to talk about Christian and Moslem relations and the bonds that had to be reinforced, especially after the long, devastating and bloody war that had taken place between Venice and Turkey. He spoke of attempts on behalf of the Venetians, who aimed at maintaining higher levels of mutual respect and understanding between the Roman Catholic Church and the Higher Gate. And finally, he referred to the sea trade and the concessions that had to be rendered by both sides for the sake of its development and progress. I could not understand, though, what kind of relations or bonds he was talking about after such war.

I translated everything Francis said. By that time, the air in the room was stuffy and so filled with smoke and incense that I almost fainted. A little while later I felt that I was soaring over the clouds of smoke that were emitted by the narghile and the Turk's mouth and nostrils.

Francis continued his irrepressibly longwinded speech, while the Bey was listening silently to him. He did not bother to comment on Francis's words, give him any answers or even ask for any kind of explanation.

After his suggestions about the improvement of relations between the two nations, he talked about the people's need to prac ice their religion freely and proposed that the restrict^ ns enforced on the exercise of religious duties should be banned.

At this point, the Bey wrenched the hose from his mouth and posed his first question.

'How many Moslem temples exist in the Vatican?'

Francis felt uneasy on his stool. He moved restlessly for a moment and then clever and resourceful as he was, he gave his reply.

There aren't any, because there is no Moslem population in the Vatican.'

The Bey as if he did not hear the answer placed the hose back in his mouth and continued his smoking.

Francis was not discouraged so he continued his speech, hoping that the Bey would eventually assimilate a few things. I continued to translate as well and fast as I could, although the smoke had affected my tongue and blocked my nostrils.

At this point, Francis's mouth dried up and he stopped his endless speech to take a breath. The Bey, ignoring his presence altogether, along with all his talk, turned to me and asked: 'And you... Where do you come from?'

I recited my lesson, the lesson that had been delivered to me by my teacher the priest. I told him that I came from Peran, where I was raised and educated and that I was the child of a Genovese couple who lived in Poli I avoided uttering the name Constantinople, fearing the Turk's anger and that I was preparing myself to become a clerical officer in the Roman Catholic Church.

'And where did you learn to speak Turkish so well?'

My village Paleokipos and my friends momentarily flashed in my mind.

'I picked it up from my friends in Peran, but I was also taught Turkish at the school I attended there.'

'Well done, indeed,' he commented, and put the hose in his mouth again.

Francis resumed his former talk about the good relations that must exist between the two sides, and referred again to the necessity of such improvement.

'Listen, priest,' the Turk interrupted, after detaching the hose from his lips once more. 'I cannot do much, singlehanded, besides, I do not care what god people believe in or pray to, as long as they are quiet and do not create trouble. As for everything else you have blabbered about, I will inform the beilerbey15 of Roumeli and we shall then officially inform you.' There were two general commanders at that time: the beilerbey of the East and the beilerbey of Roumeli. They were members of the government and enjoyed the same rank and privileges as the head of the dewan, the supreme council, during the sultanic regime in Turkey.

Having uttered that phrase, he put the hose back in his mouth assuming that vacant look he had had since the very first moment we had entered the room. His gesture was absolutely clear the audition was at an end and we had to leave. Francis and I stood up together, then we both bowed solemnly and Francis turned towards the door. I followed him keeping two steps behind.

General Commander of a region.

We returned to the church maintaining the same order and pace as before. He preceded me and I followed two steps behind him. We did not take the same way though, for we deviated and passed in front of the harbor. With heedful eyes Francis looked at the anchored ships and the fortification the Turks had made after the war, but what made a greater impression on me was the fact that we had deviated from our way, slowing down our return to the church. We could have reached the church must faster. Why did he choose tha way then? Later on the same day, I found out.

When we finally reached the churchyard, the head priest and my teacher met Francis. They headed towards the office, leaving me alone so I could return to my cell. Some time later as I was aspiring towards my return home to my village and friends they again called me to the grand office and asked me to sit in the comfortable armchair in front of Francis, who had taken over the head priest's seat once more.

'Today my son, you have accomplished a great mission,' said the headmaster. 'In recognition of your services, Bishop Francis and I, after the consent of your teacher of course, have decided that you must continue your studies in Venice. There, the seeds that Almighty God planted in your soul will fructify and flourish; there, you will be able to excel in your aptitudes and be useful to our church, the church of our Lord Jesus Christ. Your teachers, the great teachers of this church, will be happy to assist and support you. Do not forget that you are very fortunate to be chosen.

Many of your compatriots went there begging for mercy and protection after the hardships they had endured by the Turks. While you, you will go there with all respect and honor to become the personal assistant and secretary to the reverend bishop, Francis.'

I was flabbergasted I almost dissolved into my huge armchair for I did not expect such a development. I was going to find myself in a strange place amongst strange people and I would be torn away from my parents, my village and my friends.

'I do not think that would be possible,' I dared to object.

'Why not?' Francis interrupted me abruptly. You cannot reject such a generous offer.'

'But, what about my parents?'

I searched for some sort of rescue in the eyes of my teacher, but unfortunately he was looking at the tips of his shoes again, moving them restlessly here and there.

'We have already seen to that, son,' said the headmaster. 'We have called them and tomorrow they will be here. We shall announce our generous offer to them and we are confident that they will be glad to accept it.*

'I do not really think my mother will give her cons—'

I did not finish my sentence. They were both looking at me in a most austere way and I even felt sorry that I had to involve my mother in this adventure in which they had trapped me.

Your mother is a Venetian, isn't she?' Francis remarked, with a menacing look on his face.

I was speechless. His weird look and the threatening tone of his voice paralysed my existence...

'Come, come now.' The head priest intervened with a wide smile full of kindness. You mustn't be afraid. We know everything, and she knows that we know. How do you think we have accepted you in our school? When she first came here we had a long chat and she told us a few things about herself

I was slightly relieved. Perhaps she had to reveal her origin so that I would be accepted in the school, I thought. I did not really know what else to assume at that moment.

'Besides, this is for your own personal welfare. What do you expect to become here, a pirate?' Francis went on.

How did that person penetrate my most intimate thoughts? That I could never understand. Not that I had decided at that time to become a pirate, but during my games with Arouz, the idea kept haunting my mind, although I was well aware of my feebleness and physical weakness. I knew that with this body of mine I could never challenge any of the cruel giants who often appeared in my fantasies, and that I would never make my dreams come true.

'Of course not,' I objected. 'I do not wish to become a pirate, but I could become a seaman..'

'Didn't I guess so?' Francis remarked triumphantly. 'And what do you expect of such a profession? Some day your body will make good food for the fish!'

I hated the idea but I chose not to speak.

'When you come with me, you will have the opportunity to know the world, to know life! A life that you have never had the chance to experience in your village. This is the chance of a lifetime for you, my boy. Do not waste it do not be so thoughtless...'

Francis continued lecturing me on all the wonderful future prospects and the lifetime opportunities, but when he saw the expression on my face he resorted to a most effective method threat!

'Look... After your presence in front of the Bey today we have somehow exposed ourselves. I have exposed myself but mostly, you. What if one of his men sees you in Paleo... Paleo...'

'Paleokipos...' my teacher assisted, wrenching his eyes from his shoes for the first time.

Yes, Paleokipos,' Francis continued. 'What if someone sees you there and reports it to the Turkish officials? Can you think of the consequences? Your life and that of your parents will be at stake!'

That last argument was really very effective. I pictured my parents slain by the sabres of the Turks and I almost fainted. Indeed, danger was pending, and I had to make the decision alone. At that moment it did not occur to me that he was the one who had tricked me and pushed me into this fathomless pit.

'I accept.' I gave my answer at last. 'Only if my mother approves... You see, I cannot leave her that easily...'

Weaning takes place when you are an infant, my boy,' Francis remarked, with some kind of irony. 'Not when you are almost seventeen. You are seventeen, aren't you?'

Yes, Sir, I am.'

'Very well then. Besides, I do not want you to worry about anything at all. We have already invited your parents, and tomorrow morning they will be here. We shall inform them... Now you must go back to your cell and pray for the great day that is going to shine ahead of you. Do not turn your head away from the sun... You shall recall my words many times in your life.' And with a wide smile of contrived kindness, he made me understand that I had to leave and find shelter in my cell.

At night in my sleep, Satans, monsters and devils again haunted me with their fiery tongues extended to scorch my face. They had emerged from the bowels of the earth to lacerate me and then dance frantically over my torn body. At first, I was terrified and tried to run away from their grip, but then, when I thought more prudently about it, I decided that in order to avoid their scorching tongues, I had to become one of them... I got out of bed, and I ran to them. I got into their frantic circle and danced to their appalling rhythm... A short while later, I actually saw myself hurling flames from my mouth whilst my face was turning as monstrous as theirs...

I now realise how prophetic my dream was...

In the morning, I sat in my cell patiently waiting for them to call me. They had become the people who would determine my future and my life from then on.

Time went by it was almost midday and they still ignored my existence. Maybe they had forgotten me, I thought, and I felt relieved, but I was wrong. The door opened suddenly and my teacher dashed into the cell.

'Are you ready?'

'I am ready. Where are we going?'

'To the head priest's office, for your parents are • vaiting there,' he said, and turned his back to avoid my kx k and questions.

As soon as we entered the office, Francis, who was standing behind his desk, welcomed me with suavity and an innocent smile. The head priest was ostracised to a corner of the room.

'Welcome to our brother,' he exclaimed loudly, so that everyone would listen.

I did not pay any attention to him. I quickly ran to my mother and took her in my arms, kissing her many times as if 1 had not seen her for ages. My father had repressed his feelings and concealed his sorrow behind a smile.

'We have talked with your parents, my son.' Francis interrupted the family reunion. 'And to my great satisfaction they have understood and appreciated our offer. They have actually given their consent.'

I turned and looked at my mother. Although her eyes had not left me for a moment, at this particular moment tears were rolling down her face.

'If it is for your own welfare, let it be so,' she whispered.

My father was gloomy and dejected, but he did not speak. It was quite obvious that he did not agree and that he was trying to hide his real feelings, keeping his lips and mouth firmly shut. I was sure that Francis had recruited all his persuasive methods to bend my father's objections. His main arguments must have been these: What do you expect your son to become in an island full of pirates? or We shall offer him what he needs, education and social status. You cannot offer him any of the latter two, or You should not fear anything, he can be back whenever you wish...

The separation from my parents took place some time later on the same day. The priests did not allow me to return to my village to say goodbye to my friends, explaining that this might be dangerous as it could create unanticipated problems. Besides Francis was in a hurry to depart.

A Venetian commercial ship was sailing early in the afternoon from the harbor of Mitilini on the same day. On that boat Francis and I would leave this island, and God only knew when I would return.

My parents' farewell took place in the office as they were not allowed to accompany us to the harbor, besides, I did not need to take anything from home, not even my clothes Francis said he had taken care of everything. I am not going to describe the scene of separation as each one of you must have experienced it at least once in your life; however, I will only mention this: I felt my heart being violently uprooted from my body, as my mother listening to my father's urgent supplications detached her body from my arms after our last embrace. Yes, indeed, it was our last embrace. The weaning from my mother occurred at that particular moment...

As soon as they left, Francis smiled at me and said with contentment:

'Now your future lies within your own hands... A brilliant life is waiting for you in Venice. A life that belongs entirely to you, take it and tame it with your strength...'

Dear God, if he only knew...

Two

My attire provoked both the inquisitiveness and the mockery of the passersby in the narrow streets of Venice, whenever I sauntered in them after a hard day's work in the underground, humid room of the huge Venetian mansion.

I was wearing a.black costume, which very much resembled a novice's suit or that of a social servant and there was always a cloak hanging from my shoulders that touched the ground and swept the wet roads and the garbage the Venetian housewives dumped from their windows. On my head, I had a triangular hat, which betrayed the poise and gravity Γ had to display to the society of the new world to which I had been so unexpectedly and so unwillingly introduced.

I needn't mention, of course, that Francis bought this new attire from a little pawnshop in Venice, soon after our arrival. He had also bought me a spare costume, a much cheaper one, which I could only wear at work or when I did not have to accompany him at any official or formal meetings.

When we did not have such meetings, I used to hedge in my tiny lair on whose walls humidity had long engraved its fingerprints and work under the faint light of a mere oil lamp which burned all day. Every time Γ entered this dusky room, I would spread my papers on a table and start writing vehemently as everything was urgent and coercive in that place and I was always falling behind.

The documents that concerned my work formed a pyramid with asymmetrical corners, for the rest of the clerks would pile them up unevenly on the sole wooden chair in the room. Those were the papers I had to translate from Greek to Italian or Turkish...

It would take me the whole day to finish, for sometimes I would spei d hours translating a mere paragraph, especially when I came across unknown words in Turkish. The translation from the Greek language was much easier, but even then I had to comprehend a text written in Greek by a Turk! Oriental thought can never be expressed in the Greek language the result would be a disaster.

After conquering Constantinople, the Turks desired to show the world that they were worthy of the Byzantine Empire, so they chose Greek as their official language and wrote their formal documents in Greek. The result was a ghastly mixture of badly used Greek and Turkish words and translating those kinds of letters to Italian was just impossible.

Most of the time, I had to interpret letters in abusive Greek, full of oaths and promises of mutual respect and fidelity, promises and oaths profusely pledged, only to be broken at the very first chance.

That is how I had been used, as had also many of my compatriots in Venice. Both sides manipulated us, and in the end we had to pay for it all.

Francis would often come to my tiny office, either to ask for a document or reproach me for delaying an urgent report. Once a month, he would bring me an envelope with half a. ducat inside my monthly pay for the work I had offered. He never bothered to ask about my health, which was deteriorating all the time. A persistent cough would not leave me and my forehead was always burning...

At that period of time the doge of Venice was a man called Augustine Barbarigo. It seems that it was my fate to relate to people who had strange names or names that originated from 'Barba' Barbarossa, Barbarigo etc. Our ancestor Herodote had put it correctly when he said, 'No one can evade his fate, not even a god'.

One evening Francis came to my tiny office wearing a somehow different expression on his face. After the formalities we exchanged soon after his entrance to my lair it looked and smelled like a lair he announced that I should buy new black attire for an exceptional occasion! We were both invited for a dinner party held by one of the chief commanders of the Venetian fleet, who was also a member of the College of Doges.'

I was surprised by this unanticipated invitation, and I did not conceal my feelings from Francis.

'But Leo...' Leo had been my official name since we set foot in Venice. 'This invitation is a recognition of the services to our peaceful democracy...'

'It has been six months since I first came here, Sir,' I clumsily tried to justify my refusal.

'That explains it,' he answered, as shrewdly as always. 'People need time to be able to put faith and trust in you... Don't you think so? You have managed to win their trust and respect in only six months, Leo... You really deserve to be congratulated on such an achievement. Oh, and I should not forget, make sure you buy some decent clothes for the occasion. You are not a poor islander any more.'

At that time I did not really know if I had to be exhilarated for the honorable invitation and my promotion to a 'seminobleman' or to worry about the sudden trust they had shown in me. I decided not to trouble myself with questions any more and accept the invitation. The only disadvantage, though, was the expense. I was saving money for one cause to return one day to my parents and to my village, having some money in my sleeves for them and this unanticipated invitation would diminish my pocket and my efforts...

However, if I had known what would follow at this party, and whom I was gnng to meet there,. I would definitely have bought the most elegant, most expensive attire in Venice.

I arrived at the Venetian mansion with Francis. It was the first time I had entered such a majestic mansion. There were huge chandeliers hanging from the ceilings and the corridors were embellished with priceless works of art. I was utterly impressed. Francis detected the bewilderment that was imprinted on my face for he was observing me all the time and could not hide his smile.

The servants, holding silver candlesticks in their hands and with subservient courtesies, showed us to the ballroom where there were hundreds of guests. All these wonderful things distracted my thoughts and the only thing that occupied my mind was how to act appropriately in such circumstances.

At last we saw our host after passing through numerous halls to reach him. He was standing in the middle of a spacious room talking to one of his guests.

Francis after a solemn bow that I imitated clumsily introduced me to the Admiral.

Young Leonar, the soul and the body of our correspondence department. His wisdom, Andrea Griti.' That is how Francis introduced us to each other.

Griti looked at me as if weighing me up and then he smiled.

'I know, I know,' he said. 'He is already well known for his services to our democracy.'

He weighed me up again with his eyes and looked content. I had worn my gentle, kind and solemn smile that could fool anyone, even his wisdom. I did not know then that I would meet this man again along with his companion Antonio Grimaldi, as he was introduced to me years later, on a rival camp.

'Francis,' he said, after exchanging the customary compliments with the bishop. 'Why don't we use him in our decoding service? I am sure he will prove to be very useful there. We need people like him to decipher the messages sent by our men in the Gate.'

Francis made a grimace that suggested annoyance for he never liked people who advised him on his duties.

'I think it's still premature,' he uttered, behind a grin.

'Ah, if you are hinting at matters of trust, I am sure Leonar meets our requirements perfectly. I remember you mentioning something about his Gentile origin.'

At that point I sent a look full of queries to my mentor.

Yes, indeed. His mother is a descendant of the Doge Tomasso Montsenigo's family.'

Once more in my life I was flabbergasted. Listening to Francis talking about my origin and roots was something that surpassed my wildest imagination... Nevertheless, he altogether avoided mentioning my father's origin and roots.

'So, what are you waiting for?' Griti insisted, still smiling and still content. 'He is one of us and he is an exceptional case. With his knowledge and experience, Leonar will become indispensable.'

Yes, yes, of course. I see your point,' Francis muttered, trying hard to change the subject.

At this critical point, a hand grabbed my arm from behind and dragged me farther away from the company of the three men.

'If I had left you there you would die of boredom!'

I was startled. I turned my head to see who was pulling me so eagerly by my arm, and there she was, a blonde angel with deep blue eyes, a fair complexion and dressed in sheer pink.

'My name is Isabelle,' she introduced herself to me whilst I was still startled and captivated by her beauty. 'My origin is noble too. I come from... Never mind where I come from, the point is that I am Griti's nie* e.'

I introduced myself, whispering my name Leonar whilst trying to renounce the circumspect attitude I had had so far before I had laid eyes on her.

'Where have you been all this time? Have they been hiding you some place? Why have we never been introduced before?' she asked, with a dazzling smile.

I did not dare speak of my humid, tiny lair.

'I have been very busy working in my office. I do not go out much,' I explained. Then I remembered her name. 'Isabelle... It is your name, isn't it?' I asked her, shyly.

'Yes, why, don't you like it?'

- 'Of course I do. Isabelle is also the name of my mother,' I said, very moved.

'That is a coincidence that can bring us even closer to each other. They say that sons harbor a special kind of love for their mothers. They even compare them to their wives to the disadvantage of the latter,'

'A wife is destined to come second by nature,' I explained eloquently.

'What unfortunate creatures we are!'

'Yes, but you win your first place again, when you have your own sons. That is your compensation your reward for your patience.'

'You are very eloquent, young man. I like the way you have put it.'

'Thank you,' I answered with gratification and went on to impress her even more. 'Tonight's party was for me a panacea for the gloomy days I spend in the office.'

Isabelle was ecstatic. I was not sure if she understood the word panacea but the sound of the word instigated her sheer admiration and respect. 'You know, you have wonderful green eyes.'

Again the picture of my mother's face flashed into my mind she had lovely green eyes too. However, I had never noticed the colour of my eyes and I wondered why women always notice the colour of a man's eyes first.

'You have lovely blue eyes too,' I remarked politely.

'Do not be so hasty to return commendation,' she said, rather satisfied with the compliment I had given her. 'I hope in the future we will have the chance to discuss more important matters that the colour of eyes, though. Perhaps when we know each other better.'

I was paralysed. The girl was exceptionally beautiful and my heart's violent leaping confirmed this fact. It was the kind of leaping that I had never experienced before in my life. I was ready to assure her that we would definitely know each other better, when a young man overbearingly approached us,,grabbed Isabelle's hand with the pretext that he had something important to tell her and took her away from me. At that moment I hated that young man with all my heart. I had finally reached the well to quench my thirst but I could not even touch the bucket... However, something deep inside me appeased my anger and urged me that Isabelle was a consistent woman and that she would definitely keep her promise.

A few moments later I saw a servant advance towards the host and whisper something in his ear. Our host nodded as if he was agreeing with something and as soon as the servant retreated, he announced that dinner was ready to be served and that we all had to move to the diningroom.

While Griti was leading his guests to the diningroom, Francis came to me and said:

You shall sit next to me at the table. You have to be careful with your behavior and if you have any queries about the feasting etiquette you should ask me first Poor Francis. He was worried about my table manners, but I knew how to behave. My mother had taught me in my village

Paleokipos. Paleokipos! It had indeed been so long since I had brought it to my mind and memory that it felt ages away.

The host assumed his place at the head of the table and so did the guests according to their rank in the society of Venice. Francis and I were seated on the farthest end of the table, a fortunate position for myself for Isabelle was sitting right there on the opposite side. I did not care about the social hierarchy any more, it was enough for me to be able to see her at such close distance. The only thing that disquieted me though, was the fact that the young man who had stolen her away from me a short while ago was sitting by her side.

In my attempt to keep my eyes from her face, I kept them hooked upon my host. A servant had brought him a silver flask filled with white wine, he then filled his glass with the contents of the flask and waited there patiently.

Griti took the glass in his hand, sniffed in it, and then extended his red tongue into the contents. He wet his tongue with the wine and finally emptied the glass's contents into his mouth. Soon after the ritual was over, the servant served the wine to the guests, only to refill the host's glass with fresh wine. I observed the ritual with eyes wide open and Francis did not fail to notice my curious look.

You know...' he whispered, whilst fidgeting with his glass using the fingers of his right hand. 'This is a very old custom. The host tastes the wine to make sure it is not sour. Once he approves of its taste, he drinks it up, to prove that is also not poisoned.'

I looked at Francis with amazement.

'That, I never suspected!' I said.

Yes, I know. You see, in the past, our democracy used to get rid of undesirable politicians and family enemies at dinner parties, by poisoning them with wine. On that account, the host demonstrates his good intentions to his guests. He confirms that the wine is not poisoned and that they can drink as much as they wish, fearing nothing. Once the contents of the first jug are consumed, the trial process will be repeated. It has become a custom, my boy...'

Francis emphasised the word 'custom' with a shrewd grin. I did not pay much attention to his explanation, though, as I had turned my eyes to Isabelle. When Francis caught me doing so, his grin was instantly obliterated and he frowned. However, he continued.

'We shall start with white wine, as fish is served first. Then red wine will follow... They will pour it into that second glass you have in front of you, when the meat is served.'

Francis kept instructing me during the meal. He did so to protect himself in case I behaved clumsily, especially now that my attention was absorbed in Isabelle and her companion. But Isabelle was not my only concern at that point for I was burning with desire to know what else Francis knew about my mother, that I did not. However, the discussion at the head of the table was heated after the first glasses of wine, which made it impossible for me to pose Francis any questions about that matter.

I heard the dignitaries talking about a possible war that would break out between Venice and Turkey again and about the preparations they had to make so that they would 'teach them a good lesson'.

It is man's nature to talk about war when he is at peace and about peace when he is at war. He is never content...

'We have to face the apostates and renegades,' I heard Griti say. 'It is absolutely irrational for Constantine Paleologo's posterity to support and assist the sultan who massacred his own people.'

Yes, that is so very true,' Grimaldi agreed. 'Do you remember that vesir, Mezih Pasha, the first cousin to Paleologos? He caused us a lot of trouble...'

'He almost conquered the knights and occupied the island of Rhodes,' Griti added. 'Fortunately his efforts were unsuccessful. He deserved the appalling death the sultan had reserved for him on his return to Constantinople.'

Yes, but the rest of his relatives remained at his service,' said one of the guests whose name I do not quite remember any more.

'At least they did not turn against us,' said Griti. 'They only made sure they were safe and protected.'

'Don't we have a lady by the name of Anna Paleologina in Venice?' somebody asked.

Yes,' Griti, who looked more knowledgeable and informed than the rest of us, affirmed. 'She is the daughter of the Greek Admiral Lukas Notaras and the fiancee of the last emperor. She is only concerned with art and nothing except art. Perhaps her only obsession is to build an Orthodox Church in Venice, but she can dream on as we shall never allow such a thing to happen... At the time being, she is confined to her mansion and does not receive any guests.'

'And what about the brothers of Constantine?'

'They all lead an imprudent life,' said Griti. 'One of them, Dimitrios, received a feu and a manor from the sultan in Thrace and led a very extravagant life. He embraced reclusive life only a few months before he died in Andrianoupolis, in 1470. The other one, Thomas, took the skull of Saint Andreas from Patra and found refuge in Rome, where Pope Pius granted him a handsome reward. He died there in 1465. The firstborn of his two sons, who was also named Thomas, after his father, settled in Rome where he was granted the title Lord of Morias.18 Later on, he bequeathed the title of the Byzantine throne to Ferdinand the Catholic and Isabelle of Castille. The second one, Manuil, returned to Constantinople, where the sultan received him with great honors and respect and granted him a generous pension as well as a good number of servants. He had two sons with his two slaves: Ioannis, who remained Christian, and the other one Andreas converted to Islam and was renamed Mehmed'

'Mehmed!' most of the guests exclaimed with full mouths.

Yes, he still lives in Constantinople leading an overindulgent kind of life. They all sold their privileges of the Byzantine throne in exchange for their safety, pleasure and fortune.'

I was silently listening to all this gossip and I felt really uneasy. I had learned all about these occurrences and people when I was still a student at the school in Mitilini, but I did not know so many details. I thought of the deplorable, miserable people in my village who were forced, by circumstances, to renounce their religion to be able to survive in those agitated years, and I understood them completely. What kind of example or preceding ideals did these very simple and helpless people have to be able to raise objections against their persecutors from their lords.

But at this moment, Isabelle distracted me from my distressful thoughts.

'I see that you got absorbed in this talk. You do not pay any attention to us any more...'

'Yes, I don't, I mean no... It is just that I am so very interested in the history of my native country.'

'You are from Turkey, aren't you?' exclaimed the repugnant young man next to her.

'Leonar is a Venetian, and from a noble family too.' Isabelle intervened to rescue me.

I did not raise any objections, besides, I felt that I was suffocating in that place and wished to leave as soon as I could. I restlessly sat on my seat, as if it had nails on. Luckily, my torment did not last long for it was soon put to an end when the host stood up, signalling to his guests that it was time for him to depart.

We all arose from our seats and passed through the ballroom first before we made for the main entrance of the mansion. There, in the midst of grandiloquent and pretentious valedictions and wishes that this magnificent gathering would soon be repeated, Isabelle slipped through the guests and stood right by my side.

'I hope we shall see you again, Leonar...' she whispered in my ear. 'I shall call you one day to visit me at home after work. I shall be very happy to see you again... And you, will you be happy too?'

'I shall definitely be very happy, Isabelle,' I said, with a stupid expression on my face and then, gathering all my efforts and audacity, I dared to asked, *When will that be?'

'When it will be,' Isabelle answered, with a giggling laugh.

She was a woman and she already knew her role, whilst I was still an inexperienced adolescent...

Francis and I left Griti's mansion together but on our way we did not exchange one word, until we reached the lodgings where I was renting a room.

'Listen, my boy... Do not take everything you hear into serious account. It is just prattle, it is not worth taking into consideration. However, it all belongs to the past now and we want to look forward to the future. Concentrate on your work and maybe you will be able to excel in it more than you think...'

He spoke in a paternal way and I nodded in acquiescence. Francis continued affecting his shrewd smile.

'And Isabelle, isn't she a marvellously goodlooking girl?'

I did not know what to say.

'Well, you heard what Griti said,' Francis continued, without giving me the chance to answer. 'One of these days you shall also be accepted in the cryptographic service and there you must be absolutely cautious, discreet and secretive. If a word ever slips from your mouth about what is happening in that domain, the next day you will be floating, breathless, on the surface of the water of one of the canals. Have I made myself clear?'

Yes, Sir, you have,' I said, to get rid of Francis and all the heavy thoughts that were tormenting my mind.

I wished I could rest peacefully in my bed and dream of Isabelle. I thought that this was the only antidote to all the poisonous talk I had just heard at that table...

The first days in the new service were not as difficult as I had been warned. Nevertheless, although the services of translation and those of cryptography were interrelated, the secretiveness that prevailed in the latter surpassed my imagination as a veil of mystery and silence covered everything.

From my very first day, my colleagues made it clear to me that I should not ask questions that I had to be content with the things they taught me and I should never take the initiative. Such an action would raise suspicion that would result in unknown and perilous consequences.

Since the very first moment that I set foot in the service, I sensed that I was being watched closely. I felt as if an invisible eye was watching me, recording my movements every single one even those that had to do with my very private or personal needs. But this did not really bother me at all for the fact that there was somebody who was keeping an eye on me all the time actually flattered me. It was not until they saw me entering Isabelle's house that they were convinced about my loyalty to our gallant democracy.

During my work in the service I had the chance to acquire knowledge in an area that so far was unfamiliar to me. The cryptographic service was utterly fascinating and intriguing, and I was thrilled to be working there as it stimulated a new kind of interest in me. I soon realized that cryptography and especially its decoding procedures was a very captivating science.

I started with the very simple method of replacing a letter with the one that followed it in the alphabet; for example, A was always replaced by B, B was replaced by C, and so on and so forth until you reached Z, which would be replaced by A... Consequently, the word 'doge' would be written 'ephf, and 'Venice' would appear as, 'Wfokdf

There were also some more complicated methods; for example, each letter in a word had to be replaced by the one after the next. Or you could write a very simple word by placing a number that corresponded to the letter in the alphabet next to each letter.

There were numerous even more complex decoding methods for highly confidential documents or messages sent to us by our people in Constantinople and other Turkish cities. There was also a decoding device that was invented in 1470 by the architect Leon Batiste Albert! from Florence. This device had disks on, which one could replace according to the cryptographic code one used.

At that time cryptography was a very popular business. It was an effective method that was not only used by the government but also by merchants to keep their activities safeguarded from prying rivals and competitors.

Coming back to my room one day a few days after I had started my new job I found a message under my door. It was not addressed, but it was definitely sent by Isabelle. Apparently she had sent it with one of the servants who had slipped it under the door. Isabelle was inviting me to her house the following day in the evening.

Dressed in my new suit, I reached her manor at the appointed time. It was not as impressive as that of her uncle's, but it definitely had its superfluous comforts.

She received me at the door with a warm, cordial, welcoming smile and she walked me to the parlour where many of her friends had already gathered. At the same time, her parents and their friends were sitting in the main parlour adjacent to ours.

She introduced me as her 'best friend' to her parents and friends, and I soon realized that I stimulated the interest of many of her guests. Needless to say, my own attention, of course, was entirely dedicated to my hostess, Isabelle. I remained there for almost two hours and then left with everyone else. While I was saying goodbye to Isabelle, she asked me if I had enjoyed myself and if I wished to come back. I expressed my gratification for her kind invitation and my earnest desire to return and indeed that was something I did repeatedly after that time.

Her invitations kept reaching my room on a daily basis for almost a month and I kept accepting them with indulgence and delight, until that rainy afternoon when, challenging the weather conditions and the torrential rain, I decided to call at her house so as not to miss seeing her that day.

I was the only one who managed to honor her invitation, as the rest of the guests were discouraged by the storm, thus I had the chance to monopolise her company and conversation. She was always courteous and amiable towards me but on that day she was exceptionally gracious.

We sat on the sofa very close to each other. Isabelle started talking to me about one of her trips to Rome and the Vatican when suddenly I felt her hand fondling my knee. Inspired by her generous gesture, I dared to hesitantly extend my arm and place my hand over hers whilst recounting an imaginative trip to a fictitious island I presumably had been to. Isabelle was enchanted by the adventures I narrated to her and when I had finished my story, she begged me to continue. She was now rubbing my thigh with more ardour, while my hand, still holding hers, was encouraging an upward movement...

This very intimate and fervent encounter was abruptly interrupted by a servant who appeared at the door, to inform his mistress about the weather that was aggravated by a violent storm that almost shook the foundations of the house.

'Our guest will spend the night here,' she said. 'He cannot possibly go out in such a terrible storm. He shall sleep in the guest room.' Then she turned and looked at me with an alluring look. My face was glowing with both passion and bashfulness, but I managed to smile that was the most auspicious answer she could get from me.

'Good. Make sure the guest room is appropriately prepared to receive our guest and let me know when everything is ready.'

The servant bowed politely and hurriedly withdrew to execute Isabelle's command.

.. 'Do you like the idea of spending the night in my house?' she asked me playfully, when we were alone.

'I would like us to sleep in the same room,' I dared to say, shivering from head to toe. I could not believe that I was able to utter with such impertinence to an innocent young girl who had the kindness to offer me hospitality on such a horrible night.

'You can never know,' she said, with a heartening smile. You can never know what the future may bring you.'

How cc aid I know? If I had known then, or even some time later, ι laybe things would have taken a different turn maybe I would have been a different person now. But back then I did not have the disposition for this kind of philosophical thought. I only saw Isabelle's wish to keep me in her house. Her parents had withdrawn to their quarters and we were all alone in that same room.

The servant was soon back, holding the candlestick in his hand ready to show me to my room. I stooped to kiss Isabelle's cheek goodnight but at that moment she turned her head slightly and heavens, my lips touched hers! My heart almost shattered into pieces, but the long walk in the endless corridors of the manor, following that servant, brought me to my senses.

I said goodnight to the servant and closed the door. It was then that I noticed there was no key in the keyhole, but then I thought that people who belong to the same family would not lock themselves in their rooms.

I completely undressed myself and slipped into the soft bed, hoping I would dream of Isabelle once more, but that night, thinking of Isabelle whilst lying naked in a bed that belonged to her house, brought a lustful feeling that was utterly new to me.

I had blown out the candle and was looking at the turbulent sky through the window. The lightning slashed the sky and every time it did so, the room was adequately lit. The thunderbolts did not really annoy me at all, and despite their boisterous sound I managed to discern a faint screeching sound coming from the door. I was terrified, and as I was lying there naked I felt helpless and powerless. What would I do in case of a possible attack? That was the first thought that crossed my mind at that moment.

I pulled the bedclothes over my head to protect myself from the unknown enemy, and damn my luck, there was not even one thunderbolt at that moment to light up my room and help me see who the visitor was...

'Who is there?' I asked, almost out of breath. Who is there?'

'Did I scare you?'

The voice came right over my head, but I recognised it at once. The thunderbolt that finally condescended to strike at that moment revealed my angel in her transparent nightgown. She was standing right over my head looking at me with an alluring smile.

'Am I so frightful?'

'No, of course not, but...'

'You did not expect me?'

'I was hoping you would come but I did not expect it would be...'

'I came to see if you need something. Do you need an extra cover?'

'No thank you... I do not need anything, thank you,' I muttered politely.

'Oh!' she said, expressing disappointment. 'So, you do not need anything...'

The tone of her voice helped me to understand the reason for her visit.

'As a matter of fact I do feel a little cold,' I said, in my attempt to atone for my mistake.

'Then why don't you make room for me? If you let me share your bed, I can warm you up.' And without expecting any answer she got into my bed, under the same cover.

What followed in that very intimate encounter is not to be recounted in a confession. The only thing I can mention though, is that Isabelle was a fascinating woman, a woman who crouched like a puppy at a man's feet and then attacked ferociously like a wild cat. From one moment to the next she would transform into an experienced rider who knew how to tame an unbridled horse. She would not rest a moment... I followed her games, obediently and subdued. One moment I v is the master who governed her body and the next, a slave who yielded to the feral wishes of his mistress...

Everything about her was spherical her breasts, her tummy and her buttocks. You could slip smoothly upon them and find yourself falling to the floor. She was the kind of woman who, when you touched her, always had this feeling of roundness... and it was a feeling that elevated my existence and placed it in the sky next to the highest stars. I felt I was the master of the spherical universe which was the embodiment of Isabelle...

She disappeared before daybreak, and when the sun shone brightly in the sky, I got out of bed to get dressed. At that moment the servant with the expressionless face came in to show me to the door. He seemed to know everything and just pretended he understood nothing. I did not care though about what he did or did not know I was definitely in love with Isabelle.

Two days later, Isabelle invited me to her manor.again. When I reached the house I was hoping that I would be her only guest once more, but to my disappointment the house was seething with people. How could I keep her away from this crowd? However, Isabelle had changed for she looked distant and did not give me the slightest attention. That day I was not her 'best friend', I was just one of many acquaintances she had invited, and that was something that insulted me and wounded my heart...

The whole evening was spent in that boring and heavy atmosphere. When most of the guests left having run out of patience I made my way to the door. I was exasperated and confused by her behavior, but Isabelle came to me with a bright smile.

'I see you are not happy today. What is the matter?' she asked.

'How could I be happy? Why should I be happy?' I asked her.

You should be happy, because I have a surprise for you,' she said, with a cunning smile. You must leave now and be back in an hour. I will be waiting for you at the back door of the manor. You will recognize it easily as it is small and narrow. I will keep it unlocked for you. Leave the rest to me, but be careful, you shall return only when you hear the bell of Saint Mark. Do not forget what i have told you.'

I repressed my enthusiasm and my excitement deeply inside me. My heart was beating frantically, causing my chest to shake violently. I was even afraid that the beats of my heart would betray me and that the remaining guests in the house would be able to hear them, so I made for the street as quickly as possible. I did not walk on the paved streets of Venice, I jumped and ran like a little boy. If anyone was there to watch me, they would definitely have thought I was crazy. I knew that my superiors had ceased their surveillance for some time now as my regular visits to the house of Griti's niece had lifted all suspicion from me.

Time went by at a snail's pace. It seemed like a century to me more than a century... What is a century? The moment in which somebody has to wait for the utmost of pleasures... Human time is relevant, how could life be in a world without time?

I even got anxious and concerned about the bellringer of Saint Mark. I hoped that the wretched man had not tripped over in the belfry and was lying there helpless, unable to fulfil his task or had not overslept, forgetting to ring the bell...

All these thoughts crossed my mind whilst waiting for that glorious moment when I would meet with Isabelle alone...

Anyway, the bellringer was generous enough to ring the bell on time. I had never been more jubilant or exulted in my life before, not even on Easter Day in my village. I ran like a lunatic in the streets of Venice until I reached the little door of the mansion of Isabelle. I pushed it gently, as if I was afraid to break it, and I opened it ajar, then I lowered my head and passed through it to a long narrow corridor. I kept my head lowered as I had the sense that the ceiling was also very low I am not sure if it was and made my way in the darkness.

In that same darkness, a soft hand touched mine.

'Shh, do not say a word,' I heard Isabelle whispering. 'Just follow me to where I am taking you. Be careful, and watch your step. Please do not make any noise.'

I followed her like a faithful dog, to find myself going directly into her room this time... It was a spacious room with a carved wooden bed, which I soon found myself lying in. I could not make out anything else, not only because the candle was blown out, but also because all my senses perceived nothing but her existence next to me...

The bed was big enough for us... In a short while it had become a field of battle, a battle filled with pleasures and delight that overflowed both my body and my soul and gave me the sense of immense strength and power every time Isabelle breathed out that lustful sigh of exhilaration and satisfaction...

Before dawn following Isabelle's instructions once more 1 was fumbling my way back...

These secret meetings continued for many months. In the evenings I saw her in her parlour and at night in her bed.

In the mornings I would return to my service enlivened and revived. My body was brimful with euphoria and my head was filled with new ideas concerning my work.

I started inventing my own cryptographic methods, more complicated and more ingenious than the ones my colleagues used; codes that conveyed messages of love or commercial information, but in fact they hid very important government secrets. Their simplicity and straightforwardness did not stir the suspicions of the enemy, so they did not try to decode or decipher them.

My superiors were ecstatic about me. I won their trust and admiration and they soon granted me the liberty of reading the most confidential documents, since I was the only one who could decode them. There was nothing left for them to hide from me any more.

One day Francis visited me at the service. It was a long time since I had last seen him, due to the fact that I was always engrossed in my work and he made sure he put things in their correct order.

'You have to accompany me to London,' he said peremptorily. 'We have a very important meeting to attend there as very considerable issues about our region must be deliberated. England's power is expanding fast and we must pursue their partnership.'

'I do not think I would be of much help over there. You already know the codes, you may easily—'

He did not let me finish my sentence. His angry look forced me to stop. It was clear that he would not accept any objections especially from his former 'apprentice', even if he had now won the trust of the authorities.

'You will come with me,' he pointed out, bluntly. 'I will have confidential parleys and you are the only person who can keep the records for the proceedings.'

Professional progress has its advantages but also its drawbacks, I thought.

In Isabelle's bed that night, I confided in her, telling her all my worries and fears about my pending absence.

'Do not worry,' she said. 'I shall wait for you here.'

But how silly and gullible I was. I should have known that women were not to be trusted that easily... Forgive me Lord, I know they are also Your creatures but becaus * of her, I suffered immensely...

I left for England with Francis. We reached London after twenty days of travelling on the road for during our trip, we changed carts and horses more than three or four times. Not even carts and horses tolerated the dusty roads that were filled with stones and boulders.

In London, we were accommodated at the Tower that overlooked the Thames. I was so disappointed to see how unrefined the people were there. Their conversations were held in high tones and their gestures and reactions were unpredictable, especially when they ran out of patience. Their entertainment would get wild and grotesque after the first glasses of wine, and they would even draw daggers at the slightest provocation.

The Tower was surrounded by little houses where the guards of the Tower lived and a bit farther away the rest of the people inhabited small houses that looked more like shacks. All the doors if there were any were wide open and the poultry of the households chicken and ducks were roaming free on the premises. The freezing wind was blowing unremittingly. As there were no sewers or a drainage system, the crud and the refuse of the inhabitants came out through holes in the walls of the Tower or was dumped in the ground. Therefore, when the northern wind blew, the stench inside the tower was unbearable.

My reaction to all this was perceived by our hosts, since I did not possess Francis's diplomatic aptitude to conceal my real feelings.

To most of the people there, I was a haughty and arrogant young man, and this had unknown consequences for my safety. Luckily Francis's meetings were soon at an end and we left for our base with all the honors.

We barely exchanged a conversation during our return tri I was absorbed in my reveries and daydreams about my reunion with Isabelle and I did not wish to disturb the serenity that I was enveloped in once more. Francis did not stop scrutinizing my face inquisitively to establish the fact that I had changed so much since the time when he had first met me at the Catholic school in Mitilini.

Our arrival at Venice was a great relief after such a long and exhausting trip. I was yearning for the moment when I would see Isabelle again. Since the first day of my arrival, I kept walking aimlessly in the narrow streets of Venice and around her house like a famished dog that was looking for a bone to chew on. I waited outside the main entrance of her mansion, and by the little back door that I had entered so 'many times holding her soft arm. I waited for her to appear, or send some sort of signal, but there was no trace of her anywhere.

In the beginning I justified her attitude by convincing myself that she did not wish to expose her feelings towards me so quickly after my return, but, when two long weeks had passed, her certain indifference confirmed my suspicions.

At first I neglected my work and myself. I ate little, as I had no appetite for food; I scarcely talked to anyone, as I was in no mood for conversation and worst of all I had no more ideas about ciphering or deciphering codes. My colleagues would look at me with curiosity but no one dared to ask what it was that troubled me.

One afternoon I armed myself with all the courage that was left in me and knocked at her door. The servant, who knew me so well from my previous visits, answered the door and coldly announced that Miss Isabelle was busy and she could not see me. He also had the audacity to close the door in my face as soon as he had finished speaking, depriving me of my chance to pose a question.

I repeated this attempt two days later, but the answer was the same, and even more abrupt. The banging of the door as it cruelly closed in my face shattered my heart and broke it into a thousand pieces...

A few days after my last unsuccessful effort, when in my office I received a note from Isabelle that same ill-humored servant of hers delivered it to me in which she was inviting me to her house, early that same afternoon.

I was overwhelmed by this unanticipated invitation. I left the service early that day and I went to my room. I put on my new clothes and set off for her house, although it was still noon. Time seemed endless again and this longwinded wait gave birth to negative thoughts, which I tried so hard to expel from my burdened head... Why did she invite me to her house at such a time? Why didn't she ask me to meet her at the back door late in the night as before? I low could the time be consumed when I had run out of patience?

I tried to give answers to my questions, and whilst doing so, I discovered that the agony which was buried deep inside me was emerging to the surface and that my pessimistic thoughts were about to affect my future as well as my relationship with her. I was so frightened that all my doubts and scruples about her might be justified.

Time went by, and at last I made my way to her mansion. The servant opened the door and showed me to the parlor where Isabelle was waiting for me. Now when I recollect their facial expressions even though so many years have passed I realize how identical they were; both of them were as cold as the icebergs at the North Pole.

'Well...' Isabelle said first. 'Welcome back. I hope you had a good time on your trip.'

I looked around and behind me. No, she was talking to me, as the servant had gone and there was nobody else in the room except me. However, she talked to me as if I were a stranger; somebody she only met that day; somebody with whom she did not share cherished moments of love, affection and lust.

I did not grant her any answer, or rather; I could not grant her any answer. She continued, ignoring my condition and not waiting for my reply.

'I am glad you responded to my invitation,' she went on. 'I wished to see you...'

Blood ran warm in my veins once more. Yes, I was wrong I was too hasty to misjudge her and draw conclusions. She wished to see me so my premonition was all wrong. Nevertheless, an insidious little creature was still gnawing at my innermost existence.

'I wished to see you, to announce an exhilarating piece of news.'

I kept looking at her with my eyes wide open.

'I got engaged and soon I will be married...'

My apprehension was justified after all and my presentiment came out victorious and triumphant. My knees were paralyzed, but there was no chair behind me to rescue or sustain me. She had planned that I would helplessly stand in the middle of a room, whilst chairs had their backs stuck to the walls! Yes, Isabelle had planned it all. She did not want this meeting to last longer than two minutes.

'But... but this is not possible... Isabelle, how could you?' I managed to utter despite my plight.

'I do not really understand you, my dear. I am quite shocked by your reaction. You know very well that I am fond of you and I will always be. But matrimony has nothing to do with fondness. We shall certainly see each other again, and you must know that I will always remember you in the best possible way...'

The scenes of love and our games crossed my mind like a flash of light. If she could remember all these she would not talk like that, I thought. Perhaps I did not quite understand.

'But Isabelle... You... to me... you are—'

'I know, I know,' she interrupted me. 'I was your best friend, once, but now I will turn into a good memory. Or don't you have a good memory,

Leonar? Men do not usually have good memories, you see.'

'Isabelle, what are you hinting at?' I asked her, overpowered by indignation.

'But of course. Don't you represent the polygamous practice? Especially you... Eastern men...'

She uttered the last phrase with contempt and a good portion of disgust, but I did not pay any attention to that at that time.

'Isabelle...'

'Come, come now, Leonar,' she said coldly. 'Do not act like a little boy. We had such a good time together, but what we had between ourselves has to end here. There is no future in it... You are better off without me. Keep your memories if you wish...'

I was determined to defend myself, but when the words reached my lips they evaporated and disappeared.

'Leonar, the time has come to say goodbye. Soon my fiancé will be here and it is not appropriate that he finds you. Do not hate me, though. I would rather you remembered me with fondness and love. Remember the affection I gave you all those nights... Remember, Leonar, all the good times we spent together. It will be the best for both of us...'

Her voice had softened slightly, but her irrevocable decision was clearly drawn on her expressionless face. She signaled to the servant who had just come to the door and said unfeelingly:

'Show him to the door... Goodbye, Leonar.'

Then Isabelle left her seat and approached me, and stepping on the tips of her shoes to reach my face she gave me a kiss on the cheek.

'Goodbye...' she repeated.

Then she suddenly turned her back and left, running from the room. I was stunned and speechless, empty of any kind of thoughts, for I had never expected such a development. Why did I leave Venice in the first place? It is damned Francis who is to blame, it is his fault, I thought... I was ready to curse him once more when a heavy hand touched my shoulder it was the hand of the servant.

'Do you want me to walk you to the door, Sir?' he asked me, politely this time.

Perhaps he had a warmer heart than his mistress, for on his face, I saw a faint sign of compassion and sympathy.

I left the mansion but did not return home. I lurked in the darkness, not far away from the house, and watched the main entrance. Isabelle had mentioned that her fiancé was soon coming to visit her and I wanted to find out who he was. I did not have to wait long.

A short while later I saw him coming. It was that foolish young man who had been sitting next to her at the table... But was he to blame? I was the one who should have been more careful when handling the sophisticated society of Venice 1 should have known better. I should have guessed that there was no way that two people from different social backgrounds could be together for more than an adventure. Marriages in that kind of hypocritical society were carried out like business transactions.

I left as if I was chased by my fate. It was already dark and I did not know where to go. My little room would seem like a prison after the heartless, cruel sentence that Isabelle had imposed upon me, so I decided to return to the service.

When I entered my office, I saw Francis's shadow.

'Where have you been all afternoon?' he asked me, with reproof. 'I was waiting for you for over an hour.'

'I went out for a walk. I was suffocating in here and I needed some air.'

Francis looked suspicious once more but did not comment on my pretext. It seemed that he had more important problems to attend to than my inexcusable absence.

'I came to inform you that...' he paused for a short moment and then continued with a slightly trembling voice that I alone could detect. *We heard from a reliable source that... that there had been an attack in Lesvos.'

'Lesvos!'

Yes, and particularly against your village, Paleokipos.'

'What kind of attack? By whom?' I cried, in panic.

Francis maintained a kind of culpable silence.

'Please, speak to me.' I urged him to speak, grabbing him by his shoulders. 'What about my parents?'

'It is about them...' he said, with a sigh of relief because he did not have to mention them first. 'We do not know, nobody knows for sure what happened. It seems that a few houses were burnt down and a few people were killed.'

'And what about my mother... my father?'

'I do not know. As you may understand, the attack took place two or three weeks ago. There has been some kind of fray between the pirates and the natives. That is all I know so please be patient. We shall definitely enquire about it and know more...'

Patient. How could I be patient? I almost lost my senses. Patience was not a word I knew at that critical moment.

'I have to know!' I told him with determination. 'I have to know.'

'I shall make the appropriate enquiries on your behalf. Just maintain your faith and composure and we shall soon know what we must do.'

Francis rushed to the door couriers do run to the door, once they have delivered their ill-omened messages.

At the threshold he stopped and said to me, 'I shall come back in the morning. I hope I will know more tomorrow.'

Without saying goodbye he disappeared. He ran as if the Erinyes were chasing him in a bad dream.

I stayed alone in my office trying to assemble my thoughts and wondering what might have happened in Paleokipos. He had talked about pirates, and natives in both cases my father must have been involved. He was a native who also had business dealings with pirates. And sweet Mother, where could she be now? The answer to the last question was never granted.

I panicked. I dashed outside and aimlessly drifted along the humid streets of Venice, shattered and overwhelmed. At some point I thought of entering a tavern to drink a glass of wine and soothe my pain for fate had shocked me twice on the same day wine might help me. However, I had no money in my pockets so I ran to my room, took a small purse where I kept all my savings and ran back into the street. Nothing could keep me inside.

I reached the docks with the anchored ships and entered the first tavern I found on my way. I ordered wine and was brought a very poor quality red liquid it was that horrible wine they gave to the drunken seamen. I drank the first glass, then the second, and when I gulped the third, I felt the tension freeing my body as my senses were getting numb... I left the tavern and staggered along the quay. The first thought that occurred to me was to jump in the filthy waters of the canal and drown myself to death.

'Hey... Young man!' I heard a hoarse voice coming from a Spanish galliot[1] that was moored right where I was standing. 'If you jump here you will fall right into, my hold it's wide open, you see. Why don't you drown yourself farther away from my galley? They will surely find you like a frozen carcass, without giving me the trouble!' Then I heard loud resonant laughter following those words.

I turned my head towards the direction of the voice and saw a bulky, middle-aged man sitting on a barrel, in the stern of his ship.

'And who are you, may I ask?' I asked him, with the audacity of a drunkard.

'The skipper of the Spanish galliot that is sailing to the island of Chios at dawn.

---

[1] A small fast galley used by pirates in the Mediterranean.

'To the island of Chios?' I asked him, as if I was in the middle of a dream.

'And where do you know Chios from, young man?'

'It is none of your business. Will you take me with you?'

'I can't see why not if you pay me.'

'How much do you charge?'

'Three ducats...' he replied shrewdly. 'And that is as long as you know how to mend ropes...'

'It is done,' I replied, without thinking about it twice. 'I shall mend your ropes and if I do not know how, you will teach me. I will do whatever you command.'

'Put the money in my hands first, young man. Hand it over to me and then you may jump aboard.'

I fumbled in my purse and carefully took out the amount, then I threw it to him. He caught the money in the air and spoke as he was counting it.

'All right then... Jump aboard. We shall set sail just before sunup.'

I jumped aboard and landed on a sack of hay that became my bed for the night and the rest of the voyage.

The following morning I was awoken by the first rays of the sun that fell on my face. I raised my head and I saw that we had already set sail and were in the open sea. I turned my head, but saw nothing but the horizon. A sigh was released from the depths of my soul, a sigh of bitterness, sadness and despair for I felt that I was cast away from the world.

That is how I waved goodbye to Venice...

Three

When we finally reached Evriaki, I found myself cursing gods and demons for the tragic fate they had preserved for me. Forgive me, merciful God, but that was just a human reaction for I had not realized then that Your world was different to that of ours and that Your justice had nothing to do with human justice...

I disembarked from the Spanish galliot at the port in Chios. During our voyage we looted smaller galliots so as not to run out of supplies, as the Catalonian skipper had bluntly put it, leaving the marauded seamen in the middle of the sea without any food. During our first raid, I zealously attempted to raise objections to their inhumane behavior, but the Catalonian skipper ordered two members of his crew to confine me in the ship's hold for three days without food or water supplies.

During my stay in that horrible hold, I chased famished rats so as not to die of infection in there. On the fourth day the skipper called me up on deck and tried to reason with me.

You see what would become of us if we hadn't stolen the food? We would become like those rats down there and then we would have to eat each other's guts...' That was the aftermath, which I had to accept wholeheartedly unless I wished to become food for the fish.

I did not dare to raise any more objections. I kept my mouth shut and my patience alert until we reached the island of Chios. When we finally reached the port, I ran to the first shop I found, sold my Frankish clothes and slipped in my old slacks again, although I did not wish to be recognized by my fellow villagers. I sailed to

Mitilini in a fishing boat and without delay ran to my village, Paleokipos.

When I approached the village I got restless and agitated when I saw that the first houses were burnt and as I reached my house my anxiety and apprehension culminated. It was burnt to ashes too, and there was nothing left of it. The little house was burnt to the core and none of my neighbors dared to come and inform me what had happened, or explain what had become of my parents. When they heard about my arrival they avoided meeting me altogether. Others would see me from afar and would change direction, apparently so as not to be put in the embarrassing position of having to inform me first.

After my persistence, and the blabbering of the more talkative ones, I learned what had happened. Spanish pirates they were most likely Spanish, they said attacked my parental house one day and killed my parents. They plundered everything they found useable and then set it on fire.

After the first general statements, my fellow villagers found the courage to go into more detail. My father had some business dealings with pirates and it was rumored that he owed them money. The pirates got angry with him as they demanded the money, and when he resisted they attacked him, raped my mother and then cruelly killed them both.

When I heard about the rape of my mother, a dagger pierced my heart so deeply that I felt it bleeding inside me. Death did not shatter me as much as her humiliation...

I could not bear to look at the scene any more. I was suffocating my mind was blurred and

I needed to breathe some air... I ran. I ran away from that appalling scene the remains of my home and my beloved parents and while I was roaming like a wild and hungry animal amongst the aged olive trees, I kept asking myself /Why, why, why has this happened to me?'

That was how I found myself in Evriaki, the haven of Paleokipos. I kept thinking of my mother's rape and I felt that I was losing my senses I could not get the thought out of my mind.

I protested to the sky and sea; I hurled stones at invisible enemies; I cursed gods and demons... I almost lost my mind.

It was then, dear God, that I renounced You. I renounced You for the grievance I felt and the savagery of Your own creatures.

Three days passed and I could not recover from the shock. I continued wandering around in the fields like a lunatic; still hungry and confused, and avoiding the sight of any human presence. I had become the hermit of the woods, driving passersby away from me...

That was my condition when Arouz found me. He silently sneaked up behind me and grabbed me by my neck, the same way he had grabbed the dog's neck in the past. But he did not whirl me over his head or hurl me on a stone. He put his strong arms around my head and held me firmly so that I would not run away.

'What is it with you? Is this how you are going to spend the rest of your life?'

I did not listen to a word he uttered. I started hitting his arms with all the strength that was left in me, to set myself free from his steel grip. The strange thing was that I found some sort of pleasure in beating him for I felt relief, even soothed as some of my pain was discharged upon him. But Arouz was as strong as a bull and my punches did not even touch him. He laughed and dragged me to the shore, then, jumping into the sea, he pulled me into the freezing waters of the bay and pushed my head into the water. After a few moments he pulled my head up again only to repeat the process three or four times.

Although at first I believed he would drown me 1 even wished he would do so I felt all the tension leaving my body. Then he eventually decided that I had had enough and took me out of the water.

'Isaac' He called to his younger brother whilst dragging me on the sand.

Arouz's brother, the second born son of Jacob, ran to us holding a small bundle in his hand. He must have been hiding somewhere behind a tree and waiting for his brother's call.

'Get up,' Arouz demanded, but as I was unable to move, he put his hands under my arms and made me sit on the ground. Then he took the bundle, untied its sides and took out a piece of dried bread and some olives and offered them to me.

'Eat,' he commanded.

The sight of food did not stir me a bit. Arouz snatched a piece of bread and stuffed it into my mouth. He was so forceful that he almost choked me to death!

I swallowed the first piece despite my will. The second piece I managed to chew somehow, while I relished the third piece.

'Drink that.'

Arouz had brought a small jug of wine. He forced the wine into my mouth too.

'Drink some more, it will bring you around.'

And he was right, the wine slackened my nerves and relaxed me, and before the contents of the jug were finished, I felt drowsy...

'Do you want to come with us? Do you wish to sleep at our house tonight?'

I rejected his offer with a decisive shake of my head. I was still so much in pain and I could not bear the presence of people around me, especially people I did not quite know, who would start bombarding me with questions about my misfortune.

'I see...he said, condescendingly. 'In that case I shall put you up in our father's fishing boat. Come...'

He pulled me by my hand and took me to his father's boat, which was dragged up on the shore. He opened the stern cabin that was spacious enough for me and pushed me in. He also pushed a small jib, which he had for strong winds when he could not heave up the big sail to the mast.

I instantly fell asleep.

Early in the morning Arouz came back with his brother Isaac.

'Wake up,' he called in his thunderous voice. 'The sun is almost up...'

I got out of the cabin with a stiff body and legs but with a clear mind. I walked to where the water licked the pebbles and I wet my face. The water and its saltiness helped me to regain my mindfulness.

'Do you feel better now?' Arouz asked me.

Yes, a lot better.'

'Good, because there is some talking we have to do...'

We talked. He did not ask me where I had been, or why I had disappeared without saying goodbye. He did not even ask about how I had felt when I saw my house had been burnt to ashes... He was mostly interested in my health and my present circumstances.

'So what are you planning to do from now on?' he asked me.

'Take revenge,' I replied, full of confidence. Arouz derided my decision.

'Take revenge? Where shall you find those rascals?' 'I do not know,' I said, full of despair.

'Come with me,' he suggested, after a few moments of musing and reflection. 'I am going to sell my father's jugs in the surrounding islands and will be back soon. Why don't you come with me on this trip?'

I did not give him any reply.

'And if we happen to come across those rascals on our way, we shall slaughter them like animals after we have skinned them alive! How do you feel about that?'

I did not pay much attention to his words then, but later on, much later on, when I recollected those words, I said to myself, We slaughtered and skinned so many Spaniards that it was not impossible that the culprits of that appalling crime were amongst those victims. That gave me satisfaction.

'If there is a chance that I will get my revenge, then I will come,' I roared.

They say, violence is the outcome of persecution, oppression and the injustice of the strong over the weak, and at that time I had come to verify that.

You will take revenge!' he affirmed, with a hopeful disposition. 'We shall set sail with the afternoon breeze...'

At noon the two brothers I had not seen Hizr since I had set foot on the island along with a brawny young man, Arouz's new comrade, came to see me. Arouz's comrade helped him with his trips to the surrounding islands and his name was Aidini. That same young man, Aidini, was going to be Aidini reis, who fought victorious battles against the Spaniards.

Arouz was holding a sack full of ashes. When I asked him what he needed the ashes for, he refused to give me an answer.

We set off on our voyage in the early afternoon. Isaac steered the boat, while Aidini and Arouz did not stop mending its hull and sails. I made myself useful in the boat too. I helped them with the few things I learnt from my voyage on the Spanish ship to Chios.

Before we left the Bay of Gera behind us, we stole some fish from the newly mended net of an unknown fisherman, so as to have fresh food for our trip. The faint rocking of the boat by the gentle sirocco breeze lulled my pain and my memories. The boat kept dancing rhythmically in the wind that was blowing on my face, taking my mind away from my troubled thoughts. I looked at the glittering water and the waves that lapped on the sides of the hull and I stopped contemplating everything except the beauty of the sea.

Dusk fell upon us whilst we were sailing around Vatera and Saint Focas to face the northern wind replacing the sirocco that was going to follow our route to the island of Psara.

Tufts in the sky the kind that predict the change of weather, as they say in Agiasso started to appear in the sky and were heading east. This was not the only sign for those tufts were red, and I remembered what a wise old seaman had told me about them one day. He had said, 'Red tufts warn us about winds, about very strong winds.' However, I did not show any apprehension. I did not worry at all as I did not care about my fate. Even if death had emerged before me at that time, I would truly have welcomed him.

At midnight, the northern wind foreshadowed its intentions. Huge waves, almost three times my size blew frantically against the fore of the boat. Luckily the boat resisted. Arouz, who had taken over the rudder because Isaac was unable to handle it any longer, tried to ride on the waves in the squall and let them slip underneath the boat.

The whole night long the boat was left to the mercy of vehement waves as if it was a feather in the clutches of the wind, however nobody contemplated death, not even me, to whom I thought it might come as a salvation.

It was daybreak again when I saw Arouz taking a handful of ashes and thrusting them into the sea.

'What are you doing there?' I asked.

'I am appeasing the demons of the sea and shielding ourselves from being struck by a thunderbolt. Don't you know that? They have been doing it since the ancient times/ he said, assuming a mysterious look on his face.

His look was mysterious but also triumphant. It was the first time he had taught me something I did not know.

We decided to forget about Psara as the craze of the wind would not permit us to go there and sail with the winds to the north. The sea would wash us ashore somewhere, anyway.

From our position, in the middle of the sea, we saw the island of Chios from afar, but Arouz wanted us to continue our voyage. He then announced that we would sail to Patmos, where we could sell his father's jugs... But we never reached Patmos.

At dusk, when the storm was assuaged, we saw a ship sailing along the horizon. That is, Arouz saw it for he had the eyes of a hawk.

'We have to watch out for that ship, it might be a piratical ship with Berber pirates,' he warned us.

And he was right. The first rays of sunlight clearly revealed that it was a tsarniki, a kind of light and fast boat with pointed ends. It was three times the size of our boat and was sailing quite far away from us.

'Take the oars!' Arouz cried out loud. 'They are African pirates, who will plunder our boat. They will kill us all!'

In the meanwhile the ship sent us its signals urging us to advance towards them. When they saw that we did not obey their command they took their oars and started to row towards our boat. When they were at a distance of only fifty yards from us they started crying out inconceivable words that disclosed their anger and savage intentions.

'Aidini, Arouz cried. 'Go to the front cabin and open a hole on the left waterline of the boat. You, the two of you, get to the stern.'

'What are you telling him to do?' I asked him. We shall sink.'

'That is what we must do,' Arouz cried. We must sink!'

Aidini took the chisel and a hammer and got into the front cabin in which I had slept two nights before. He started breaking the beams and joists right on the waterline as the head of the boat was rising because of our weight in the stern.

When his job was done he came to the stern and waited for Arouz's command.

'There are only seven people on the ship,' Arouz cried. 'As soon as their boat touches ours you will grab the gunwale and jump over on to their boat... Do you understand?'

We all gave our consent, but my heart was beating hard. It was my first experience of attacking and I forgot about my desire to die. Self-preservation is such an unbeatable emotion after all...

In the meantime, the pirates exposed their rage and fury whilst they were still on their gunwale. With frantic gestures and wild cries they notified us that we had to draw alongside their vessel as it was more convenient for them to jump aboard us in that way. Despite their urging cries Arouz went ahead with our prow raised. The Berbers got mad at our challenging behavior and got ready to jump on to our boat as soon as we approached them.

At this point, our hollowed head hit the side of their vessel. The Berbers holding daggers and scimitars raged with fury at our contemptuous behavior and frenetically started to hurdle on to our boat. The stern was raised slightly by the weight of their stout bodies in the prow but also because of the water that had started to flow into the vessel through the hole.

We managed to get ourselves hooked on to the bulwark of the gunwale of their boat and get on to their deck, leaving behind four of the Berbers whom we terrifyingly watched sink along with the vessel, for they had been unable to reach the stern and attack us.

Three of their fellow countrymen were still aboard. They were slaughtered instantly with the expression of surprise still printed on their faces. The first one received a stab right in the heart by Aidini and the other two were killed by Arouz, who, with a very dexterous movement cut the throats of the two men at the same time.

The rest of them, trapped in our sinking boat, were crying for help. When they saw Arouz's head emerging from their previous boat, they started to curse and swear at him in the foulest way.

'Son of a whore, bastard, you were born in a dirt pit...'

They cursed off some more vilification, the sort of which, dear God, I should not refer to as I am addressing You and as it has no place in my confession...

When Arouz heard such abuse being addressed to him, he completely lost his mind. He grabbed one of the dead bodies that was lying listless on the deck, ripped its stomach and took out the liver, hurling it to the men at sea. His wrath was so vicious that he went on ripping the rest of the bodies and threw the intestines at the faces of the Berbers.

'Eat their guts, you bastards. It will be ages till your next meal. That is if you do not become a meal for the sharks!'

But it seemed that he had not had enough.

'Now you shall see...' he roared.

He grabbed the two lacerated bodies with his bare hands and threw them into the sea, then he threw the third.

'On second thoughts, I'd rather watch you being torn apart by the sharks,' he yelled, like a lunatic.

A huge red stain from the blood of the slaughtered covered the sea. The sharks did not waste any more time. Ai the horizon, the fins of four sharks made their appearance on the surface of the water. They slit the calmness of the sea. We saw them from our deck and they saw them too. It was then that they started crying out and imploring.

'Pity, have pity on us!'

But Arouz commanded Isaac who had taken over the rudder of the boat to make circles around them, so that we could enjoy the view. The sight was horrible. The sea, at that spot, got rough from the frenzied sharks, while the rest of it was calm. At first we could hear their screams, then only splashes. A few moments later we saw parts of their bodies emerging and floating on the surface of the water, only to sink again along with the fins of the sharks. We could not see much anymore but we could imagine what was going on beneath. Besides, this was not sea we were looking at, it was a red puddle, on the surface of which pieces of torn clothes were floating.

When satiated, Arouz ordered Isaac to sail with the north wind and the rest of us checked our winnings.

We discovered that the boat had been stolen by the Berbers from some merchants of unknown nationality and fate... It was transporting wine, olives, oil and raisins and we assumed it belonged to a merchant from Kalamata. After reading the log of the boat kept by the former skipper I found out that it had been looted only two miles away from Monemvassia.

I reported what I had discovered to Arouz. He was glad to get this information and commanded me to look for any documents I could lay my hands on, but I found no more documents, except a few letters written by the unfortunate merchants to their families.

We threw the letters into the sea, and after cleaning the deck of the blood and dirt the Berbers had left on the boat, we drank a glass of wine from the good wine that was left in the hold and washed it down with some raisins. It was a banquet that we relished that night, celebrating our victory by moonlight, but this bliss did not last long.

At dawn, a magnificent galley appeared on the horizon. Arouz said that he suspected the ship belonged to the Knights from Rhodes who were apparently chasing the Berbers...

We were unquestionably in great trouble. We took the oars to flee but the grand ship supported by its huge sails rifted the water with haughtiness and was advancing towards us steadily...

What would become of us? I thought. Would we pay the price for what the Berbers had done? How could we prove that we were innocent and that we had stolen the ship from the Berbers and not from the legal owners?

Frightful thoughts overflowed in my mind, when suddenly a cannon shot wrenched me crudely from my ruminations. Those Knights were definitely good aimers for with the first shot they pelted our mast. Before we realized what was happening a second cannon shot beheaded Isaac who was standing at the rudder. The headless body of Isaac writhed for a few seconds and then fell into the water, following its head. We did not have time to mourn Isaac's death for we had to think about ourselves first and our own survival had we known what it would cost us, we would have envied Isaac his fate.

Immediately afterwards, the ship reached our boat and some lancers hurdled upon our deck. We surrendered. They chained us with heavy buckles and hoisted us on to their ship using a strange type of crane. Then they dumped us in the bottom of the hold, which was the filthiest part of the ship. There, all the impurities of the oarsmen above fell on us their refuse, their urine and their vomit.

During our interrogation the Knights did not believe a word we said about the Berbers. They were not interested in our origin for to them, we were just pirates, the scum of the earth. Besides, their only concern was to lay their hands on the goods that we had in our boat. The only thing they insisted on knowing, with utmost precision, was how much of the goods we had consumed... We naturally pretended that we did not know a thing...

For the first two days, Arouz was trying to recover from his brother's death and the debacle that had befallen us. On the third day, the soldiers came upon us and after thrashing us with their whips, put us in the place of three oarsmen who had died the previous day whilst on duty. They chained us to our thwarts and after welting us on our bare backs they had stripped us of our clothes and warned that if we ever stopped rowing they would instantly have us cruelly killed.

At this point I must describe the conditions in the hold for they surpassed the wildest imagination... It was a floating hell, where people wished that they could die, hoping that in the hell of the underworld the conditions would be more humane. You see, hope never leaves man, even for life after death...

Much later we found out that the ship that had captured us was the flagship of the Saint John's Knights, who had fled and settled on the island of Rhodes after their expulsion from Jerusalem. Ironically enough, the flagship was called the "The Immaculate Conception of the Virgin", and was openly and indiscreetly making rounds at sea or more correctly, piratical forays against the infidels: Moslems, Turks and Orthodox Greeks.

The hold was one of the most ghastly, most appalling in the universe, defying the sacred name it bore so crudely.

No captive had ever survived that hell, unless of course he had relatives who could pay his emancipation ransom. Otherwise a slave was doomed, like the three oarsmen we had replaced and some more whose death we witnessed during our captivity.

As I have already mentioned, we were chained with heavy buckles. That is, one leg was chained whist the other was free to press against the bench ahead for resistance whilst pulling the oar. On each bench its length was about eight open palms there were three, four or even five oarsmen, who were 'accommodated' according to the size and weight of their oars. The benches were covered with hides so that our bottoms would not bleed and on these benches we sat, slept and did our needs. Because of the fetor in this area the officers of the galley on the upper deck were always carrying small handkerchiefs soaked in perfume and holding them to their noses. Not even the sea wind could dissolve the stench on the boat...

The unbearable heat during the summer made it impossible for us to work under the scorching rays of the sun unless we were completely naked, and in wintertime we were only allowed to wear a pair of slacks and a red woolen shirt.

At sea our hands were cuffed to restrict our movements and annihilate the chances of rebellion when our ship fought against another... The officers were always afraid of a mutiny for they knew that in such a case we could capture and chain them to the oars and take command of the ship. That was perhaps the only reason that justified their ruthless and aggressive behavior towards us. They would often fall on us like bees and tear our backs with their long whips or lashes, with or without a reason at all.

We rowed according to the pace commanded by the captain. He would pass his command to his junior officer who would advance it to two pipers, one on each side of the hold. The pipers would then use their whistles, which were hung around their necks, to determine the rhythm we had to follow.

Consequently, you can imagine the awkward picture. Five naked men chained to their bench, holding huge oars four or five times the height of a common man and bending their bodies with stretched arms so that the oars would pass over the backs of the slaves in the front benches, who would also bend theirs in the same way and then throw themselves back again to pull the oar once more...

During sea storms things were getting even worse. The waves would make it difficult for us to handle the oars or bring them back to their former positions. In such circumstances the oars would be jumbled up with the ones in front or behind, causing great confusion. In these cases the junior officers and the pipers would fall upon us like wild dogs and whip the hell out of us for the mess we had created. The same happened during a sea battle, our oars would get muddled up with the enemies'.

If one of the galleys sank it would drag the slaves still chained to their benches to the bottom of the sea. Only the captain and his officers could get away for they could jump into the water and swim to the shore.

We pulled the oars all day and the greatest part of the night until our backs were scorched from the sun and the saltiness of the water our skin was always prepared to open like that of a roasted pig. The sweat would trickle on our faces and bodies, and our eyes were always in pain as we had nothing to wipe them with.

If the officer or the piper happened to see a slave taking his breath or his time, he would slash his back with a thick rope that had been previously soaked in sea water. The slave had to endure all this brutality patiently and uncomplainingly, and if he ever dared to protest or even utter a moan then he would be beaten even more severely until he lost his senses.

'Son of a bitch! How dare you complain?' That is how the junior officer often addressed me or the rest of us in the hold.

We were full of lice and fleas but we could not feel their bites as our skins had lost all sense of feeling. We were fed on two pieces of rancid bread every day. If we had to face an enemy vessel then they would douse the bread with wine to boost our strength and courage. Very often we would row interminably for ten, fifteen and sometimes twenty hours according to the captain's needs. When there was no urgency we would rest in turn or in shifts. Sometimes, during our short breaks, we would carve small pieces of wood given to us and create items that we could sell to the natives when we reached a port.

At each port they would unchain us and set us free but always under the supervision of the officers. There, we could sell our little objects and make some money with which we would buy food and coal to use for cooking on the ship. Only then could we eat properly. Sometimes we even knitted socks or mittens and sold them in exchange of some small pieces of meat.

Alas to the slave who endeavoured to escape! This was something that Arouz tried once and paid for it very dearly.

A coastal village on the northeastern side of Kos. I do not remember the port we had disembarked at, but I think it was the port of Kos, near the Turkish coast. Arouz had run out of patience and could not tolerate the ordeal and suffering any more. He escaped from the supervision of the guards and ran towards Lambi, planning to swim to the Turkish shore and from there to reach Karamania on foot as he had told his friend earlier but his attempt was a gruesome mistake...

When the captain was informed about the escape, he called the dignitaries and priests of the island to come aboard ship and warned them that if they did not find the fugitive before sunset they would all be sent to the hold of the ship. Terrified, the priests and dignitaries ran to notify their fellow villagers who were soon searching the island to locate the fugitive slave. They caught Arouz before he had reached the sea and brought him in chains to the captain.

What happened next was a hair-raising experience. Arouz was cruelly beaten up until unconsciousness and then he was whipped on his back and the soles of his bare feet. After that he was hung head down and an officer set a fire underneath his head until his hair almost burnt. Then they took him to the hold and whipped him again...

When Arouz reacted to pain no more, they threw him next to our bench like a bag of bones. No sooner had he recovered slightly, than they seated him on the bench, chained his legs and hands and forced him to pull his oars. Arouz was not released until his ransom was paid a few months later...

It had been almost a year and a half since our captivity in that hideous place, and there was no spark of hope for freedom or our future left in us anymore. Personally, I had believed that I would spend the rest of my life I hoped it would be short in this hold and that someday I would become prey for the beasts of the sea, after cutting my left ear off that was the custom when a slave died, to affirm to the captain that a piece of his merchandise had been lost. We were nothing more than merchandise, you see. They could use us in any way they wished they could sell us, exchange us for other goods or barter for a handsome amount of money paid for us by the rich on an island. I had nobody to pay the extravagant ransom the Knights demanded for my emancipation; therefore I had no hope...

One morning the three of us were called up on deck. I appeared before the captain, believing that I had done something I should be punished for. The only thought that soothed my tormented mind then was that death might come as redemption from my misery, but to my great surprise I saw that the captain was saluting us with respect and unprecedented kindness.

He was seated on a couch that had been placed in the centre of the main deck, and received us with a smile whilst inspecting our faces attentively, as if he were studying our features.

We stood before him and did not dare to speak, move or even look at him. Aidini had directed his eyes to the mast of the ship; Arouz aimed his gaze at the horizon while my eyes kept piercing the wooden deck.

'So, you are the lucky fellows who are to be released from captivity at last!' the captain exclaimed.

We were dumbfounded, flabbergasted and stupefied. Those words had been completely erased from our vocabulary all that time. What had happened? Released from captivity? How could that be? How could it possibly happen? God, am I witnessing a miracle? I pondered.

But the captain was absolutely solemn.

'Well, your ransom has been paid. The priest brought the money to the ship this morning. You are free!'

Only then did I notice the Roman Catholic priest who was standing behind him with his hands crossed on his stomach a stance that I soon remembered.

'And you, Barbarossa...' The captain was addressing Arouz. Apparently he had just contrived that nickname to tease him for his red beard and to sound friendlier in the presence of the priest. You must love your friends very much.'

Arouz did not reply. He still had his eyes fixed on the horizon.

That was the first time anybody had called him Barbarossa and that was the sobriquet he afterwards adopted until the day he died. His brother Hizr inherited the name although he did not have a red beard.

'I admire your faithfulness to your friends! You insisted that you would only be released when the ransom was also paid for your friends...' said the captain in a buoyant tone. Seemingly, he was more than content with the generous amount he had received. 'How long have you been friends?'

'Since we were children, Sir,' I replied on behalf of Arouz, fearing the captain's anger because of his unresponsive and apathetic attitude.

'Friendship! What a valuable virtue!' the captain asserted, with a melancholic smile.

The priest approached Arouz and put something in his hand.

'This money is sent to you by your brothers,' he explained. 'A small amount that can get you on your feet, my son...'

The captain signaled to one of his officers to unhoist one of the lifeboats into the sea and then he ordered two of his junior officers to get us to the shore and to our 'fortunes'.

And so it was done. When we got to the shore we stepped on firm land and lay down for hours. It had been a year and a half since we could lie on our backs like real people. The seamen who accompanied us to the shore reluctantly informed us, before they departed, that we were on Turkish land right across from the island of Rhodes.

'Why did you do it, Arouz?' I asked him, when were left alone on this foreign land.

'Do what?'

'Why did you demand that our ransom be paid as well? You could have been released a long time ago...'

'The son of a bitch explained it to you, didn't he?' Arouz said, somewhat indignantly. 'We are friends, aren't we?' Then after a few moments of pause 1 e added, 'And I do not wish to discuss it any more... It is over now...'

That was Arouz! Ruthless and cruel to his enemies but faithful and loyal to his friends, perhaps going as far as self-sacrifice, as his death verified years later. He possessed the qualities of a genuine, unquestionable leader qualities that sultans and kings failed to have.

We lingered on that coast for three days. We had found a cave near the shore, and had made mattresses of dry moss and slept comfortably on them.

When we woke up on the first day I cannot tell for sure after how many hours of deep, uninterrupted sleep we were famished. We climbed a short hill and saw a wild goat that, with his ploys, Aidini managed to trap. We skinned it and roasted it in the embers of the fire we had made on the beach. It was such a long time since any of us had had a decent, lush and delicious meal, that we enjoyed it to the last bite even though we swallowed the ashes as well!

Our wounds started to heal fast and our skin was cleansed of its bugs and dirt due to our frequent swimming in the sea. We would then lick our bodies like cats, or rub our wounds with saliva, using our hands wherever our tongues could not reach. Soon the cuts and scars that the whips had left on our bodies almost disappeared.

It was then that I noticed the changes in my body; I was a completely different person now. I was not the thin, feeble young boy I used to be in Venice with the white skin and delicate, refined features. Now I had become a man with strong hands and arms from pulling oars, despite the scarcity of food on the ship. My skin was not soft anymore; it had roughened and was almost black from the effect of the sun on it. I looked more like the Berbers we had slaughtered before our captivity, than that young fair boy of Paleokipos.

Even my innate characteristics had changed, judging from the way I had slaughtered and skinned the goat with my bare hands. I was amazed at myself and the dexterity with which I had handled the dead animal and I felt as though I had always been a butcher or a skinner all my life.

When we regained our strength and vigour, we decided to leave the place. Arouz led the way, although he was unfamiliar with the paths. After a day's walk we finally reached a village the name of which I do not recall now and spent the night there at an inn. We ended up in real beds with three beautiful slaves who reminded us that we were still men for we had almost forgotten sex after all the hardships we had suffered.

The following day, Arouz bargained for the purchase of three horses and asked the peasant who sold us the livestock the way to Karamania. The peasant gave him the directions.

'Is Korchoud still there?' Arouz asked him.

Korchoud was the brother of the sultan, Selim the Cruel, as everyone called him. At that time his father, Vayatzit the second, had conceded him the right to rule Karamania.

Korchoud, knowing what his brother would do to him once he took the throne, tried to organize a fleet in the Aegean Sea mainly constituting of piratical galleys so that he would profit from their looting and at the same time create a reliable sea force that would enable him to confront his brother. He did not wish to experience what his uncle, Zem, had endured from his own father.

When Mehmed the Conqueror came to the throne, his first concern was to choke his half-brother to death whilst he was still a baby in the cradle so that he would not have to face any challengers in the future. A few months later he issued a firman[21] in which he announced:

After longwinded deliberations with my advisors w have reached the decision that it is permissible for whoever succeeds me after my death to kill his brothers, sons or even grandsons so that he will secure peace and serenity for his people. My successor should act according to this suggestion...

Thus, his firstborn son, Vayatzit, was persecuted and fought against his brother Zem, who was also known as Zizim or Zizimi. Zem eventually took refuge in the west, trying to persuade the Franks to wage war against his brother. However, Pope Alexander to maintain peace and the good terms with the sultan imprisoned Zem in the fort of Saint Angelos, where he was found dead a few days later.

Korchoud was afraid that he might end up with the same fate as his uncle Zem. It was then that he sought out, and actually found, Arouz. It seems that he had heard much about his extraordinary aptitude at sea and his unrivalled strength probably because of previous piratical action that had taken place during my absence in Venice. He sent him to the Kati in Smyrna, with a written order that he would be armed with a fully equipped galley and an efficient crew whom he would personally select.

Financing pirates was a flourishing and profitable business at that time both in the west and the east. The difference lay in the ways the western and eastern sovereigns disposed of the winnings from their piratical ravaging.

The Eastern investors would take their winnings for themselves, they would not give anything to anybody, whilst the Western investors 'beautifying' the act of piracy endowed a part of their winnings to charity.

Thus with the funds allocated by piratical activities and the endowments of dogmatic, orthodox Christians and antichristian Moslems, they built imposing cathedrals in the name of Our Lord, Jesus Christ, as if He was exclusively their own property.

Even popes contributed to these charities. Their majestic galleys manned by dogmatic Christians and Moslem slaves sailed the Mediterranean, reaping the fruits of its sea trade in the name of The Lord, His Son and the Holy Ghost.

Having the endorsement and blessing of Korchoud and also his order to receive a fully equipped galley ready for piratical action, we met the Kati of Smyrna. From our pillage winnings we had to pay a handsome sum to the Kati himself, who naturally considered it a gift sent from God for the faithful Moslems, of course.

Arouz did not raise any objections to the amount set by the Kati and very soon he received his galley. We set sail from Smyrna with twenty sailors, most of whom were unemployed men or Greek renegades.

We lurked for merchant ships in the Capes of Chios, Lesvos, Lemnos and Samos and our winnings were always satisfactory. Whenever we saw a Frankish galley especially if it was smaller than ours we would rush upon it like drones and exterminate everyone on board. Our hatred generated from all the torture we had endured at the hands of the Knights was so intense and fierce that we did not let anyone escape our blades. Even the veterans upon our ship were dazed at our rage and our obsession with not leaving anyone alive.

When we had slightly satiated our thirst for revenge we started to act more reasonably. We would leave a few captures alive to be able to sell them in the slave markets.

Much later, when our rage appeased even more, we would even treat the survivors with generosity. We would feed them and treat their wounds so that we could sell them at better prices, as adept and experienced pirates did.

But things were not always so easy. Many times we had to confront mutinies and rebellions on the ship, especially when the hours of lurking behind Capes for merchant ships were prolonged extensively. 'An idle mind is the orchard of the devil' they say, consequently, during the long hours of inactivity, inertia, waiting and boredom, the men on ship would end up rioting against each other or even against us. In such cases we always ran the risk of ending up behind bars.

It was then that Arouz would become very violent. He did not tolerate treason or any sort of treacherous behavior that 'would bring us back to the holds', as he often said. He would hurl himself upon his mutineers and eliminate each and every one of them singlehanded... He would even cut off their heads or other parts of their bodies and throw them into the sea.

His reactions were savage because of the fear that had nested in his heart fear of experiencing captivity once more and this was mainly the reason why we never sailed farther away from Samos. The memory of the Knights was still vivid in his mind as it was still engraved on our bodies...

On one of our voyages we sailed off to Lesvos, to the Bay of Gera. There we met with Hizr and the rest of the members of Jacob's family. Jacob had been dead for some time, and Elias his second born son had taken over his workshop. He, like Hizr, was married and had two children. The two sisters were married to Christians for it was the will of their mother Katerina.

Katerina, Hizr and Elias received us with joy and offered us everything they could get for us, but we did not need anything, we had everything we could wish for. Hizr could not hide his admiration and envy for what we had been transformed into and what we he even wished he could join us on one of our trips. He expressed his astonishment when he saw me for I did not remind him of the boy he had known in the past.

You have become so strong! I almost did not recognize you!' he told me, his eyes sparkling.

'Do you want me to expose my strength to you?'

I took a thick rod and bent it with my hands.

Hizr was speechless. He had not expected all these sudden changes.

'I will join you on your next trip,' he said.

Arouz did not encourage him.

You are a married man now, Hizr, and you have a family to look after. One pirate in the family is more than enough.'

'If you do not take me with you now I shall have to join you later...'

Arouz laughed and did not add another word. He thought Hizr was only dreaming about the safe Bay of Gera.

During our stay in Evriaki I remained on our ship. I did not have the courage to go to my parents' house. My fellow villagers had told me that the burnt remains still lay there as no one had dared to approach the place after the massacre.

In the meantime our crew had started to grumble again about the sluggishness and inactivity we had put them through. They started with mere complaints, and then exceeding their limits, went on to steal from the surrounding olive groves. When they ended up having squabbles with our fellow villagers, Arouz decided to dismiss them all, but they soon found other piratical ships that were looking for men.

As soon as the men left, Arouz asked for help from our old friends in Paleokipos. He told them that whoever wished to join us would be welcome but they should not anticipate quick repatriation. Many of our friends those who were more susceptible to escapade and venture followed us. They desired, as they said, to experience a new adventurous and challenging life at sea.

Thus, young, strong recruits like Pirros who later became Pirri reis and others, formed our crew and bade farewell to the Bay of Gera one warm afternoon. It was the last time Arouz ever saw the Bay he left behind for more adventure and the new conquests his mind was brooding on...

'What is there beyond the Mediterranean, besides chaos?' he asked, as we were taking the northwest direction through the Cyclades islands towards the Cape of Mallias, in Peloponese.

I smiled at the old memory and replied:

'Just a few islands that they have now called the West Indies. I hope you are not planning to take us there...'

'No, but we could sail to the border of former chaos,' he replied.

The fore of the ship was now pointing to the west, leaving the White Sea where we were all brought up behind us.

We sailed for many days and nights following the stars, the magnetic needle and the charts that we had stolen from a ship we had once looted near Smyrna.

We were following the winds and heading towards Apoulia, the northern part of the Italian peninsula. If we happened to fall upon a Frankish merchant ship smaller in size than ours, of course on our way, we would plunder and then continue on our course, unhindered.

'In these seas the ships are bountiful,' Arouz used to remark very often. 'They have opulent merchandise. They are nothing like the niggardly ones in the East... Here the crop is richer.'

And it was true for the first raids brought us a lot of winnings, more than we could ever imagine getting in the East. Our vessel was filled with all sorts of goods from the East that we sold secretively in the remote villages in Italy or to the Arabs in Libya. I say 'secretively' because if the sheikh in Tripoli had found out about our business dealings he would have asked for a generous share and this was something Arouz would never tolerate.

When we had had enough of small and helpless galleys, we decided to move on and attack bigger ones for bigger winnings. People are never satisfied, dear Lord, but I guess You already know that...

One of these ships that we attacked was a galley that we had come across in the Adriatic Sea when it was heading for Venice. We employed our tactics and in less than an hour we had snared it. When we got into its cellars to examine the merchandise, we discovered to our disappointment that the ship was transporting only a few reels of cheap fabric and wines of inferior quality from Marseilles. This merchandise was useless to us for it could not possibly be sold easily in the small markets of the coastal Italian villages. The local people did not appreciate such goods, moreover, they were fearful to obtain them as they were afraid of being punished by the authorities.

However, as I was searching the skipper's cabin I found some letters, one of which was written in code. I laughed when I saw that the Venetians still used the cryptographic methods I had invented. At first I looked at the letters with pride and admiration but I soon realized that I was unconsciously decoding their contents... and it was quite a catch!

One was a message sent by a Genovese merchant to his Venetian colleague, who lived in Rome merchants did not have rivals when business was involved in which he was informing him that two galleys, with a rich merchandise of silk and other rare and precious goods from China, were sailing from Genoa to the Italian port Civitavecchia, in ten days. From there they would transport the goods by road to some place in the southern part of Rome. It also referred to the fact that the greatest part of the merchandise belonged to the Vatican; to the Pope. The merchant from Genoa was urging his Venetian colleague to attend to the process of unloading the merchandise as well as to the other procedures involved, so that the delivery to Pope Julius the Second would not be hindered or delayed in any way.

I read the letter to Arouz and he was enraptured by the news.

'Do you know how much we can earn by selling the silk in Tripoli?' he exclaimed, with the utmost enthusiasm, and before I could give him any answer he added, 'A fortune!'

Wasting no time, he gave orders to his men to get prepared at once and set sail to the Western Italian coast. He even set the ship's captives we had seized free, except for the merchandise and the crew that is! That incident occurred in 1504.

We changed our course to the south and sailed around Scylla and Charibdi to the narrow pass of Messina following a good wind and then we headed to the north.

We reached the passageway that separated Elba from the mainland of Italy; the channel at that point is relatively narrow and there are a lot of reefs.

As the waters were not deep, we lurked behind some steep rocks across from a small island. We anchored our ship behind one of these rocks and with Arouz, Aidini and I climbed the highest rock to watch the Sea of Liguria.

Two white dots appeared on the horizon. Each of the two papal galleys had twenty oars on either side that were all moving rhythmically in and out of the water. They were so huge that it stirred our fear...

As we were now even more experienced, we estimated that the ships were over laden, not only with cargo but also with an army that we could not confront easily.

Aidini and 1 tried to persuade Arouz to call off the expedition as it was dangerous and risky but Arouz wouldn't listen.

They will capture us and throw us into the holds, I insisted.

'It is a gift from God,' Arouz replied. 'Can't you see? God wants to reward us for all our hardships...'

Aidini and I had to accept our fate. We knew of Arouz's stubbornness, so whatever we said would not affect him.

We returned to our ship, which looked like a small mosquito in comparison to the two stately galleys we had just watched and Aidini and I were very discouraged and alarmed. Personally, I cursed myself for having been able to decode the letter. If I had not read it to Arouz we would not be running such risk now...

Aidini approached me. He was terrified and looked at me gravely whilst handing me a dagger.

'Take it,' he said. 'If we happen to get, caught, stab it right here in my heart. I could not bear becoming a slave in the holds once more...'

'Neither could I,' I said, taking his dagger. 'Do you have one for me? I want you to do just the same for me.'

'And how could I stab you after I have been stabbed?' he asked, with a somewhat clumsy expression.

I did not have time to answer his question for Arouz's harsh voice thundered ferociously from the deck.

'Posts everyone! No one will stir a muscle, unless I give the signal... Are you listening?'

Some of the men nodded.

'We shall wait here behind this rock,' Arouz went on. 'When the first galley comes into sight, I will give you the signal to attack...'

The galley was advancing right towards us. The pipers and oarsmen got ready to obey Arouz's orders. They were supposed to pull their oars abruptly with all their strength and then raise them so that the rest of us could leap upon the enemy's galley.

Aidini came to me with the apprehensive look of a person who was about to be executed. He showed me another dagger that he had taken from the ship's armory and whispered with a bitter smile:

'Whoever stabs first and then the other should have to turn it to his own heart.'

Despite my uneasiness, I managed to smile. We separated and each one of us took up his position. Aidini stood at one gunwale and I at the other. Arouz took his position by the steering wheel alone, crying out the last instructions for our assault.

The first galley reached the rock behind which we were hiding and was just venturing its fore out. It did not take any notice of us and it would almost have continued on its way had our oarsmen not rowed as fast as Arouz had commanded and collided with its hull. They then raised their oars as they had been instructed and our vessel drew close to the papal galley. Our crew screaming their souls out and with boisterous commotion jumped on to their gunwale and then upon the Pope's spears men who were at first stupefied by the sudden attack. No sooner had they regained consciousness than a ferocious battle took place on the papal galley's deck.

Our men with the fury of beasts and their unquenched eagerness to steal the merchandise recklessly fell upon the soldiers and obstructed them. As a result many of the spearsmen hurt or even killed themselves with their own spears as the others fell upon them with frenetic fury. Some of the soldiers leaped on to our ship and now fought with Arouz who was all alone on the deck. He confronted them singlehandedly, assisted only by his vehemence and fearless strength. He managed to disarm and immobilize five stout men all by himself, with his arms of steel.

However, the battle was not going well and I imagined myself chained in the hold that was if I ever survived the massacre... I even heard myself moan in anguish and pain under the piper's whip.

It was at this particular moment that a fine idea suddenly flashed into my mind. I looked for Aidini. I saw him lying down on the deck with two spearmen standing over him, ready to rip his guts apart. I jumped on them with my dagger and managed to stab their backs exactly at the point of the heart. The two spearmen fell lifelessly upon each other leaving Aidini alone.

'Quickly, come with me before the rest of the soldiers see us,' I urged him.

Aidini managed to stand on his trembling feet and followed me whilst I crawled along the deck. I found the stairs that led to the lower deck of the hull of the ship and Aidini was always behind me. I pointed to the piper who was ever watchful standing on the left side with his whip in his hand, and Aidini received the message right away. I chose the other piper on the right side.

We vaulted upon them from behind and stabbed our blades into their backs. They were instantly killed.

Wasting no time I unchained and uncuffed the slaves. They were all Arabs, Algerians and Moors former inhabitants of Spain who were chased away by Isabelle and Ferdinand years ago. Amongst them there were also a few Christians who were sentenced to a lifetime of imprisonment for their debts or other crimes they had committed. When they were set free they grabbed whatever they could find and ran to the stairs that led to the upper deck.

On the other side of the deck, Arouz had done with his enemies... Now the battle was in our hands. When the soldiers saw the released slaves they started screaming with terror and soon cried out that they were surrendering they had little chance of survival anyway. But the slaves did not listen to their cries for they jumped upon them with blind rage and would have torn them apart if we hadn't stopped them; not because of charity or sympathy but because of the money we would make if we sold them in the markets in Africa...

When the massacre was put to an end, with great satisfaction we estimated the human prey that was lying between our hands, beside the merchandise that now belonged to us. But our joy did not last for long.

'We must run away!' we heard Aidini shouting behind us. 'The second galley is on its way to us.'

Arouz turned to him with his arrogant look and roared, 'I am the commander here. I do not take orders from anyone!'

Arouz had already been sitting in the armchair of the captain of the papal galley and with a pompous gesture he added, 'Decisions and orders are only made by me.'

Aidini recoiled and did not utter another word for he had never raised objections to Arouz before; nonetheless, I had to express my opinion.

'Aidini is right!' I blurted out. 'We have to run away as soon as possible for we will not be able to combat the second galley; it's much bigger.'

Arouz looked sternly at me but maintained his composure; after all I was his best friend. He was thoughtful for some moments and then addressing the crew, he said. 'Get ready for the second attack. We vanquished the first galley; we shall vanquish the second as well!'

I was shattered by his reckless decision. I tried to dissuade him, even to beg him change his mind.

'We will lose everything. Greediness will kill us. Please come to your senses, Arouz.'

But Arouz remained aloof and disinterested in my supplications.

'It is a gift from God so we shall not reject it... Gift from God, gift from God.'

He repeated this several times until we had to yield to his wishes and orders. Nobody was able to contradict Arouz anyway, not even his friends, and not even me... I realized then that even friendship had its boundaries.

We were resigned to our fate and with heavy hearts resumed our posts for the second attack. We had so many captives on the ship that we were also afraid of a mutiny at that critical moment. How would they react if they saw us slaughtering their compatriots? But it seems that Arouz stole my thoughts from my head.

'Get the captives undressed and send them to the hold. They will pull the oars from now on. On each bench four of them will be seated observed by one of the former slaves, a Moor or Arab. Do I make myself clear? The rest of them should wear the clothes of their oppressors. I want them to look like perfect Franks.'

Arouz's plan was extraordinary. I could not believe how this uncouth person could perceive such a devilish scheme under all this pressure.

In a few minutes the deck looked like a theatrical stage. Some men got undressed and others wore the fine clothes of the soldiers. The naked ones got down to the hold and the dressed ones took their places on the deck. It was pandemonium a hullabaloo. The gentlefolk became slaves and the slaves became the masters of the ship.

Only one captive remained dressed and handcuffed on deck. It was the wretched galley's captain who was standing behind Arouz.

You,' Arouz thundered, turning to him You have a special mission. I will inform you in due time. Do I make myself clear?'

It was then that I noticed the use of this question 'Do I make myself clear?' being repeated with special intonation and formality. Arouz was somehow changed and looked grave and more serious than ever.

'Do you have any objections?' he politely asked the captain again.

'No, no objections at all,* he replied, shattered and overwhelmed.

'Excellent,' Arouz commented, and to our surprise, he started to unchain the captain!

After he had also uncuffed him, he adjusted his suit and his belt and dusted off the battle's dust. He even demanded that they would find him his hat that was lying somewhere on deck and he personally placed it on his head.

'Now you look as perfect as before,' Arouz said. 'A perfect gentleman and an officer,' and, turning to the rest of the crew he asked:

'He looks perfect, doesn't he?'

We nodded for we were all dumbfounded. We did not understand what he was aiming at.

'Come here, Ermoleo!' Arouz called to me. 'Find him the clothes of a junior officer.'

Some of the men ran to get me the clothes.

'Well, listen to what you must do,' he said to the poor captain who felt as though he was playing with a tiger. 'As soon as the second ship comes into sight, you will signal for help and assistance. Ask them to draw near our vessel so that they can give you the help you need. Do I make myself clear?'

The poor man tried to swallow his saliva but he could not.

'You are commanding me to betray my men?' he muttered.

'Ah! Do you consider this treason? Do you prefer that you betray us instead? I granted you your life, you bastard. I shall rip your throat apart with my own teeth for your being unfaithful to God and to me. You should be thankful that you are still alive!'

Arouz turned to the two Moors, who were eagerly standing to catch their expresser in their hands, and signaled to them. When the captain had deciphered the signal, he fell on his knees and implored him.

'For God's sake, don't! Have pity on me and I will fulfill all your wishes. I shall do whatever Your Excellency commands.'

The last compliment gratified Arouz.

'All right, all right,' he said, with gestures of magnanimity, and immediately demanded that the crew who were gathered on the deck were to take the dead bodies away, along with the wounded, and pile them up on the left bulwark of the vessel. He said that they might be useful there, for they could be trodden upon during the final raid against the second galley. He also commanded his men to rinse the blood off the deck so that nothing would stir the suspicion of the captain of the other ship whilst drawing near our vessel.

The operation proved to be easier than the first one and was an absolute success. Our 'captain's' signals were received and very soon the second galley was there right next to us. As soon as the two ships were bound, the Franks witnessed an inconceivable scene. They actually saw their 'colleagues' attack them with the ferocity of wild animals.

The first few men, who tried to resist, were immediately killed but the rest surrendered with their mouths still wide open. Their astonishment was wiped away when they were taken to the hold to replace the former slaves.

We caught the new captain alive, but he, unlike the first one, was stubborn and conceited. When he came to our deck where Arouz and I were standing next to his former associate, he jumped on the latter to bite him because he could do nothing else with his hands chained behind his back. The only thing he managed to do, though, was to spit in his face and call him 'treacherous!'

The captain's disrespectful behavior towards the prisoner excited Arouz's wrath so he drew his sword and aimed it at his nape. However, at the last moment he changed his mind for another fiendish notion had crossed his devilish mind.

'I will not send you to God, yet,' he said. 'I will keep you for myself...'

We knew what was going to happen. He grabbed him, completely undressed him of his clothes and underwear and asked for a whip soaked in sea water. He hit him three or four times and every time a new gory slit was notched on his white bottom, then he sent him naked to the hold to be taken care of by a Moor. We could not even tolerate the screams from the torture inflicted upon him by the Moor and in the end we had to throw him into the sea to find his peace and we, our quiet.

When the other captain witnessed his colleague's misfortune he fell on Arouz's feet and implored him once more.

'Have pity on me! I beg of you to have pity on me and I will do whatever you wish. I have nowhere to hide they will tear me apart down there. Keep me next to you. I know these seas very well and if you give me the chance I will prove to be useful on your voyage. I will navigate your ship and I will take you anywhere you wish... I beseech you, have pity on me!'

Arouz looked at him with sympathy; after all, he had helped him with the raid against the other ship and had already proved his loyalty and obedience.

'All right, all right,' Arouz mumbled. 'From now on you will be the navigator of my flagship. But beware of my anger if you ever betray me! I will have you bound between the two ships and I will rip your body apart...'

The new navigator shriveled at this thought.

'I swear to God I will never betray you. I will be your devoted servant, forever.' He gave him his solemn word and he was truly sincere. Before the year was over, he was one of the most reliable, trustworthy men of Arouz, one of the most faithful reises we had in our fleet.

Soon afterwards, Arouz inspected the captives with his expert eye, setting apart those who could pay for their ransom from the ones who could be sold in the slave markets of Africa. Then he examined the oarsmen and made sure that no bench would remain unguarded by at least one of the former slaves of the galleys. They had to listen to the 'prattle' of the slaves and report it to the pipers who would therewith notify the junior officer. The junior officers were mainly responsible for the ambiguous activities of the prisoners and they alone had to take their 'measures'. Usually they whipped them and in some cases as instructed by Arouz they eliminated them altogether.

When we searched the other ship, we found some women from the aristocracy of Genoa hiding in the cellars with their servants whom we promptly took to our cabins to safeguard and protect them. We had an enjoyable time with them and forgive me Lord and judging from their moans, I even gathered they had a better time than us!

Arouz appointed Aidini as commander to the second ship and ordered him to follow ours at a close distance. The third vessel, ours, looked so small and petty compared to Arouz's aspirations, that he conceded it to one of our friends from Paleokipos. Later, when it impeded our voyages, for it was slow and heavy in comparison to the elegant and fast galleys of the Pope, we towed it behind Aidini's ship.

I remained with Arouz as it was his wish. He invariably needed me by his side as if I had become his sublime self or perhaps the completion of his inner self.

'And now/ he commanded his navigator, 'we shall set sail to the south, to Tunisia. We shall reach the port of Goletta to pay our respects and offer our gifts to His Excellency the Sultan Muhammad.'

Sultan Muhammad was well known for the sanctuary he offered to the pirates in that area, in exchange for extravagant tributes of money and precious goods. He took one tenth of the value of the pirates' looting as he had to maintain the fortification built around the port of Goletta, which safeguarded the piratical ships that took refuge there.

We set sail to the south, keeping Sardinia on our left-hand side whilst avoiding the western edge of Sicily, and entered the port of Goletta unobstructed. But in Goletta, a surprise was waiting, a surprise that determined not only my fate but the fate of a whole world.

In the palaces of Tunisia we found Sultan Muhammad with Hizr the brother of Arouz expecting our advent.

Four

Thus, we penetrated the domain of the Berbers, where Arouz and his brother Hizr were destined to become the supreme masters of political change and the regulators of the conflicting interests of kings, tyrants, leaders of states and religious dogmas. That disorderly and turbulent part of the world was the 'underbelly' of Catholic Europe and its rulers, who had always had the ambition to keep it under their 'control' or rather under their domination so that they could be engaged in the wars and skirmishes between each other, were unruffled and undisturbed.

We disembarked in the port of Goletta, where Arouz exhibited both his unrivalled qualities in promoting his goods, and his decorous manners, which he assumed every time he met or dealt with the powerful men of the region. He bought two fine horses and ordered two of the most beautiful female captives after he had dressed them in fine woven clothes that divulged the finest parts of their bodies to ride them, for he had selected them to be offered as gifts for the sultan's harem. They were the ones who led a pompous procession that proudly strutted to the sultan's palace in Tunis. The rest of the women, in transparent white robes as well, came next, followed by young boys and the captives. They were all going to be sold in the slave markets.

On both sides of the procession he had placed pirates in elegant garments, which we had stolen from the papal galleys. They all strode with a submissive gait except for Arouz, Aidini and myself who haughtily rode on three black Arabic horses whilst wearing our suits of armor also found in the hold of the galley and had our swords and sabers protruding from our belts. The sultan had to witness with his own eyes that we were not a rebel asker but an orderly and organized army and also had to sufficiently understand that we were not prepared to negotiate commissions that might exceed the limit of 'one tenth of the winnings' he demanded in return for his protection.

The sultan was thrilled with the parade that stopped right under his palace and his enthusiasm culminated when we presented him with his gifts. We knew that monarchs always cherished and appreciated gifts; the more you offered them the more congenial their friendship would be. Two astounding gifts exhilarated Sultan Muhammad.

'With these birds of heaven, Allah rewards his brave men!' he exclaimed with admiration, and sent them right to his harem.

The sultan was stupefied! He was not given the chance to ask for his share for we gave him pouches filled with diamonds and semiprecious stones that we had collected from the papal galleys and our previous assaults against other ships. He granted us his permission to spend the night in Goletta and other ports in his country.

The rest of the slaves both men and women were taken to the slave market to be sold at the best possible prices. The female slaves, whom we had deprived of both clothes and jewellery they only had on transparent white robes as I had previously mentioned, were obligated to disrobe every time a zealous buyer made his appearance. If the buyer after a meticulous examination of the body was still not satisfied with the merchandise, the slave would wear the robe again and have to wait patiently for the subsequent buyer to repeat the process. This would happen many times a day until the 'piece of merchandise' was sold. It was a longwinded and tiring operation for both us who had to watch the slave getting dressed and undressed numerous times a day and the slave herself; for she had to tolerate physical inspection which most of the time was disgraceful and humiliating.

As far as the male slaves were concerned their prices varied according to their corporal vigor and strength. Most of them were sold for cultivation purposes and fieldwork whilst the old women when no one would buy them would be bestowed upon rich homes because their sojourn with us would cost us money and time. Consequently we preferred to offer them as gratuity rather than have to drown them in the sea.

Goletta, with its fortress, was a peerless shelter for us and our ships, especially in the wintertime, since our piratical ventures would stop around the middle of October and start again in the spring. In the winter the sea was rough and stormy and we could not handle it with our small ships and, accordingly, neither could the skippers of the merchant ships. So even if we had wished to go out to the sea, it would have been useless because no ship would leave its haven.

However, Arouz was dumbfounded and did not believe his own eyes when he saw his brother Hizr standing next to the sultan.

'I thought you would listen to my advice and remain at home!' he demurred, with an angry look on his face. You have no business in this place.'

'I have always wanted to be with you' Hizr explained, knowing that with this sort of coaxing he could bend his brother's disinclination and objections. You will have your brother on your side. Your brother who cherishes you more than anything and anybody else in the world and will never betray you...'

Hizr was the only person who knew how to manipulate this magnificent, stupendous man. He knew that Arouz would feel insecure with so many pirates around him and that he would always lead the effort against the menace of mutiny and treason.

'I do not wish you to be here, but since it is your desire, you may stay for a short while and then we shall have to decide,' Arouz succumbed.

But nothing is more permanent than a temporary condition as the Greeks say and Hizr was well aware of that fact.

'I will grant you three ships,' said Hizr, with pride. 'Those I have pillaged on my way to Tunisia... They will now belong to you...'

Arouz's face gleamed, not because this was the first gift ever conferred on him but because now he would own three more ships as well as the ones he already possessed. Now he would be the master of a small fleet! A small piratical fleet!

'Well done, well done,' said Arouz. 'And I shall appoint you commander of one of them. As for the other two, I will have to select two reliable and competent skippers, but you must know that you shall enjoy the same privileges as the rest of the reises. If you do not approve you can leave now...'

Hizr expressed his acquiescence at once and with his approbation, the groundwork of a new partnership was simultaneously set; a partnership that dominated the seas beneath Italy, France and Spain for the following decades.

Hizr had also to seal approval for my fellowship. Although we had known each other since we were children, I had never forgotten his abusive behavior towards me or his look which was constantly drenched with envy and contempt, but now he was a new adherent, and as a new adherent he was inferior in rank to me and the rest of his brother's associates.

But here I have to relate a short story about Hizr, and I heard it from his own mouth a few days after his arrival in Tunisia. This story bore a lot of significance as it had an effect on the development of the events thereafter and also illustrated how a mere coincidence may result in major changes in a person's life whilst leading him to totally different routes.

Before Hizr reached Goletta, he had wreaked three piratical raids on his way, as he had explained to his brother. However, besides those piratical pillages he had also perpetrated looting on land. He attacked small and helpless villages in Southern Greece and Italy, burnt them to ashes and captured their people to sell them in the slave markets in North Africa.

In one of those raids, on the coast of Sardinia, a little boy courageously appeared in front of him holding a dagger in his hand and threatening to kill him. The boy would have stabbed the knife in his belly, if Hizr, with dexterous movements, had not evaded the blow. Before the boy could run away after his unsuccessful attempt Hizr grabbed him by the neck and whilst trying to restrain his anger asked him:

'What were you going to do? Do you know who I am?' Yes, I do. You are the chief of the pirates,' said the young boy.

'And you are not afraid?'

'Why should I be?' said the boy fearlessly.

The boy's intrepid answer captured Hizr's admiration.

'What is your name?'

'Pepino,' the boy replied unabashedly, probably shielded by his unawareness.

Hizr, either because he was impressed by his dauntless attitude or because he reminded him of a son he had left behind in Paleokipos, kept the boy with him instead of sending him away with the rest of the captives. However, despite his paternal feelings he did no* hesitate to castrate him so that he would be certain that th< boy would be loyal and devoted to him. He also circumcised him and called him Hassan.

Many years later it was rumored that Hassan was Hizr's real son an illegitimate son he most probably had with a slave but I never believed these rumors as the true story was the one that Hizr himself narrated only a few days after his arrival in Tunisia, when he introduced the boy to me. Twenty-five years later, the boy, Hassan, became the Sultan of Algiers, succeeding Arouz and Hizr, and ferociously fought the expeditionary armies and the fleets of the unified powers of Europe. There were not many times indeed when they managed to be united.

But we have still a long way to go until we reach that time. As for now we must only refer to the fact that Hizr became one of Arouz's commanders, and that he was treated as equally as the rest of us, with no special favors, preferences or partiality on the part of his brother.

At that time, Arouz had ten captains who ran his ships. Most of them were Christians who had renounced their religion for safety reasons. They were not good Moslems either, for they were debauched and drank in taverns all winter long.

His first captain was Aidini, who now had become Aidini reis and our friend in both good and unfavorable times. He was a faithful partner, a competent navigator, and he had no ambition whatsoever apart from pleasing Arouz by successfully accomplishing all the missions he had entrusted to him.

Then there was Okiali reis, an Italian who was born in Calabria. Although he was much younger than the rest of us, he managed to become one of the most notorious captains, instilling fear and awe into the hearts of his former compatriots.

There was also Dragoud reis, born of Greek Orthodox parents in the East. A Turkish pasha who kidnapped him when he was still a young boy had him circumcised and forced him to convert to Islam. When Dragoud became an adult he ran away from the Turk and fled to Tunisia where he became a pirate. He fought many battles and was always victorious.

We also had a Jew amongst us, Sinan reis, who was also Islamized. We used to call him the Jew of Smyrna because he was born there. He also had the sobriquet 'the magician', because he could locate our 'stigma' with exact precision and the place where we were heading, without using the astrolabe or any other instruments that could help him to measure the height of the stars above the horizon. In my humble opinion, Sinan must have known the height of stars in a certain season or area by heart. Nonetheless, he would nourish the rumor that he was using magic in the nautical art to inspire fear in the hearts of his crew and rove about securely on both his ship and any place he wished in the harbor. Sinan was a remarkable captain, but he would become ruthless whenever he fell upon his prey...

There was also Kara Hassan, the Turkish pirate and one of the strongest men of Arouz. He did not remain with us for a long time though, as he deserted us. Sometime later, he was killed in Algiers by Arouz's hand.

Every time our fleet expanded, new captains would be added to our list. Our captains were mainly from Greece but we also had skippers from France, Genoa, Sicily, Naples, Spain, Calabria, Corsica and even Albania and Hungary. Except for the Greeks who would come to us mainly to escape the oppression and cruelty they endured under the Turks in Greece and in the islands the rest of them, the majority of whom were Franks, were former convicts who were condemned for debts they owe and other 'heavier' criminal acts. By recruiting themselves into our piratical fleet they were in fact signing a treaty with freedom, especially since they knew that if they were caught again they would have to face the guillotine or the scaffold. That is exactly why they fought with such fierceness and fury against their ex-compatriots when they confronted them in battle.

To stand a chance of survival in case they were captured, they even converted to Islam and changed theirs or adopted new Moslem names so that they would be taken for Berbers or Turks.

Only then could they shun death after resuming their seats on the benches in the holds.

My position in Arouz's piratical fleet was weighty and significant. I had also adopted a new name, but this time it was an Arabic name as the language we used in Tunisia to be understood by the inhabitants was Arabic. Therefore, I named myself Erm, with a throaty E as in Arabic most vowels are pronounced either gutturally or glottal. Next to Erm they added the attributive title, reis, because they always saw me next to Arouz. Hence, after Ermolaos and Leonar I adopted a third name, Erm, which was soon modified to Arm or Arm reis. I have to admit that this name proved to be 'advantageous' for me as it induced the pirates' respect and shielded me from the anger and vindictiveness of Venetians...

I reported directly to Arouz and I avoided having business dealings with any of the other captains including Hizr. Arouz trusted me and relied upon me on his expeditions, especially after his success with the papal galleys, which he owed primarily to me and my interpretation of the letters. Accordingly, he assigned me to read and decode the correspondence transported by the ships we looted so that we would be able to know, in advance, what kind of ships would cross the narrow passageway between Tunisia and Sicily, and consequently, after proper preparations, could decide upon the appropriate time of attack. That was a task that I continued to carry out all my life in the piratical galleys and which secured my protection from the rest of the pirates and their unpredictable behavior.

I was only close to Aidini after what we had been through on the benches in the hold of the galley of the Knights. The bond of friendship gets tighter when two people share hardships and difficult moments and this happened with Aidini, Arouz and myself...

In the meantime Arouz became famous in most of the Christian countries. His success with the papal galleys was so outstanding and unrivalled, that not even the doges could believe or accept the enormity of his victory.

The expansion of his fame was mainly due to the captives we released after receiving their ransom. They returned to their countries, narrating their experiences in the slave markets of North Africa, magnifying the events and describing the notorious pirate as a monstrous creature with red hair and beard. Thus the sobriquet of Arouz, the red bearded pirate or Barbarossa, accompanied him all his life and was bequeathed to his brother Hizr after his death.

But let's take the events in their correct order.

Our 'partnership' with Muhammad, the Sultan of Tunisia lasted for three years. He would receive his share and let us spend the winters in his country. In springtime, when the weather had improved, we would abandon our slothful and idle life on the land of Goletta and in other harbors in Tunisia and we would spurt out on to the sea.

The sea passageway separating Tunisia from Sicily was the best trap for the overloaded trade ships that were coming from the East and heading for the harbors of Italy, France and Spain in the West. Our piratical ships had become so many that every time new pirates detected our rich prey, they were joining us. They all exposed their loyalty and faith to Arouz so that they would be accepted into our fleet.

Arouz, my childhood friend and fellow villager from Paleokipos in Lesvos, had become the most powerful and awesome tyrant in the area. Everyone feared him but most of all the captains of the merchant ships, who, every time they heard his name, 'Barbarossa the pirate', would change course that is if they had the time to do so, otherwise they would surrender unconditionally, for they would choose captivity over death.

The fame of Barbarossa spread all over Europe and sovereigns despite their childish disputes amongst themselves started to deliberate ways that would annihilate the red bearded pirate. The first action they took was to intimidate him. Intimidate who? Barbarossa? He was not afraid of anything and they knew this fact very well. Their second thought was then to turn to the Sultan of Tunisia and warn him that if he did not expel him from his harbors they would attack his country and annihilate everything in their way.

The sultan, despite his admiration for Arouz and his men, considered this ultimatum several times. In the end, fearing the consequences of an imminent war, he decided not to employ his 'gallantry' against the Europeans but resort to diplomacy instead.

He indicated to Arouz that he would grant him the island of Jerba, in the southeast of Tunisia, providing he desisted from marauding in his territorial waters. Arouz, who had become restless and impatient with the sultan's never-ending stipulations, accepted, but in fact he had something else in mind. As soon as we reached the island separated from the mainland of Africa by a narrow stretch of sea he proclaimed himself the 'Sultan of Jerba.

The local people of Jerba, mainly peasants, acclaimed his decision and accepted him with enthusiasm. The poor islanders even predicted a brighter future as they anticipated the marketing of slaves to be developed on their island, and dreamt of treasures and rich ransoms as well as ventures being initiated from the pirates' dealings. Arouz demanded that his men treated them with kindness and generosity so as not to have them as adversaries, and we gave them an ample portion of the treasures we had brought with us.

No sooner had Arouz set foot on the island than he took the captives out of the holds and transformed them into builders. They built a fort around the harbor of the island, towers, and even a palace to accommodate the first reises, including myself. Thus, Jerba was metamorphosed into a powerful fortress that no European warrior would dare to penetrate.

I was trusting that with this conquest endowed to us by God we would at last find our serenity and peace of mind, since Arouz had satisfied his ambitions and became a sultan. However, forgive me, Lord; man, whom You created, bears an inexhaustible amount of greed and vanity. Before the year was over, Arouz was satiated with his small sultanate and sought more.

Jerba was too small for Arouz's never-ending ambitions, and he desired a chance for greater conquests and the chance he had been expecting came just in time, a chance that if he had known beforehand what it would have caused him, he would have cut his own hand before signing any agreements.

But I should recount the events in their right order.

It was the spring of 1512, when the emissary of a tribal chief called Mehmed arrived in Jerba. Mehmed used to be the Sultan of Bizana, a city to the east of Algiers, which we simplified and renamed Bouzi for its articulation in Arabic was difficult for us to pronounce.

This city was renowned for its thriving commercial activities but mainly for the fact that it had mastered all the seaways between Spain, the passageway of Gibraltar, and the whole centre of the Mediterranean Sea, including Italy and Sicily. Its position was much more advantageous than that of Jerba's, which was somehow isolated, and our ships needed a much longer trip to be able to reach the routes used by the Venetian and Frank trading ships.

Mehmed had, been dethroned by the Spaniards two years before when they captured his city for their nautical needs. He was therefore asking Barbarossa, through his emissary, to help him to repossess his city, offering him tax free refuge in return, right after he had taken power again.

Arouz accepted immediately and signed the contract of agreement expressing his support and solidarity to the tribal chief.

'He is so naive to believe that I will seize his city to deliver it into his hands,' he said to me with a cunning smile.

We loaded our ships with cannons, battering rams, catapults, and all the artillery we kept in the fortress of Jerba and we set sail for Bouzi. Mehmed was waiting for us on the shore and was jubilant and elated for he was confident of the outcome. We unloaded our armament in a small bay near Bouzi and started the preparations for the attack. However, things were very different compared with our experiences in assaults and raids at sea and we were absolutely ignorant of fighting wars on land.

Very soon we realized that our cannons were ineffective as they were too small to break open the impenetrable fortification of the city. The iron cannonballs, along with the rocks, fell on its walls and were shattered into a thousand pieces without causing them the slightest damage or fracture, and worst of all, the Spaniards, well organized and more than adequately equipped, confronted the piratical crews with the adroitness of expert warriors. When they witnessed our unequivocal defeat which very shortly befell us they started to jeer and boo from the top of the walls, aggravating our anger. They were actually only a handful of soldiers who were appointed to defend and guard Bouzi by the Count Pedro Navaro after he had seized the city.

Arouz was full of resentment and indignation, for this notorious pirate did not expect such ridicule. In a short while the ridicule reached its limit. The Spaniards sent a herald carrying a message to Arouz in which the Spaniards asked him to surrender and in return they would spare his life.

This provocative action was the last straw for the wrath that was devouring Arouz's heart all these scorching days of August. He apprehended the emissary, stuffed him in the cannon and sent him back to his people!

You want an answer? Here I am sending you the answer!' he cried out loud.

I did not know what had become of the wretched man who was flung in that inexorable way the last time I saw him he was high in the sky flying over the walls of the city. As Arouz had exceeded all his limits he demanded his men to invade the city.

Naturally the leader of the invasion was Arouz himself he was always the first to dash against our rivals followed by the rest of the pirates who ran gasping for breath behind him. The Spaniards did not anticipate such a heedless attack. At first they were baffled by our recklessness but then they employed their dexterity against us, as soon as we reached their launch site. We left many dead and casualties behind us but no one dared to retreat or abandon the battle because Arouz kept marching ahead.

The first pirates managed to ascend the walls using the ladders they had brought with them, followed by the rest of us. They confronted the Spanish soldiers.

We would have won the battle if something totally unexpected had not hindered our impetus. He was fighting a long way ahead of us with his sword when a shot, hurled from a launching machine, hit Arouz's arm, mutilating it from its elbow. The Spaniards would have mangled him if we had not run to rescue him just in time. The only thing we managed to do, though, was to take him away from his slaughterers and carry him back.

When our comrades saw the mutilated hand, they lost faith and courage and retreated with us. In the end we ran to avoid the shots of the Spaniards, who fortunately did not come outside the walls of the city. This was a lesson we learned.

We transferred Arouz to the fastest ship and selected the strongest, most efficient oarsmen to get us back to Tunisia before it was too late. Hizr remained behind to collect what was left over from the havoc.

It was a complete disaster that nobody had foreseen. Only I had had some presentiments and doubts about our competency to fight a war on land that was different from our raids at sea in so many ways. But no one had listened to me...

I tied Arouz's arm using ship's yarn, so that haemorrhage would be stopped, but his hand was bleeding incessantly. Arouz did not regain consciousness until we reached Tunisia and there we got him ashore and ran to call the quacks of the area.

At this point, I should mention that in Tunisia the art of surgery was very popular and that there were many 'surgeons' who excelled in it their aptitude having been acquired from experience with pirates. Due to the urgent and recurrent demand in Tunisia there were many surgeons who knew their job perfectly. They would cut the numb member of the body and put herbs and other therapeutic ointments in the place of the wound to stop the hemorrhage so that it would heal as fast as possible.

Hizr amassed all our ships and joined us in Tunisia. On his way, however, he ran across a galleon that belonged to one of the richest merchant families in Genoa, called Lomelini. The galleon transported sapphires, rubies and a crew, and the passengers were even dearer than the prey itself. He plundered it so as not to waste such a chance and sailed to Goletta to see his brother who was still unconscious.

The plundering of the Genovese galleon proved to be disastrous for it brought about negative consequences. The Genovese were ruffled by this action, because they saw that the fate of commerce in the centre of the Mediterranean was at stake, and since the eastern part of the Mediterranean was mastered by Venice, their rival state, they decided to take measures against the handful of Berber pirates who had arbitrarily settled in Tunisia. Members of their senate called upon the Genovese captain, Andrea Doria, giving him ten galleys and ordering him to sail to Tunisia to eliminate the pirates' wasps' nest.

It was in December 1512 when Doria's fleet made its appearance on Goleta's horizon. When we saw it, we ran to take weapons but we had no leader to direct us. Arouz was still lying unconscious in his bed and none of the other commanders were able to confront such a grand fleet without guidance and instructions. Moreover, in the midst of our agony and confusion Kara Hassan, one of our chief commanders and able men, deserted us. He took his four vessels, set out for an unknown destination and disappeared.

In this predicament, Hizr had to take command and make fast decisions. As all our ships were still in the harbor, Hizr had to sink four of them the best ones so that they would not fall into the hands of Doria. He set sail with the rest of the ships there were still six of them left to confront the Genovese opponent. However, Doria's galleys were more adequately armed than ours by far, and his cannonballs immersed three of our ships before we could even advance, forcing us to jump into the sea and swim to the shore to rescue ourselves.

Doria did not restrict himself to this success. He discharged his troops on land and chased us to the walls of Tunisia where we managed to enter and lock ourselves in. His soldiers halted there, for the Genovese captain did not intend them to besiege the whole city. Instead, he returned to Goletta and destroyed the fortified installations that Sultan Muhammad had erected there. He demolished the wall that looked over the entrance of the harbor and seized of all our ships, including Lomelini's, and returned to his country triumphantly.

That was the most rigorous and painful blow we had ever received. Doria's success against Hizr the first and the last were astounding and stupendous. Hizr tried to extenuate and with his spirit overwhelmed did not dare to meet Arouz, for he was afraid of his wrath. He knew that his brother would not hesitate to take his head off for the havoc he had caused, although I must admit he did not fail because of ineffectiveness or incompetence. Nevertheless, as soon as the Genovese departed from Goletta, Hizr left and, humiliated, took refuge on our island, Jerba.

In the beginning, he confined himself to his quarters, refusing to see or meet anyone, whilst Doria was being received with honors, applause and enthusiasm in his birthplace by his people who appointed him Admiral of all the galleys in Genoa.

When Arouz heard about this ignominious defeat, wrath and resentment against his brother overwhelmed him. With his left hand for he had no right hand any more he uprooted half of the hairs on his chin. He disavowed and disclaimed Hizr, and it took him a very long time to be able to forgive him, and even then would not assign him with any leading tasks concerning the fleet or what was left of it. The person whom Arouz never forgave was Kara Hassan, the deserter and traitor, but fate was predestined though, from the very first moment that he had set sail and left us to face the ordeal alone.

During this time when Arouz still held the grudge against his brother Hizr did a lot of work in Jerba. He hauled up the ships that were sunk in Goletta and transported them to the island, where he rebuilt them to become able to fight again. He constructed a gunpowder factory and erected warehouses around it for storage, so that we would not have to rely on the European merchants. With the help of his slaves as well as his brother's, he also constructed some new ships.

In the meantime, we were being confronted with a lot of problems in Tunisia. The sultan, either because he was afraid of the Genovese warnings that they would destroy his country if he continued to offer his protection to the pirates, or because he had lost faith and trust in Barbarossa, who was now physically disabled, instigating no fear and awe in anyone, started pressuring us to leave his country.

On Arouz's instructions, two or three times I managed to postpone our departure from the island until he had completely recuperated, but when the sultan's patience was exhausted, we 'packed our things' and returned to Jerba where Hizr received us with honors. Arouz did not speak to him for a long time. He ignored his existence and I knew that Hizr suffered because of that for he loved his brother so much.

Whilst we were in Jerba, we received a new message from Muhammad of Bouzi, in which he was informing us that he was prepared to undertake an expedition to reclaim his city once more and was asking for our support. He had created a new army of Moors, Arabs and Berbers, which would help to storm and seize it from its occupants.

'Ignore his persistency and do not pay any attention to him,' I said to Arouz. 'He is just a jinxed man who has already caused us a lot of damage.'

'And what shall become of us?' he asked. 'Are we going to spend the rest of our lives in isolation and hampered by the rest of the world? Don't you see that we are far from the routes of the merchant ships? We have to make our living farther north where there are better chances...'

I raised some more objections, and so did the rest of the captains, except for Hizr who was still apprehensive of expressing an opinion after the irremediable affliction he had put us through. But Arouz's decision was irrevocable so we loaded the cannons on to our ships once more and set sail for the cursed city of Bouzi. However, we had to experience the intolerable burden of utter failure once more, despite the fact that this time Arouz exposed his strategic excellence.

It was in August 1514 when we bombarded the walls of the city until we broke open a part of them. However, we could not invade until we had widened the breach so that our men could pass through, but this was a major mistake and unfortunately it was not the only one. We wasted precious time and as a result, we fell into the same pitfall as before for, in our attempt to avoid failure once more, we committed a number of unforgivable blunders.

We continued bombarding the walls until the autumn in the same year. However, we had not realized that during our absence, the Spaniards had built a new fortification on the sea side so that they could be provided with supplies continuously. Thus, whilst we were engrossed in our efforts to violate the fortification on the desert side, five grand ships under the command of the Spanish captain Martin de Retheria were sailing unhindered on the side of the new wall. They would anchor unobstructed and unload their provisions as well as a few thousands soldiers, ammunition, and all kinds of war supplies...

At this critical time, our indigenous allies Arabs, Moors and Berbers who were under the command of Mehmed deserted us. They abandoned us on the absurd pretext that they had to sow their land. Arouz could not believe such justifications in the middle of a combating venture. Some others left without any excuse at all and eventually, even Mehmed disappeared out of sight. If I had ever laid hands on him I would surely have strangled him with my own hands for having put us in this plight... Merciful God, forgive me!

Arouz, eradicating the rest of the hairs on his beard and a few from his cheeks since not many were left on his chin any more gave me the order to cease the siege of the city. He also commanded us to embark on our ships so that we could save ourselves and what was left from total havoc. I was hoping that we would return to our safe haven in Jerba, but Arouz had different plans.

You are being unreasonable!' he objected. 'What are we going to do there all alone?'

'We cannot stay on this coast anymore,' I insisted.

We shall stay!' he contradicted abruptly, showing that he would not tolerate any more of my objections.

And how could one raise objections with a man who was groaning like a wounded animal ready to rend whoever came near him? Still, I was the only one who had the courage to express my dissent. Our lifetime friendship and all the hardships we had been through were the weapons that empowered me to oppose him when necessary and express my opinion freely. The only thing Arouz could do was to groan whilst disagreeing.

'And what are we going to do in these waters?' I insisted. We will be aimlessly drifting in the rough seas and in the end everyone will abandon us.'

Arouz pondered over my last words and said, 'Do you think I am a fool who has never contemplated this possibility?'

'Hei, you are the one who insists that we stay in these waters.'

'These are the waters that lick the shore, Erm. We are going to Tzitzeli.'

'Tzitzeli!' I exclaimed. 'But that is a desert area.'

'We shall go there,' Arouz said stubbornly. We shall build our bedrock there. It is going to be our hideout, the base of our operations; this is from where we shall attack,'

Sometime in the past we had visited Tzitzeli to get drinkable water and we knew it well. It was a small and barren peninsula in shallow sea waters, accessible only to our ships with shallow draughts. The enormous galleys of the Spaniards and the Genovese could not reach or even approach it. They would run aground in the shallow waters. I then realized that Arouz had more reasons than the one I had given him...

Thus, around the end of September, 1514, shortly before the storms of the Mediterranean burst out, we resorted to Tzitzeli with twelve ships and about a thousand pirates who remained by our side.

Tzitzeli was not far from Bouzi and this fact gave me the impression that Arouz's stubborn mind still heeded the possibility of a new expedition against Bouzi.

When we reached Tzitzeli, Arouz proclaimed himself a sultan as he had made a habit of doing extending his title to 'The Sultan of Jerba and Tzitzeli'. This title we made sure by his order of spreading quickly and making known to Europe through the slaves who were liberated, so that the doges and kings would know with whom they were dealing. However, the Europeans had their own preoccupations to attend to at that time.

The Spaniards had achieved transatlantic conquests and brought slaves and gold from the West Indies of Colon, and the Genovese still rivaled the Venetians as far as trade was concerned. The latter had even faced problems in the Aegean Sea, for they were engrossed in their attempt to maintain their dominance in the islands from the Sultan of Turkey who tenaciously claimed them and recruited pirates to conquer them, although without considerable success.

Arouz directed all his efforts into organizing a great piratical expedition before the weather worsened, as it was already autumn. We embarked in our twelve galleons and set sail for the open sea, but this time we had a plan to follow.

We spread our galleons in the sea just like fishing nets, and the captains received the order to maintain the ships within visual range of each other, so they could exchange messages and promptly offer help to their neighboring ship when needed. Consequently, with twelve ships we occupied a great portion of the sea between Sicily, Sardinia, the Balearic Islands and Spain. In this huge net great fish were caught!

Three majestic, fully armed Spanish galleys they were huge merchant ships that could each transport a treasure of merchandise, a hundred soldiers and two hundred slaves to handle the oars made their appearance in the horizon heading for one of the harbors in Spain.

The venture was much easier than we had anticipated. The soldiers were unaccustomed to sea battles, and they were already worn out after the nausea and vomiting they had endured during a stormy night at sea. Moreover, the slaves, taking advantage of the soldiers' impairment, revolted and rebelled against the crew and managed to liberate themselves. The rest of the passengers, with fear imprinted on their faces, waited peacefully up on deck to surrender, hoping that their relatives would pay us for their ransom.

We towed the ships to our aft and set sail to Tzitzeli in the high winds. We imprisoned the slaves in the caves of the surrounding hills until the Catholic priests would negotiate their ransom, and we unloaded the merchandise.

Arouz treated the natives with exceptional generosity. They were poor people cultivators of land. He assembled them in the harbor along with the highlanders of the nearby areas who had heard about the distribution of wealth and had come down to the shore and gave each one his share of the pickings and the wheat we had stolen from the Spanish ships. The local people were thrilled with the goods they had so bountifully received and they declared Arouz the sultan of their area. He accepted their kind offer and gave them a few diamonds that we had stolen from the ships.

In the days that followed, Arouz devoted his time and effort to the people of Tzitzeli. He gave orders to his slaves to build works to make life easier for the natives, who were enchanted by his charming and docile nature after all they had endured from the previous sheikhs who occasionally ruled the area, and the expeditions of the Spaniards. To them he was a brother and savior who detached them from poverty, hunger, hardship and suffering.

This illiterate man from Mitilini knew how to establish authority in a country. He had to affiliate himself to its native population and win their respect and trust. He implemented this strategy with great success in Tzitzeli and the natives worshipped him.

It was then that a Kadi called sheikh, Aben el Kadi, made his appearance with his men to protest against the trespassing on his land and the insulting disregard of his supremacy in Tzitzeli.

Arouz heard him, at first, with dissimulated patience and understanding, but the sheikh kept on groaning and grunting, hoping that he would persuade Arouz and drive him away from his country. When Arouz had had enough of his persistent complaints, he suddenly leaped from his seat with a flushed face, grabbed his sword and with a flashing movement cut his head off in front of the eyes of his thunderstruck men and compatriots. Arouz made it clear that he would not tolerate any more grumbling.

Following a 'democratic' process, he asked the Arab's men if they wanted to follow their sheikh or their new ruler. In unison, they all conscripted for Arouz, who was kind enough to grant them their lives and placed them in the holds of his ships, as 'free' oarsmen to be sufficiently trained in rowing.

Soon after that, he demanded that the sheikh's head be hung on one of the walls of the city, to remind the natives of the incident so that no one would succumb to the devil's temptation as he said and rebel against him.

'Is this how we are going to live from now on?' I remarked one day. 'Haven't you had enough?'

'What do you have in mind? Aren't you satisfied with what we have achieved so far?'

'It isn't that at all. It's just that I miss home. I think the time has come for us to return home.'

'To Mitilini?' he asked, almost bewildered.

'No, to Paleokipos...'

'And from kings you wish for us to become fishermen again? Is this your ambition in life? What are we going to do in Paleokipos, unless you want us to reduce ourselves to petty pirates, drifting around the Aegean and stealing fish out of the fishermen's nets? Here, we are kings!'

'Kings who try every day for survival...!'

I continued in the same way, whilst Aidini and Hizr were following the conversation. They did not dare to interrupt us or express an opinion for they knew that only I had that privilege.

'And shall we continue to eliminate people in this way? Where are we heading to with such gruesome tactics?'

'And what do you expect us to do? If we do not kill them first they could eat us alive!'

Forgive me, Lord, but I found his argument reasonable. As Your creatures have this imperfection, they have a stomach that needs food all the time and if they cannot find it, they steal it from other creatures sometimes even along with their lives to survive. However, let Your wish be so...

'They won't even have us cooked...' Hizr suddenly intervened with a faint smile on his lips. He just wanted to sound witty.

I turned and directed a harsh look at Hizr, who recoiled instantly, for he knew at which point he should stop when I was talking to his brother.

To my surprise Arouz smiled. However, ignoring his brother's remark he turned to me.

'Pick yourself a pretty slave. Only a woman will disperse your nostalgic mood... It seems that you are getting emotional lately, but have you forgotten what you have been through in Paleokipos? Do you want me to remind you?'

The sweet face of my mother flashed into my mind. I was tearful.

'See, I have warned you...' Arouz went on, observing my reaction. 'Go now; fetch yourself beautiful lass and soon your fervent burden will dissolve. I shall speak to you again tomorrow.'

We did not tackle this issue ever again. We did not need to since the events that followed were thrust upon us with such speed that we did not have time to think about anything else but our survival. Still, as I have mentioned before, Arouz had changed. He was not a mere pirate anymore; now he had become the master of a whole country; now he was a monarch and a leader. He had received the title of The Sultan bestowed upon him by his people very seriously and behaved accordingly. Besides, he was not worshipped for his intelligence, but for his strength and potency and his efforts to secure and maintain a good life for his people.

Arouz was a realist; he knew that he had to do everything he could to maintain what he had accomplished. Therefore, he behaved like a genuine leader in the area and ordered works to be done for the benefit of his people and forts to be erected for their protection and the safe keeping of his dominance.

In a very short while, he had mastered the waters of the Mediterranean Sea, and he was unrivalled. Very few ships could cross the sea of Tzitzeli, and the Genovese merchants were mainly the ones who had to withstand the consequences and tolerate the damage caused by our expeditions. I am certain that many of them started to react against their admiral, Doria, who did not dare to sustain his assault on Tunisia and did not take advantage of the opportunity to exterminate us when it was given to him. From the information I received from the slaves, we knew that there was still much vexation held against him.

Still, it was too soon for the senate of Genoa to decide on a new campaign against us. They were well aware that they would have to risk a great deal, since the desert expanse could be used as our sanctuary in case the Genovese admiral persecuted us. Thus, their irresolution and indecisive less on one hand and their friction with neighboring countries on the other, gave us both the opportunity and the time to reinforce and intensify our new position.

But, as I have repeated many times before, Arouz was rapacious and his ambition was never satiated. His title 'Sultan of Jerba and Tzitzeli' was not enough for he always desired a bit more, and this 'more' came with a momentous event.

In 1516, the king of Spain, Don Ferdinand nominated by the Catholics who had annihilated whole populations such as the Moors and the Saracens and those wretched ones in the West Indies of Colon beyond the Atlantic, died at the age of sixty-two. Spain mourned the death of Ferdinand in Algiers, but the rest of the Berber territories celebrated the death of the infidel with songs and dances, especially the Moors whom the late king, and queen Isabelle, had driven away from Spain. Most of the expelled Moors found refuge in Algiers, where they were forbidden to endeavor any kind of professional activity, and worst of all they had to pay onerous taxes. Isabelle, Ferdinand's respectful wife who had helped him to exterminate two populations had died a few years earlier, conceding her place to a beautiful and tender young woman.

But if you, my reader may ask me, what is the association between Barbarossa, Ferdinand and Algiers? Well, I shall answer you this:

Reality sometimes surpasses fantasy for there, in Algiers, a game of passionate love and power took place with this ferocious and ravenous pirate in the leading role!

Five

Three months after the death of Ferdinand, Prince Selim, who was domiciled in the environs of Algiers, sent his emissary to Barbarossa...

But before I narrate what resulted from this encounter, I should first include a few historical events so that the mission of the emissary, as well as the course of events in which we were involved, are well understood.

When the news of Ferdinand's death had spread to the coasts of Barbary, the population of the area did not conceal their rapture and gratitude to Allah, who had redeemed them from such a tyrant. The death of the Spanish monarch was especially celebrated by the Moors the so-called Saracens who, as I have stated before, the late king and his wife had ruthlessly exiled from Spain.

These Moors, who had seen their possessions disappear in one day and themselves banished except for a few of them who remained on the Spanish coast as slaves to the Spanish lords held an unquenchable grudge against the king, his wife and the Spaniards in general, who would attack them every now and then on the North African shores, showing their fear of their expansion and new attempts of aggression against their country.

After their expulsion, the Moors found refuge in Algiers, a small settlement then, and cohabited peacefully with the Arabs, Berbers and other natives. They remained Moslems since the Catholic monks did not have time to lure them to Christianity as they had done with the populations in the West Indies of Colon adopting the traditions and customs of the native population, but maintaining their particularities and vehement temperament as well as their aversion towards the Spaniards.

Algiers was not far from Tzitzeli; in fact, it was near Bouzi, which always reminded us of our misfortunes and failure. It was us the pirates of Barbarossa who attributed this name to the settlement, for its real name was El Tzazaier which means 'the islands'. The Arabs may have rendered it such a name because of the morphology of its shores, or perhaps because of the ancient Roman city, Caesarea, which is near there. I really do not know for certain; however; we named the place 'Algiers' and were through with its difficult pronunciation.

The Moors of Algiers, who were obligated to pay a tax of subjugation and servitude to the Spanish and at the same time were deprived of any kind of business activity, heard about the death of their persecutor and rebelled. They refused to pay their taxes and declared their independence, despite the fact that right across from the harbor of Algiers lay in a small island on which the notorious Spanish fort of Penion, manned with a powerful Spanish garrison, was threateningly real.

Some of the most estimable Moor families, after deliberations with the natives, called upon emir Selim who had temporarily settled in the area and asked him to protect them and become their leader. The Arab monarch accepted their offer but as he felt 'weak' in the number of his soldiers, he searched for allies in the surrounding areas it was then that he found us.

His emissary appeared before Barbarossa and explained the cause of his mission. If we accepted to support the emir and move to Algiers, we would have free access to the harbor in defiance of the fort of Penion. We would also procure everything we wished for without having to pay anything in exchange.

Arouz thought carefully about the offer and very soon he expressed his acquiescence to the emissary.. However, he had other insidious intentions on his mind that he did not reveal to anyone, not even to me... He gave his brother, Hizr, orders to load the cannons on to our boats and transport them to the harbor in Algiers. Arouz, Aidini and I had to follow him on land and we would meet him in a few days.

We marched across the desert with eight hundred pirates, three thousand natives and two thousand Moors who had volunteered and sworn revenge on the Spaniards. Before we reached Algiers as instructed by Arouz we deviated and went further north to the town of Shershell.

There, we paid a 'friendly' visit to our former cooperate, Kara Hassan, who had abandoned us in the critical moments in Goletta and Tunisia. Kara Hassan had domiciled in the area soon after his desertion and had proclaimed himself the Sultan of Shershell, whilst ravaging across the sea from his town.

He graciously welcomed us to his palace, for he was well informed about the last events concerning the insurrection of the Moors and vainly believed that we had gone there to solicit his assistance. However, he did not hold this optimistic attitude for long, for right after the salutation formalities, Arouz changing his disposition sternly asked him why he had deserted and betrayed us in Tunisia. Kara Hassan was startled for he had not expected such an interrogation from his guests in his own palace and tried to digress.

'Kara Hassan,' Arouz interrupted him, harshly. 'Do you know how I reward traitors?'

The Sultan of Shershell was speechless.

'Why don't you answer me, Kara Hassan?' Arouz insisted.

Kara Hassan did not know what to say although he knew the answer. He knelt before Arouz and beseeched him to spare his life whilst promising from now on he would remain faithful and loyal to Barbarossa.

Traitors always remain traitors, Kara Hassan. Once traitor, always traitor, Arouz thundered. Once they have committed treachery, they never change. So, answer me, do you know how I punish traitors?'

Kara Hassan's face flushed as he was thinking about traitors and treason.

You cut them into pieces and give their flesh to the dogs,' he said breathlessly.

That's right, Kara Hassan,' Arouz replied. 'And that is exactly what I am going to do right now.'

And before anybody could think of moving, he flashed his sword in the air and directed it with force on the nape of the defector. His head rolled over on the floor before our dumbfounded eyes. Then Arouz turned to Kara Hassan's men who were breathlessly watching the appalling scene without being able to react, and commanded them to take the headless body, tear it to pieces and give each piece to the dogs of the town. As for the head, he had it hung on the wall of the city so that it would set an example to whomsoever had Obscure' thoughts on his mind.

After that he assembled the people of the city of Shershell and following his unvarying 'democratic' procedures, he asked them to give allegiance to him unless they preferred to follow their leader. The people of Shershell voted for him unanimously and started to cheer and applaud for Barbarossa, the new sultan of their city thus Shershell was added to the sultanates of Jerba and Tzitzeli.

We recruited new men, mainly selected from the local people, and purloined the cannons, ammunition and the other supplies of Kara Hassan after we had appointed a powerful garrison formed of reliable and trustworthy men in Shershell and we set out for Algiers, where Hizr was waiting for us.

Prince Selim received us at the gate of the city himself, leading a forceful army formed by a thousand Moors who had reserved a very cordial and enthusiastic welcome...

Right after the festivities, Arouz took control of all the significant posts in Algiers, and naturally appointed his own guards at its walls. Being even more knowledgeable and experienced now after what we had gone through in Bouzi he sent a delegation to the fort of Penion, to the leader of the Spanish garrison, proposing a thoroughfare to the sea, providing that they surrendered.

The Spanish, however, were obstinate and arrogant. They were not used to surrendering effortlessly and their answer exasperated Barbarossa.

Neither your threats nor your offers can entice us, they wrote in a message that was launched over the walls of the island. They did not dare to send an emissary after the 'flying' episode in Bouzi. They also added, Do not have any illusions about fallacious victories and do not forget what befell on you in Bouzi. The wisest action you can take is to depart from Algiers at once, before the situation gets even worse.

Arouz was outraged by the provocative content of their message. He set the artillery around the walls of the fort and set off a barrage of cannon shots that lasted for twenty days. Nevertheless, despite the prolonged siege, no substantial damage was done. Our cannons were still small, and powerless to cause the slightest breach in the Spanish walls. For them we needed bigger, more powerful cannons; thus, we decided to suspend the siege until we were supplied with new and more efficient cannons that would either be bought from the French or plundered from piratical raids upon Spanish galleys.

Nevertheless, our withdrawal from the fort of Penion was followed by a period of stagnation and inactivity, which gave Arouz plenty of time to plot and contemplates our new adventures. As I have mentioned before, 'An idle mind is the orchard of the devil', and Arouz's head was seeded with new treacherous thoughts; thoughts of becoming the king of Algiers.

He knew that with more subjects and followers, he could achieve the seizure of the fort of Penion much more easily if he was also supplied with greater and more efficient artillery. But in order to accomplish his goal and become the king of Algiers first he had to eliminate Prince Selim, who had committed one more tragic mistake, besides inviting us to Algiers. He had introduced Arouz to his wife, Princess Zaphira, a ravishing woman of noble Arabian origin thus, a game of love and power took place in Algiers.

Since he was still in Tzitzeli, Arouz was scheming to exterminate the prince and marry his widow, for only then would he become the indisputable sovereign of Algiers whom every king in the Mediterranean would esteem, honor and glorify. Hence, he put his plan into operation, with complete secrecy.

One day, when the prince was having his bath in the public Turkish bath, Barbarossa dashed in finding him all alone, naked and defenseless. At first, he tried to strangle him with a wet napkin he had found, but when Selim managed toward him off, Arouz drew out his yataghan.

The poor and helpless prince had to confront the mighty Barbarossa completely naked and unarmed. In the beginning he tried to defend himself, but having no clothes on something that made him feel at a disadvantage before his puissant opponent he began to run helplessly in the chambers of the hamam. The scene was repulsive: a completely naked man running in panic with his private parts oscillating; crying his heart out and beseeching the powerful Barbarossa for mercy.

Eventually, he did not evade his double-edged weapon. Two blows and were left listless. However, what was most awkward in that moment was the fact that Selim right after the first stab had an erection... We were all amazed, except for Arouz who never paid attention to these matters. One more stab right in the heart confirmed to the stupendous pirate that Selim's erection was momentary and that he would not budge from the place where the yataghan had nailed him. His body lay spiritless in one of the corners of the bathhouse.

Arouz rinsed his hands of his blood and hastened out of the bathhouse, ordering us to follow him. I was the last one to leave the place and Arouz was irate at my tardiness.

As we left the premises of the bathhouse, Arouz saw some Arabs who had probably come to bathe approaching. He signaled us to get back into the hamam again and led us to where the body lay. As soon as he reached the corpse, he affected a mixture of great surprise and concern at the death of the prince. He even started to scream and howl that some traitors had brutally assassinated the emir. He gestured to us to do the same and we started to bellow over the body, so that the rest of the people were persuaded that we had nothing to do with the assassination. However, none of the inhabitants in Algiers believed us. They did not have the slightest doubt that we had committed treachery and that we harbored the same fate for them.

No sooner had the news of his death spread in Algiers, than the people locked themselves in their houses leaving the field free for us to act. If at that point they had amassed in the streets or attacked us, none of us would have remained alive.

We immediately took hold of the critical posts of the city, fearing the insurrection of the mob once they had recovered from the sudden death of Prince Selim.

In a very short while, the citizens behind the closed doors and windows of their homes heard the clatter of our horses that ferociously ran in the streets of the city. We were screaming slogans against the Spaniards who allegedly schemed against the benevolent prince and actually killed him in a most cowardly way.

At the same time we sent our heralds to the neighboring cities to announce that there was external danger impregnated by the infidel Christians, and that it was wise for everyone to remain shut in their own houses to protect themselves from being massacred by the Spaniards. They also announced that Arouz, because of the predicament that had befallen Algiers after the conspiracy and assassination of the emir, was taking over the authority to safeguard and protect the city from an impending attack.

Arouz appointed me as the eyewitness of the slaughter of the prince and made me write a proclamation to the citizens which the heralds read to the people of Algiers so that everyone would be informed about the course of events that had taken place in the bathhouse.

In this upheaval I wrote the following proclamation:

After the assassination of the faithful and benevolent Prince Selim, whom Allah had placed on his right side, the commander in chief, Arouz, submitting to the holy will of Allah and the order he has received directly from the Prophet, succeeds the emir and therefore is proclaimed the king of Algiers.

Long live Arouz, the commander in chief whom God has chosen to liberate the people of Algiers from the oppression of the Spaniards, and may he rule with prudence and clemency. Curse and havoc to whoever tries to dispute this charismatic and lawful king.

I added the last phrase so that the people of Algiers would understand clearly that Arouz would not tolerate any kind of opposition and place before them finished facts as the new 'sultan' had wished me to do. Arouz had already settled in the great parlor of Selim's palace surrounded by his most reliable and faithful pirates waiting for his subjects to appear before him, pledge him loyalty and devotion and congratulate him on assuming his new duties. However, only a few turned out most of the people avoided coming altogether. Arouz was outraged by their behavior and sent his troops to bring them to the palace by force.

The ritual of recognition and expression of devotion to the new sovereign lasted for three days. Last of all came the reluctant dignitaries of Algiers, for they were left with no other choice. They were even compelled to sign the edict of his ascending to the throne and promulgate him king of Algiers. After the ceremony Barbarossa read a new proclamation which stated the following:

You must all return to your regular and peaceful activities without fear or apprehension because now you must know that you have a father who will look after you. I, Arouz, am the sole protector who will encompass you with tenderness as if you are my legitimate children and I will always act like a genuine father.

In the meantime the young son of the assassinated emir, fearing that he would have the same fate as his father, managed to escape to Oran, accompanied by two domestics. When Arouz heard about his flight, he was enraged. In the beginning he held me responsible for his escape, and issued orders to his men to behead the two wardens who were guarding his quarters. However, having listened to my advice once more, he repressed his exasperation so that no more suspicion or negative impressions would be raised in the heart of the boy's mother, Princess Zaphira, with whom Arouz fell passionately in love.

The young boy, however, was received in Oran with honors and royal tributes by the Marquis Gomares, governor of the area, who pledged animosity and revenge on Barbarossa.

At first, Arouz did not pay any attention to Selim's son's childish activities for he felt powerful and confident. Through coercion and violence, he had established authority whilst at the same time he had bolstered up the fortification of the city, especially its fortress, which was now armed with appropriate artillery and a very strong garrison.

He had money coined in his name and his portrait was engraved on both sides along with the phrase: The King of Algiers. He promoted works of common welfare and reinforced the walls around the city, using the funds of the wretched Moors. Eventually, he restored the fortress of Kasba, for he intended to turn it into his centre of operations right after he had annihilated the Spaniards who still held the fort of Penion.

The people of Algiers the children of the 'tender and affectionate father' very soon realized the impasse in which they had been trapped.

Not long after the new king had assumed his new duties, Arouz gave orders to his most trustworthy soldiers to execute anyone whom they suspected was a danger to his safety. Then he accused the victims of being accomplices of the murderers of Selim and expropriated their property, evicting their families from their homes.

He resorted to his cruel piratical ploys once more, despite my persistent warnings and exhortations that he could receive whatever he desired from his subjects using less violent methods, such as imposing heavier taxes, fines and other tactics that kings in Europe applied in their kingdoms. But it seems that piracy was in his blood...

Arouz's spies were spread everywhere, reporting every furtive or obscure movement of the citizens. His followers' murdered men, whom they presumed to be conspirators, sold their wives and children in slave markets and confiscated their properties. The people of Algiers were exasperated and they could not believe the lethal mistake they had committed in bringing him over to their country. They even wished that the previous situation could be restored, when the Spaniards' only concern had been to collect taxes, leaving them in peace.

Thus, the Moslems started to look forward to the Christians' help and support to deliver them from Arouz's tyrannical grip. They abhorred him so much that every time he appeared in public, passersby would disappear from the streets and run off to hide in their homes.

Nevertheless, despite the miserable conditions that prevailed, Algiers started to develop into an international trade centre. All kinds of merchandise, obtained from piratical expeditions, was transported there to be sold in the local markets. Moreover, many Spanish, French and Italian convicts who had escaped penal servitude found refuge in Barbarossa's land and became legal citizens of Algiers. They would not return to their countries except as pirates to avenge the hardships they had endured at the hands of their compatriots. Most of them converted to Islam and adopted Moslem names to feel more secure.

Amongst the new settlers there were many European slaves who could not be repatriated as their relatives, right after their capture, had appropriated all their possessions and wealth, leaving them with no resources to live on most of them would even die as slaves in Algiers for their ransom was never paid.

Here, I have to mention that in Europe there were laws against those heirs who renounced their relatives and refused to redeem them from captivity in order to usurp their property. These laws even predicted the forfeiture of their wealth as punishment, but they were often violated and very few snatchers were ever penalized. Consequently, many European slaves remained in Algiers, forming a peculiar kind of society with four or five formal languages: Spanish, Italian, Arabic, Turkish and of course Greek because of the pirates. Thus, ironically enough, Algiers was transformed into an international communications centre.

In the meantime, Arouz had started his romantic advances towards Princess Zaphira, who had already rejected many of his offers and persistent invitations to his chambers allegedly to pay her his respects.

The delicacy of her virtue and chastity foreshadowed that only unhappiness could be expected from such a bloodthirsty tyrant, who was also a usurper and assassin of her husband and her people. Consequently, she turned down all his efforts and attempts to approach her. She had also been supplied with a poi nard that she hid beneath her clothes to kill the assaulter of her virtue or at least protect herself from being ravished or disgraced. None of the spies Arouz had placed around her ever found out about it. The women who accompanied her discouraged her from such actions and advised her to remain shut in her quarters until the vehement passion of the pirate was assuaged. Later, when his impetuosity got even more intense and he had to be refused by the princess, they suggested that she should request permission to go to her parental home in the town of Perfon.

Her tenacious refusal exasperated Arouz, but having repressed his anger, after my suggestions of persevering, he allowed her to go to Perfon. He had to affirm as I had recommended his good intentions, his respect, as well as his devotion to her by such a generous action so that she would accept him with free will. I also counseled him that he should resort to milder methods, such as bestowing her gifts and demonstrating submission.

Therefore we offered her all the comforts and sent her many gifts hoping that we would mitigate her aversion to Arouz that she harbored because of the death of her husband. Along with the gifts we offered her slaves who were actually infiltrators. They would inform and report to us in every possible detail everything that took place in the princess's quarters. The only thing they never discovered was the poi nard...

At the same time I convinced Arouz that he had to act like a lovesick man and that he should write love letters to his adored.

At first, Arouz ridiculed my advice, for it seemed awkward for a pirate to employ such romantic methods. However, when he had carefully reconsidered my suggestion, he yielded and at once ordered me to write a letter on his behalf.

I succumbed to his wishes as I always did and wrote my first letter, and the translation of it from Arabic is exactly as follows:

Arouz Barbarossa the King of Algiers, to Princess Zaphira.

Charming Zaphira, image of the sun, whose transcendent qualities are still more charming than the radiant luster that encircles Perfon. The most fortunate and most intrepid conqueror of the world, to whom everything yields, to thee alone becomes thy slave. I have the tenderest sense of your loss and affliction but passion, which your charms have kindled in my breast, b still stronger. Charms which our great Prophet might behold with admiration were he to return to Earth.

I am rejoiced beyond expression that you have stood the torrent of affliction which at first was comprehended would quite overwhelm you, and that there is hope for your speedy and perfect recovery.

Praise be to the one Almighty God, Who governs all things from eternity. Adore His decree and do not offend Him by any extreme passion. Since He is the disposer of the lives of mankind which is without beginning and what He has ordained from the beginning must come to us whether good or evil. Do not entertain any fears that I shall employ my right of sovereignty to force you to be mine, but I advise you to give me your heart freely. Your station, lovely Zaphira, will raise the envy of all the women in the world. You shall reign like the real queen of thy king and thy subjects in the fullness of absolute authority.

I hope that shortly my velour, seconded by my invincible troops, will enable me to lay all Africa at your feet. Until your elevation is accomplished, you will be mistress in my palace and all your proceedings will be approved. And whoever is the one who shall presume to disobey you and not prostrate themselves to kiss the dust of your feet: such being my supreme order to all my subjects.

Arouz was delighted with the letter and believed that it was only a matter of time before he would put his arms around the beautiful princess. Thus he ordered me personally to deliver the letter to her in Perfon and perhaps escort her on her way back to Algiers. I had no other choice but to accept.

Arouz had grown so impatient that no one would dare to deny him a request.

I reached Zaphira's home late at night. At first her women refused to let me meet the princess but I strongly insisted upon delivering the letter from the king of Algiers into her hands. Zaphira appeared before me. When she saw that the letter was sent by her husband's assassin she could not conceal her grief and anguish. With a heavy heart she opened it and read it. At first she denied me the reply, but then a wise elderly woman advised her to answer his letter so that she would not torment his temperament even more. They spoke in their language, but I well understood everything they said for I had learned excellent Arabic after spending so many years in Barbary.

They asked me to wait until the princess had written her response. My waiting was not prolonged and I soon had the princess's letter in my hand. I did not hesitate to open and read whilst I was on my way to Algiers. I had to know beforehand what kind of reaction I would expect from Arouz.

It stated the following:

The unfortunate Zaphira to the King of Algiers.

Sire,

Any other swayed by glory, greatness and riches, more than by reputation wherein true glory, supreme greatness and the most valuable riches consist would with transport give themselves up to you, to enjoy that shining fortune that you generously offer me.

But for me to accept it would be eternally rendering myself the abomination of all true believers. Allow me, Sire, to remonstrate to you that my husband has lately been taken from me by a violent death in the judgment of all who have viewed his venerable body. Scarcely was the horrid act perpetrated, barely had his dear last breath expired, when you forcefully seized the city.

Your soldiers committed the most shocking cruelties; they have killed, ravished and plundered. In a word, it is by violence alone that you reign, for freedom has no share in your exaltation, and the miserable condition to which the public is brought by your tyranny, affords strong suspicion that you are the murderer of my husband. In complying with your offer I should be chargeable with a share of your guilt and that you and I concerted his death in order to commence our marriage and advancement.

For my part, Sire, I do not think you capable of such a crime, but that is not enough. You must give me the utmost proof of your innocence. I could not bear to live under the least suspicion and would meet a most cruel death rather than stain my character. I must, Sire, entirely justify myself, that your own honor and acquittal is concerned in leaving me herein the mistress of my own conduct.

Few refuse a kingdom when it is within their reach. As a demonstration that you do not reign by the enormous guilt of having murdered a prince who had received you into his house as a brother and an ally against his enemies and likewise, to convince the public that I am as pure and innocent as a harmless lamb make one virtuous effort, if it be true that you love the unfortunate Zaphira. Allow me to return to my native plains of Mutija with the companions of my misfortunes deprived of my dearest person. Allow me to alleviate my sorrows in the embrace of those who, next to the Almighty God, have given me life.

This, Sire, I request in the name of the Sovereign of the Universe; to whom nothing is hid; who enjoys probity, benevolence and the universal practice of virtue and is the avenger of all wickedness. May the Holy Prophet, his well beloved Mehmed, incline you to grant my request and extinguish your passion which would be highly criminal in me, and consequently implicate us both in untaught misfortunes!

As I had anticipated, Arouz was enraged by Zaphira's reply; however, her rejection aroused his passion and rekindled his desire towards her even more. He revenged his wrath and disappointment on everybody in his quarters and if I had not intervened, none of his guards would have remained alive. In the midst of his fury, I implied that he should write to her again as one letter is not enough to influence a woman like Zaphira.

'What more we can write to her?' he thundered. 'There is nothing left to say for we have exhausted all issues in the first letter. I am holding you responsible for this humiliating situation... You are the one who advised me to take such ludicrous action!'

'Patience, patience. We have to persuade her that we are innocent of her husband's blood,' I said breathlessly as I had sensed the extent of his indignation. 'We must send her a new letter in which we shall promise her to hold long interrogations in Algiers until we lay our hands on her husband's murderers and that we shall inflict the cruelest punishment upon the perpetrators.'

Arouz pondered over my idea for some time, for this new contrivance really tempted and entranced him. He could win by using diplomacy for the very first time in his life.

'And where shall we find the perpetrators?'
'We shall recruit volunteers.'
'Volunteers?'
'Yes, volunteers. We shall give them gold and then help them to flee secretively to Egypt that is if they agree to publicly confess that they are the murderers of the prince and that they have committed their crime for theft...'

Arouz grew even more amenable to the idea.

'And where shall we get hold of those volunteers?'

'We shall select the worst members of our crews; those whom we intend to get rid of anyway.'

His eyes flashed at the devilish thought.

'Sit down at once! You shall write the letter,' he commanded.

I wrote the letter, which this time, was delivered by a slave.

The King of Algiers to Princess Zaphira.

Incomparable Zaphira, I was extremely shocked at the part of your precious letter that suspects me as the murderer of Prince Selim God knows how unjust but since it is the bar to my happiness with you, I will clear myself from such an imputation, even if it means the loss of my kingdom. My honor and my love are my concern and if it be necessary, I will discover the guilty party even by causing a torrent of innocent blood. I will immediately give orders to detect him, and terrible shall be his fate and that of his accomplices, if he had any.

That I seized the kingdom upon the death of the trustworthy Prince Selim is true, but where was an equal competitor? Were not the Christians on the point of becoming sovereigns and my courage checked their progress?

Time, I assure myself, will show me to be as innocent as you have accounted me guilty, and then, without the least reluctance you will accept the kingdom I offer you in which you will be adored by all your subjects in imitation of their king.

Whilst the letter was being delivered, we issued an order requesting that anyone who knew anything about Selim's murder was to testify in exchange for a handsome reward.

At the same time, one of Arouz's trustworthy men was negotiating with a man called Ali the price for recruiting people to publicly plead guilty and sign on a special list we called the 'guilty list'.

The men he selected were all Egyptians who were persuaded that by signing a kind of deposition, and publicly confessing their crime, would be helped to flee to Cairo after they had spent some time in prison along with a handsome amount of money as compensation for their services.

The holy month of Ramadan had already started when we decided that the trial would be held in public. Ali testified before the incredulous eyes of the people of the city that he had found out about the conspiracy against the life of the prince by chance, but it was too late for him to hinder it or prevent it from occurring. Then he designated the murderers. The 'criminals' publicly confessed their abominable action and some of them even started to bemoan and express sorrow, to substantiate their repentance for the abhorrent action.

Of course the verdict was condemning and they were all sentenced to death, but instead of being driven to the dungeons of the palace as they had been promised they heard Arouz issuing the order for their instant execution.

The condemned men were flabbergasted for they had not expected such conduct from the man whom they had tried to exonerate. They begged for mercy and beseeched his compassion, but Arouz was relentless. With their immediate execution, he would fulfill his promise to Zaphira and at the same time save the reward he had promised the Egyptians. Then, with a haughty expression, he signaled to his executioners who had been lurking there amongst the crowd to carry out the sentence.

The heads fell off one after the other, before the eyes of the overwhelmed people who feared that the executions might extend to them.

The scene was gruesome. When the executions were over, the heads were spread everywhere in the streets of Algiers and the headless bodies were piled up like sacks.

Ali was the last one to receive his punishment. Arouz did not have him beheaded, instead he had his tongue cut off because as he explained he did not use it to warn us against the conspiracy. In fact he cut his tongue off so that he could never divulge the truth about the devilish scheme of the tyrant and the real cause of the slaughter. Ali was illiterate if he had known how to write he would also have had both his hands lacerated.

Then Arouz commanded that the heads were to be amassed and hung on the walls of the city whilst the bodies were thrown into the sea. Thus, justice was done... After this appalling ceremony, Arouz commanded me to write a new letter to Zaphira.

The King of Algiers to the Princess Zaphira.

Lovely and incomparable Zaphira, now I am cleared of the monstrous crime which had been charged upon me so insolently. The accomplices have been put to death upon their own confession which has saved a great deal of blood for not one of my subjects would have been left alive if my honor and your scruples were not satisfied. Now, nothing can withhold you from giving me your hand. Make haste to reign with splendor and power unknown to you before, and upon your union with me, restore to your illustrious ancestors those vast countries which their velour formerly subdued.

The princess, who had expected these words, was under no difficulty when replying.

The unfortunate Zaphira to the King of Algiers.

Sire,

The death of those wretched men, executed by your orders, has not quieted my scruples.

My husband's ghost is ever in my sight. Last night I dreamt that it appeared to me by order of T\ie Prophet and informed me that all were poor, deluded, innocent victims. So, Sire, I freely declare to you that I shall prefer death to your offer; nay the end of such a distressing life as mine will be welcome if you presume to act the tyrant in love and force a marriage. But if justice be of any real weight with you, confine me no longer as a slave but send me to my country, in the manner becoming my birth and quality…

All the letters cited in this book arc authentic. They can be found in the book by J Morgan, The History of the Piratical States of Algiers, Tripolis, Tunisia and Morocco.

That was the last letter[27] written by Zaphira.

When Arouz read it, he got so incensed and cholic that nothing could restrain him anymore. Despair had turned him into a beast and converted his love into hatred. He cursed Zaphira and promised himself that he would not comply by gentle methods anymore and that he would use violence. He ordered fifty of his horsemen to accompany him including myself and, giving her no notice, we rushed to her palace.

When we reached Zaphira's quarters, the soldiers took away all the women whilst five captains including myself followed Arouz to the princess's chamber. At the doorway we wavered and had to halt, whilst Arouz darted inside like an arrow. We held our breath as we did not know what was going to happen; however, from our position we were able to watch everything in detail.

When Zaphira appeared in the room, Arouz seized her violently with his sole hand and set forth to undress her he was determined to impose himself upon her at any rate.

Zaphira was resisting and begging him to have pity on her and respect her, but Arouz would not listen.

'Kill me, kill me if you do not wish to respect me,' she beseeched.

But now Arouz had already disrobed her, unveiling her ravishingly fair skin before our bewildered eyes the scene stimulated our senses, let alone Arouz's...

'I am ready, to die, Sire,' Zaphira cried, with resolution. 'Keep your promise and apply your threats for I will never surrender. My husband is watching from above and he will be waiting for you. There, you will pay for your crimes!'

Zaphira's last words checked Arouz's impetus. It seemed that the gullible man must have believed her, because he immediately raised his eyes to see if anyone was watching. When he realized that no one was there, he lowered them again.

The flesh below her voluptuous tummy as well as her black citadel brought his blood into his head and rekindled his vehemence once more. He rushed upon her and tearing her underwear, he opened her legs using his sole hand and his left knee. As he tried to penetrate her, Zaphira stretched out her hand and grabbed the poi nard from a nearby table and endeavored to plunge it into his heart. Arouz warded off the blow and only received a wound in his left arm. He withdrew to bind up the wound, still more exasperated at such an attempt and fiercer in his resolution to overcome her. If he had had, two arms he would not have become so violent but with only one hand his wrath could not to be subdued any more.

In the midst of this short interval and before Arouz could do anything, Zaphira took some poison out of her cloth that was lying there beside her and drank it. The poison operated immediately, depriving Barbarossa of the satisfaction of revenge. She died in his arms before he could satiate his passion for her.

At first, Arouz was flabbergasted and speechless for he had not anticipated such an action from Zaphira. When he recovered from the shock and realized the magnitude of the evil he had executed, he revenged his despair on the princess's women, whom he strangled and buried secretly along with their mistress; the report which was given out later was that they had escaped in disguise.

Very few believed our story, but nothing really mattered any more. The inhabitants of Algiers tried to save themselves from the cruelty and persecution of Arouz's troops. However, after

Princess Zaphira's tragic death, Arouz's days started to count irreversibly.

The great conspiracy that the Moors were preparing was going through its last phase of preparation. The information I was receiving from my informers was very alarming and disturbing. According to it, some people from the most eminent families in Algiers had come into contact with the Spanish garrison in the fort of Penion and had agreed on a mutual operation.

The Moors were going to set our ships which were anchored at the shore outside the walls of Algiers on fire. Whilst we would be extinguishing the fire, the Spanish would get out of the fort, enter the city and lock the gates behind them, leaving us outside. The plan would have been successful had we not found out about it promptly.

We decided to counterattack, taking our measures with great precaution. The operation was scheduled for the night of the second Thursday of the month, so that on Friday, the following day, everyone could go to the mosque to pray and thank Allah for the victory.

On the appointed evening, we sent our trustworthy soldiers to hide amongst the vessels, with strict orders not to harm any of the conspirators and not to use arms unless there was an absolute emergency. The order was to avert arson. And so it was done.

When the sun set and the conspirators emerged within close range of our vessels, our men came out from their hiding places and surrounded them. The Moors were taken by surprise but they justified their presence by using the stupid explanation that they were being watchful of our ships, for the sultan was anxious and concerned about a reciprocal attack by the Spaniards.

Conforming to their sultan's orders, our men did not harm anyone. They just listened to their explanations condescendingly, pretending that they gave credence to them and eventually allowed them to return to the city. The Spanish, however, did not dare to abandon their fort since they had received no signal for attack from the conspirators. Thus, they had to postpone their operation...

The following day, the Moors and Arabs gathered for the Friday prayers in the city mosque. When they all entered the mosque, we thronged outside and firmly secured all tl e gates, placing our guards at them. Only Arouz with some of his most reliable men went through the main entrance.

Having a list with the names of the conspirators in his hand, he interrupted the prayer and started reading out the names one after the other. For each of the men whose name was mentioned, two soldiers ran to him, unfolded his turban and bound his hands with it. Then the conspirators were led outside to the sloping courtyard of the mosque. There, they were all beheaded without being granted the chance to stand trial.

Twenty dignitaries of Algiers lost their lives on that day. Their heads rolled down the main road by the mosque before the eyes of the passersby, who watched the scene with eyes full of wonder, awe and alarm, for they did not understand what was happening.

When the executions were over, Arouz read to the apprehensive worshippers a short speech that I had prepared for him the previous day after his instructions:

Following these unfortunate circumstances and my condemning decisions against those brainless people who, having been brainless, did not need to have their heads any more I call upon my beloved citizens to contribute to the advantage and prosperity of our nation, and voluntarily donate half their property to the treasury of Algiers, so that the works of common interest, which my virtuous administration has planned for your benefit, can be carried out.

Amongst the crowds of worshippers were people who had just lost their sons and brothers and now the tyrant was demanding that they should endow their property 'at their own discretion'. However, no one dared to raise any objection and they all conformed to the spirit of Arouz's speech.

The truth of the matter was, that Arouz in only six years despite his unfortunate expeditions in Bouzi and all the misfortune that had followed him in Tzitzeli had managed to become the indisputable leader of Barbary, the vast desert territory that in the past had never been governed or controlled by steady or constant leaders, except only occasionally and partially by the Spaniards, Arabs and Berbers. This area was of a high strategic significance for it included the routes of the merchant ships in the centre of the Mediterranean Sea.

Arouz became the sultan of the whole country that encompassed Algiers and he was the one who established and built its foundation so that the area survived in the future. He did not live long to enjoy his achievements though. His irresistible inclination for attainments and accomplishments caused his destruction.

In May 1517, if I well recall, a galleon brought us the news that the Spaniards were preparing a powerful fleet with the ultimate goal of attacking us and annihilating us altogether.

According to these pieces of information that I mainly received from the persecuted Moors who had remained as slaves on the coasts of Spain the Spanish Admiral Diego de Vera, after exhortation from Cardinal Himenes of Toledo, boarded ten thousand soldiers, massive artillery and ammunition on his ships and set sail for Algiers to exterminate the 'bees' nest', once and for all.

At first we panicked! The military force of the Spaniards was too tremendous for our potential defense and the prevalent thought was to abandon Algiers, temporarily at least.

When Arouz heard about our resolution he was infuriated. He thundered loudly and stated with determination:

We shall fight back like men!'

It seems that Arouz took immense pleasure in fighting and no one dared to express ' heir scruples to him.

We estimated the time Diego needed to reach the African coast and we prepared ourselves for the attack.

Arouz ordered his brother, Hizr, to guard the walls of Algiers whilst he, with his toughest pirates, camped near the shore, where he conjectured the Spanish would drop anchor and spread a net of sentinels along the length of the African coast. The distance between each sentinel was such as to allow them to convey messages to one another, until they finally reached him.

Soon the ships of Diego appeared on the horizon. It was quite clear that they were heading for the shore where we had camped which incidentally was near the walls of Algiers. Apparently, Diego had planned to disembark his troops there and then advance directly to Algiers.

Arouz summoned all his pirates and gave them orders to hide behind the sand hills that were situated along the shore. Then he ordered them to hurl stones and arrows against the Spaniards as soon as they approached the shore, just before setting foot on it.

'And woe betide anyone who shoots his arrow before or after their landing,' he thundered with the wild temperament that always overpowered him every time he had to wage a battle.

Arouz was well aware that the most crucial point of any military landing was the moment the soldiers came to the shore, right before taking up their posts on land. If they did, then it would have been almost impossible to wrench them from their positions...

Diego gave his landing orders and the first wave of Spaniards fell into the sea. However, just before they reached land, a rain of arrows hindered their way. Most of the soldiers were instantly killed whilst others tried to return to their vessels. However...

As if the devil had known, the stubborn Diego persisted in his attack. To support the first wave and hamper the withdrawal of the ones who survived, he released a second wave of soldiers, who swept the survivors along towards the shore.

Still, none of them was able to get ashore for they were once more impeded by the dense swarm of our arrows. They endeavored to withdraw again but they were prevented by a third stream of soldiers whom Diego sent into the battlefield to reinforce the first two waves. In a few minutes, chaos and confusion predominated in the shallow waters of our coast...

It was then that Arouz ordered a comprehensive attack, which he himself led whilst crying out vague and inarticulate rumbling screams against the Spaniards. Not a head remained erect; anyone who refused to surrender was instantly killed.

Here, I have to cite a report that fell into my hands long after the battle. It was a report written by Bishop Santoval of Pablona, who had witnessed the battle from the Spanish flagship, whilst blessing the wretched Spanish soldiers who were being ruthlessly eliminated one after the other. The bishop quoted the following:

Barbarossa, observing that the waves of soldiers had dispersed, dashed with viciousness and fell upon them with his men, crying out incomprehensible war cries. When our soldiers saw the tyrant in this frenetic condition, they were overwhelmed and overpowered, and tried to withdraw to their ships. Without much effort, the barbarians killed three thousand soldiers and captured four hundred of our men...

The impact of this victory on our reputation was tremendous. Everyone talked about the great hazard the red bearded pirate represented against the welfare of Spain, the mistress at sea, which, although she had managed to settle in the West Indies, had her African 'underbelly' unshielded.

Therefore, they started deliberating ways to obliterate us...

In the meantime, Arouz received a message from the inhabitants of Tlemsen. Tlemsen was a town in the hinterland of Algiers, on the southwest side of Oran, where Zaphira's son had found refuge and who persistently goaded the Spaniards to attack us, so that he would be avenged for his parents' tragic death.

The inhabitants of Tlemsen had declared their submission to Barbarossa, providing that he saved them from their indigenous leader whom they detested. Arouz took advantage of their request and without giving us time to repose, we set off to Tlemsen. Arouz had already sent a note to his brother, Hizr who was still in Algiers to dispatch his artillery via the sea.

We reached Tlemsen in MidAugust and set our artillery in front of the walls of the city, which the sheikh was defending with a military force far greater than ours. The only difference was that his men had never waged a battle before. After the first barrage from our artillery, the defenders of Tlemsen ran away, along with their sheikh. The inhabitants of the city who were now alone received us with great enthusiasm and naturally declared Arouz their sultan.

Arouz was now dominating the whole coast of Barbary, except for the city of Oran, which was governed by the Marquis Gomares and guarded by the fort of Penion, at the entrance to the harbor of Algiers.

The latest news about the seizure of Tlemsen incited the fear and terror of Spain. Barbarossa was now the unquestionable sultan of Middle Barbary with Algiers as its capital. In addition to this situation, the Sultan of Turkey Selim the Cruel, as he was called sent a message to Arouz, in which he acknowledged him as sultan of the area and the beilerbey of Algiers. This endorsement by the sultan the leader of the Ottoman Empire disturbed the Spaniards and their allies even more...

King Charles of Spain who was later promulgated to Emperor of Spain and Germany and was known to the world as Charles V received Gomares at his palace. Gomares expressed his concern about the rapid expansion of the territories under Arouz's dominion.

'We have to act before the Barbarossa brothers take full control of the territories,' Gomares insisted. 'If we do not take immediate action to overturn them as soon as possible, they will isolate Oran on the sea and land side, causing immeasurable damages to both our trade and prestige...'

Here I have to clarify that the Spaniards attributed the same sobriquet 'Barbarossa' to Hizr as well, despite the fact that Hizr's beard was brown with a few grey hairs.

Because of his young age and ardent desire to obtain a military triumph right after ascending to the Spanish throne, seventeen year old Charles agreed with Gomares and organized a new expeditionary force comprised of ten thousand well trained and experienced Spanish soldiers and sent them off to Oran.

Having acquired knowledge and wisdom from the previous failure, the Spanish organized and disembarked the military force on the shore of Oran with utter secrecy. Unfortunately, only when the force was already on its way to Tlemsen where we had settled with Arouz and our comrades, still rejoicing at the trophies of our new conquest did we know about their advent...

When we realized the danger, it was already too late. The advance guard of the Spanish army had already reached the walls and was preparing their unrivalled artillery to set upon the city.

We only had two alternative solutions. The first was to remain in Tlemsen and resist the attack, which was extremely unattainable for the walls of our city were small and frail they would collapse after the first salvo fix m their cannons and the trampling of the soldiers would sweep away everything in their way. The second was to flee in the middle of the night. We opted for the second...

However, luck had already turned its back on us and especially on Arouz.

The Spanish had anticipated our moves and predicted that the red bearded pirate, along with the rest of his men, would take the mountainous hinterland paths to reach Algiers. Thus, they waited for us on the side of the mountain near Tlemsen where their army encountered us. It was then that a fatal chase took place...

Arouz ran before everyone urging his comrades to follow, but the Spaniards had cavalry that was supported by powerful forces of infantry.

As it was midsummer, we were all soaked in sweat and our tongues were burning of thirst, however, we continued to run in the scorching desert to save our lives.

Arouz, who had filled his pockets with diamonds and other jewels from Tlemsen, took them out and threw them behind him in the hope that the Spanish soldiers would be tempted by their luster and interrupt, or at least relax their pursuit to collect them. But Arouz's 'generosity' was to no avail... Gomares fiercely exhorted his men to overlook the bait and persevere in their chase.

At some point we reached a river, the name of which I do not recall. Arouz and our comrades those who could swim fell into the water and crossed to the other bank. The ones who did not know how 'to swim remained behind. When the Spanish troops reached them, they rushed upon them, exterminating them all...

When we reached the safe bank, Arouz heard the cries of the ones who had remained behind, as they were being massacred mercilessly by the Spaniards.

Arouz would not tolerate this ordeal. He had never abandoned his men before in his life, and desertion was not in his nature. He was tough with the men who betrayed him but he never hesitated to help and support his loyal co warriors. Therefore, with a cry full of pain and anguish he dived into the river again and returned to help his comrades who were being brutally massacred. When he reached the bank of the river and before he even got out of the water, he raised his yataghan and dashed upon the Spaniards with unprecedented fury. His attack did not last long. The Spanish soldiers, who kept swarming, set upon him and I lost sight of him for ever...

On the other side of the river after the scene we had watched and, with our hearts encumbered by remorse and guilt, we ran away.

The Spaniards seized Tlemsen soon after Arouz's death. They established their headquarters there and imposed heavy taxes on the natives, taking twelve Arabian horses and six hunting hawks that were endowed as a gift to the King of Spain.

Much later, I found out that the man who had killed Arouz was a Spanish officer called Garcia de Tineo, who, after piercing his heart with his spear, had maimed his head. This man was later honored by the Spanish king himself, who allowed him and his family to obtain the head of Barbarossa and place it amongst their other trophies.

Arouz's mantle inlaid with gold that he was wearing at the time of his assassination was transported to the church of Saint Bartholomew in Cordoba, where it was displayed for the public for many years, under the statue of the saint.

Thus, Arouz Barbarossa never returned to his birthplace: the island of Lesvos. Arouz Barbarossa was acknowledged by many, even his enemies, as a man who left his mark on the history of that era. The Spanish even dedicated poems and epics to him, and a tragic play about his death. Much later he was recognized as the founder of the State of Algiers. The Roman Catholic monk, Abbot Diego de Haedo, who settled in Algiers many years after Arouz's death, met many of his collaborators and servants who had known him well and were able to describe him. In his book, Topographia e Historia General d'Argel, that was published in 1612, Abbot Diego de Haedo writes about Arouz:

Arouz Barbarossa, although a man of middle stature, was exceptionally strong, fearless and inexhaustibly restless. His eyes were moist, sparkling and keen sighted and his nose was crooked like a hawk's beak. His complexion was dark from the sun but the features of his face were refined and gentle. He was courageous, decisive, defiant, generous, reckless but extravagantly liberal. He would get violent and bloodthirsty only when he dashed into battle. He would turn into a beast when he met treason or insubordination... He was loved and respected by his men, soldiers and servants. When he died he left neither a son nor daughter. He lived in Barbary for fourteen years, during which time, the hardships that he amassed for the Christians cannot be described...

Fourteen years had passed since he, as a petty pirate, departed from the Bay of Gera, only to develop into one of the greatest menaces to the Catholic leaders in the West and become the tyrant of Algiers. He was barely forty-five years old when he met with his death...

Six

Haunted by feelings of guilt and remorse, I was compelled to return to Algiers.

After the death of Arouz Barbarossa, the Spaniards believed that they had ultimately defeated the Berber pirates and consequently they returned to Tlemsen. The rest of us those who had survived the massacre, that is burdened and impaired by fear that we might run into Spanish squads once more, took the rough paths in the scorching desert plateau and, famished and exhausted, reached the central gate of Algiers.

I was so fatigued that I did not pay much attention to the bustle and commotion that was taking place in the city. Cannons, ammunition and war supplies were being transported outside the walls of Algiers towards the shore. I did not observe the anxiety that was engraved on the faces of the pirates or the gloating and exultation in the smiles of the natives, who had gathered in their hundreds in the streets of Algiers to watch this tumult and exchange ironical remarks about it.

Straightaway I went to my home, for my only wish was to be shut inside it and to let my slaves take care of my physical and spiritual recuperation, after all I had been through and witnessed.

And so it was done. In only two days, I was well again. Their knowledge of and expertise in a man's body was very effective for both my corporal as well as my spiritual shape.

On the third day, I received a message from Hizr in which he was requesting me to visit him at his palace. Meeting Hizr was something I had hoped to avoid doing, at least for some time after my arrival. However, I could not turn his invitation down, as I did not wish to be misunderstood and then have to face new adventures and new problems once more.

I reached his palace with a torn heart, but Hizr seemed to be sharing the same feelings. I sat on a stool facing his armchair without saying a word to him or even saluting him as if we had been together all this time. We were both immersed in deep pensiveness and lost in our reflections.

As I observed him, I tried to compare him to his brother, my childhood friend, Arouz. At that moment, I became aware of the fact that Hizr was looking very like his brother. He, also, had an imposing stature, even more grand and impressive than that of Arouz who was not as tall. His manners were more refined, courtly and dignified. He was exceptionally hirsute, with dense, long eyelashes and eyebrows. His hair was reddish before it grew greyer with the years and light. That is perhaps why he kept the sobriquet Barbarossa that actually belonged to his brother. Most people in the West thought that it was their family name or title, and many others believed that they were the same person. Hizr, having been aware of the awe and veneration that the name stimulated, retained the sobriquet since he had outlived his brother.

I do not remember how long we were both silent, but I do recall that Hizr eventually spoke first.

'I see that the death of my brother cost you as dearly as it did me...'

'At least as dearly...' I said, knowing that Hizr was an intelligent man and that he would understand what I was implying.

'I quite agree,' he said, showing that he had grasped my allusion. 'You have lived with Arouz many more years than I did and you had been so intimate...'

Yes,' I replied, with a somewhat offensive attitude. 'Do you want me to give you an account of what happened after our departure from Tlemsen?'

I was prepared to recount everything that had taken place even my cowardice and decision not to dive back into that river and help Arouz. As a matter of fact, this thought kept torturing my conscience for it had permanently settled inside my head.

'No, no...' Hizr replied, with a deep sigh. 'I know everything, but nothing could be done, Erm. Even if you had crossed the river, the only thing you would have achieved was to have yourself killed...'

Hizr was therefore well informed about everything, I thought, and strangely enough I felt immensely relieved of my burden.

'And what are you thinking about doing now, Erm?' Hizr asked me, after a few moments.

'I do not know. I have not even had time to think about it... I cannot think about anything any more...'

'Do you know the prevalent condition in Algiers now?'

'No, and to be honest, I do not care either. I have been shut in my home since the very moment I set foot in Algiers. I do not really wish to know...'

'But you must know, because it concerns you as well,' Hizr said. 'We heard that Gomares is returning to Algiers to launch a new attack. He intends to obliterate the rest of us, leaving no pirate alive in Barbary. As a matter of fact, we are packing everything and shall depart from Algiers as soon as possible. We are contemplating going back to Jerba where it is safer... In Algiers we are exposed to unequivocal danger...'

In my mind, I justified the precipitous transportation of the war supplies outside the city they were definitely loading them on to our ships.

I was thoughtful for some time and Hizr was kind and prudent not to interrupt.

'I do not think Gomares would be so reckless as to endanger the triumph he has achieved so far, especially after killing Arouz Barbarossa,' I said. 'I believe that he will be yearning to go back to his country to announce his victory and receive his reward from Charles. Men like him tend to boast about their achievements and swell the events, in anticipation of countless prizes and honors. He will maintain that by killing the leader of the pirates and dispersing his men, he has actually redeemed the sea passages in the Mediterranean from piratical assaults. If we leave Algiers then we will be affirming and endorsing his triumph. Whilst...'

'Whilst?'

'Whilst, if we remain in Algiers, we shall deflate the enormity of his victory and avenge Arouz's death...'

Now that I am writing these words, I do not know for sure if I was articulating all of them or if Arouz was speaking through my mouth!

Nevertheless, Hizr followed my words with vigilance and fascination.

'Are you insinuating that we should stay in Algiers and confront them whenever they attack us?'

*Whenever we attack them,' I stressed. 'In the meantime we could fortify our walls and reinforce our ships. The Spaniards will have to think very seriously about a new aggression, for they will take their previous failures into consideration...'

I paused for some moments for suddenly my friend Arouz flashed in my mind and then I proceeded.

Of course, when they had to confront the mighty Arouz Barbarossa who raised their terror and fear...'

Hizr did not utter a word about my allusion. He scratched his beard whilst considering my words.

'Do you mean you do not have faith in me?' he asked, with no sign of malice.

'Arouz was a great warrior,' I said, spontaneously. 'He dashed into the battlefields heedlessly and impetuously without giving it much thought. He did not even consider his life... You are different.'

'In what way am I different?' he asked, becoming more interested.

You think twice before you dash into a battle,' I replied, adamantly, showing that I did not fear the consequences of his reaction. *You contemplate everything and calculate the results before you take action'

'And which of the two temperaments do you think is more appropriate?' He interrupted me for the first time. 'Dashing into the battlefield impetuously without considering the consequences, or entering the battle after circumspection of the advantages and disadvantages of the anticipated outcome?'

Hizr had inverted the problem and put me into the difficult position of having to answer. The truth of the matter was that Hizr was a completely different man to Arouz, as if they had not come out of the same womb.

I had described Arouz many times before as a brave but impulsive and reckless hero. Hizr was more analytical and crafty. If he judged that the outcome would be to his benefit he would dash into the battle with the same vehemence and vigour as Arouz. It was obvious that he had qualities that his brother lacked, and that he was a good leader and warrior.

You did not grant me an answer,' Hizr said, with a smile. 'But I do not really mind. I will wait for it for as long as it takes...'

That was Hizr's character. He was patient and wise enough to give his interlocutor the chance to speak freely and then suggest his own ideas and advice but taking his time to evaluate and decide. He bought the counsel of his men freely he never interrupted them and was never critical of their thoughts even if their opinions were senseless. He knew that someday their words might prove to be prudent and advantageous. He was not pompous about his knowledge and never demonstrated any signs of superiority. He respected his partners whom he selected with care and gave them his trust and protection whenever they needed it...

'I believe prudence is always more effective,' I replied.

Hizr was speechless for some moments and then he changed the subject.

'What are you going to do? Will you stay and support me or do you intend to go back to Mitilini?'

It was my turn to ponder over his words. I had never thought about this option, but before I could answer he added:

'I would like you to stay here with me for we have known each other since we were children and we have been through so much...'

I recollected the day he had attacked me. Once more the scene was enlivened in my memory and it seemed that Hizr penetrated my mind and my thoughts. A smile was soon engraved on his face, then he suddenly left his seat and approached me placing his head underneath my arm.

'It's your turn, Erm. Take your revenge, so that we will be even once and for all.'

I withdrew my arm from his head quite muddled as his action had really taken me by surprise.

He stretched his back and said, 'Do you see how much trust I put in you? I gave you the chance to strangle me. Do you know any pirate who would do such a thing?'

I did not give him a reply.

'Well, are you staying here with me?'

'I thought you were loading your ships to depart from Algiers.'

'I was, until you suggested that we should stay here. I have embraced your advice as my brother always did and I really hope we will continue this way...'

As I desired to satisfy myself and assuage my worries concerning the responsibility I was taking upon myself by giving such advice, I asked him if this decision was final.

'It is final...' he replied.

We remained silent for some time. In my mind, I was looking at a new cycle of adventures which I, so imprudently, had started myself.

'Of course,' Hizr continued. *We must first pick out a leader. Arouz's place has to be filled in...'

I looked at him for a moment and then said, 'Arouz had declared himself Sultan of Algiers, and therefore we must choose a sultan...'

Again silence reigned between us, but sensing Hizr's aspiration I added, 'I would propose that you succeed him. Arouz did not have any children or heirs except you. You are the only one who can replace him according to Western practices and customs.'

Hizr smiled at me rapturously.

'Are you suggesting that I should become the new Sultan of Algiers?' Yes.'

'Well, but what about the rest of the pirates? They must ratify your proposal.'

Without further delay, he sent his servants to call all the reises to come to his palace. Fifteen captains came at once to the chamber where Hizr and I were waiting.

'Erm reis propose that I should succeed my brother and become the Sultan of Algiers. Do you approve?'

Without giving it much thought, they all started to cheer and acclaim the new sultan. When Hizr had received their approval, he announced:

There is something else I have to inform you... After deliberating with Erm reis, I have reached the decision to remain in Algiers. We will fortify it more effectively and bolster up its walls, in case the Spaniards endeavor a new attack. Our departure is cancelled. Bring the artillery and all the ammunition back to the city and...'

He continued issuing his orders, demonstrating his organizational aptitudes. However, no one could make me believe that he had not planned everything beforehand and was just waiting for my sanction.

When everyone had left, Hizr ordered me to stay for he was apparently expecting more of me.

'We must now liberate a few of our slaves and send them to the West, so that everyone will know that the succession took place peacefully and is unanimously endorsed by all our men.'

'I agree, but the only thing that troubles me is that we are still very weak and there is always the hazard of a sudden attack.'

'We have had some contact with the Sultan of Turkey before. Why don't we send him an authorized delegation secret to announce my succession and ask him for help? He is the only one who can offer us his support.'

Hizr measured the value of my idea and said, 'I believe you are right, Erm. Write a message at once and we will forward it to the sultan with our emissary. I hope he will accept it. I will make sure he receives many gifts, so that he is tempted...'

The Sultan of Turkey, Selim the Cruel, received the message we sent with our trustworthy reis Hatz Houssein, who also brought us the reply a month later. In it, Selim accepted our request and officially appointed Hizr Beilerbey of

Algiers not as its sultan though. Selim was still absorbed in conquering Syria and Egypt and had no time to thoroughly consider our problems. His only concern was how to maintain his own sultanate, which he did not intend to share with anyone, not even the 'minor' sultanate of Algiers, as he had it. His answer was plain and bestowed titles that were only convenient to him.

I pointed that out to Hizr, but he did not pay much attention.

'Let him state whatever he wishes. We are here in our country and I am the Sultan of Algiers. Let him attribute to us any names or titles he wishes. He can achieve nothing at this distance. Soon he will fall at our feet begging us for succor and then we shall think about how much of it we shall confer on him.'

He was prophetic; whatever he predicted came true. But Selim was not the one to fall at our feet for he died only a year later. It was his heir, Suleiman the Magnificent who, despite the name, begged for our help.

Nevertheless, we had more serious problems to attend to now that we had no substantial help from the Turks. Hizr, after fortifying the walls and other citadels, needed to safeguard himself from the natives of Algiers, who started to hide their money in their cellars progressively. They transported everything valuable that they owned outside the walls of the city and many of them even absconded from the country.

To deter these operations, Hizr and I wrote a proclamation that was announced by our men in the streets of the city, warning the natives that if they did not stop their hideous actions and continue to operate as before, the punishment would be most severe. We concluded the proclamation with the following words:

There is no fear whatsoever; the enemy of the nation will be annihilated.

And so it was done. The natives, who had gained experience in the ruthless punishments we imposed upon them and the massive executions outside the mosque, conformed to Hizr's wishes and ceased fleeing from the city.

Once the internal problems were settled, we started to prepare ourselves singlehandedly for the impending attack of the Spaniards. Only the Greek god, Zeus, was on our side when he commanded his inferior gods of the sea and winds Neptune and Aeolus to stand by our side... But before he could send them forth to us, we had to undertake a great deal of work and exertion to fortify the walls of the city and other citadels.

With successive raids we plundered many ships and pillaged a good number of cannons that we placed around the walls of the city. In addition, we expropriated arms and other war supplies from Spanish and Genovese galleys. We took the slaves out of the holds and compelled them to enhance our fortification works of the city.

From the fort of Penion at the entrance to the harbor where the Spanish garrison invariably sojourned, we received messages full of mockery, and threats that we would very soon be annihilated and vanish from the surface of the earth. Despite their intimidation and threats, we persevered with our work, although some operations were delayed, as always.

In the same year, the southwest part of Europe was getting ready for a comprehensive attack against us. However, the whole summer passed with deliberations and conferences in which the Pope, the kingdoms of Naples, Monaco, Spain and the Saint John's Knights were involved.

According to the secret messages we received from the Moors of Spain, the battleships that had been amassed by the Franks were fifty, and about three hundred merchant ships were transporting war supplies. Of these vessels, fourteen were commanded by the Genovese admiral, Andrea Doria, and seven by the Spanish, Ferdinand de Gotzaga. Only France did not participate in this allied fleet for it was consistently on bad terms with the rest of the Catholics in the West...

Summer had already gone by when all the ships of the fleet were assembled, and the Western captains did not take the weather conditions the strong winds and sudden storms that burst upon the Mediterranean in early autumn seriously into consideration.

It was on August the twenty-fourth, Saint Bartholomew's Day, when the unified fleet of the 'Christian forces' as it was called appeared menacingly in the waters of Algiers. Before it reached land, however, the ships had withstood a tempestuous night and the crews were already debilitated. Nonetheless, the landing of the first squads took place immediately.

It was at this particular stage of the battle that Aeolus and Poseidon intervened promptly and concurrently. The former discharged his vehement winds, whilst the latter released colossal waves that hindered the landing of the Spaniards. Gigantic waves eroded the coast of Algiers whilst the ferocious winds eradicated everything in their way.

The first Spanish soldiers to get ashore were left undefended on the coast as their co warriors prevented by the weather conditions were not able to follow and support them. Wasting no time, Hizr gave his orders to his men who were patiently waiting on the shore to attack the enemy. Very soon our troops exterminated each and every one of them.

The rest of the soldiers on the ships, dumbfounded and appalled, could only watch the massacre of their co warriors on the shore, for landing was now quite impossible. Their adversity reached its height when the ships because of the violent storm started to collide and smash into one another, throwing them into the sea unarmed. Those of who managed to swim to the shore had to face our spears...

The massacre of the Franks was attained by both our rage and the fury of the elements of nature.

Shortly after the massacre, and having received Hizr's orders, our men started to apprehend the captives to secure their ransom. Hizr himself intervened to liberate a group of Spanish officials who were caught by the raging Moors.

When the battle was over which was one of the most shattering for the Western fleet at that time Hizr, who spoke five languages perfectly, Greek, Italian, Turkish, Arabic and Spanish addressed the Spanish officials.

'Do you believe that noble and honorable people like yourselves should always keep their promises?'

Yes, of course,' they replied.

'Then why did your leader, Gomares, not abide by the agreement he had signed with my brother? Why did he not spare him his life and let him leave Tlemsen? Why did he have to chase and kill him?'

I did not know that such an agreement had been signed between Arouz and Gomares. When I heard about it I was astonished, but I kept my mouth shut and did not express my feelings. Arouz belonged to the past and now there were new circumstances to be confronted.

'It was not the fault of the Spanish, Sire,' one of the captured officials replied. 'It was the Arabs who killed him.'

'Gentlemen, I could make the same allegation,' Hizr scoffed. 'I could have had you killed and then accused the Moors... However, as a nobleman who keeps his promises and word of honor, I will grant you your life and freedom soon after your ransom has been paid. All the money in the world cannot compensate me for the loss of my brother or any one of my faithful men. These ransoms will be but a symbolic atonement for the evil you have caused. When you return to your country, make sure to convey my message to your sovereigns regarding the commitment of honorable men to abide by their word of honor. You will convey everything you have heard to your people...'

And indeed, this short oration to the Frank captives made its round in Christian. Europe, elevating Hizr's reputation in the West...

Hizr, indeed, had the qualities of a genuine leader, just like his brother. No one had ever taught them although they both knew how to impress the civilized world in their own unique way.

The havoc in the Catholic Christian army was immense. Hundreds of soldiers were drowned in the waters of Algiers. Over twenty ships either ran aground or sank and the price of the slaves in the markets fell because of the copious supply. Doria was among the Spaniards who survived. He had kept his ships farther away from our coasts and returned to his base only to recount what had happened and spread the news of our victory.

Despite our triumph, the defense works in Algiers continued as if no damage had been done to the unified fleet of the Europeans. Flizr promoted the organization of his nation, taking severe measures to safeguard and preserve his supremacy in Algiers. He signed coalition agreements with the majority of the Arab tribal chiefs whilst he forced the few obstreperous ones to submit to him, eliminating the most dangerous and riotous ones altogether. He firmly consolidated his mastership, so that he would not face any insurrection from within the country.

At the same time he managed to achieve a sort of 'administrative decentralization', He stopped leading piratical raids, and only coordinated them. He did not expose his life to danger anymore and preferred to plan for the expeditions and then demand full reports from his captains. He had a harem of twenty-four women; a garrison comprised of a thousand devoted men and led a quiet and safe life.

Thus, after the Spanish expedition against us, ten years passed peacefully.

In the meantime Charles of Spain the strongest of all the nations at that time was preoccupied with wars in central Europe, mainly to fulfil his desire to be crowned as Emperor of Spain and Germany by the Pope himself.

I followed Hizr's example and embarked our ships only when I had to make contact with my informers on the Spanish shores. On one of these voyages, with my old friend Aidini who was now the Admiral of Fleet the Spanish feared him so much that they gave him the nickname, 'sock of the devil' and the vice admiral, Salah reis who descended from a noble European family I met with someone from the past. That shattered me and wrenched me from my cycle of thoughts and the serenity with which I was shielded at the time...

We had sailed from Algiers with fourteen galleons to plunder the Balearic Islands. On our way we encountered some commercial ships that belonged to merchants from Naples and Sicily. We marauded the ships and sequestered everything that they transported, including the passengers whom we sent to Algiers.

However, we remained in those waters, knowing that Charles, along with the fleet of the Spanish Armada and seven warships, was sailing to Italy, to be crowned Emperor by Pope Clement the Sixth, in Rome.

We continued our forays in the Bay of Valencia when we received a message from the Moor slaves of a Spanish estate owner, called Count de Olivia. They were requesting us to grant protection and transport them to Algiers on paying us a stipulated fee. We agreed on the price and arranged to receive them on an isolated coast in the bay of Valencia.

The Moors, who had fled from the estates of Olivia with many of his jewels, gold and other possessions, turned up at the appointed time. When they had all boarded on our ships, we realized that there were too many of them, and that our needs for water and other food supplies had become urgent with so many more people on board. Therefore, we decided to deviate and get provisions from the small island of Formedera, south of Ibiza, which we had visited in the past and so knew that it was a haven for other independent pirates.

When the Count de Olivia was informed about the flight of his slaves and the misappropriation of his treasures, he decided to find ways to capture them. He contacted Admiral Portudo the leader of the armada of eight Spanish galleys that had transported Charles to Italy whilst he was returning to his base in Barcelona.

He dispatched him a message in which he offered him an enormous reward if he arrested his slaves alive and brought him back his jewels and gold. He also informed him that his slaves had found refuge on the island of Formedera. No one ever knew how he obtained this piece of information.

Portudo decided to seize the opportunity and get the handsome reward. He changed course and sailed for Formedera, sending his son ahead with four ships, whilst he remained farther behind with the rest of his fleet. Later, we found out that he had commanded his son not to bombard any of our galleys before he reached the island.

Apparently, he was afraid that the blasts might sink the ships, dragging the Moors and the treasure to the bottom of the sea.

When we saw he ships coming from afar, and because we were ignorant of Portudo's instructions, we panicked. Our ships were overloaded with Moor refugees and facing the Spanish ships would have been disastrous if the enemy had started a salvo. However, Aidini the sock of the devil left the Moors on one of the coasts of the island and ordered them to wait there until he returned to collect them, then sailed off towards the north. On our way, we fell upon the ships of Portudo's son who, according to his father's orders, did not use his artillery. Aidini, presuming that the Spaniards feared us, was high-spirited and encouraged. He decided to approach them even more and since Portudo's son still remained inactive, he issued an order to approach the Spanish ships. Without meeting any resistance on the part of the Spaniards we stormed their decks and seized the galleys. It was then that Portudo's fleet appeared on the horizon.

When Portudo saw that our ships had drawn near the Spanish galleys, he thought that his son had succeeded in arresting us and approached us without taking any precautions. When he was within the shooting range of the galleys we had seized, he received a merciless barrage from our cannons. No sooner had he recovered from the shock, and then another barrage pelted down his masts and spread terror and panic amongst his men. At the same time, our small ships were detached from his son's galleys and became hooked on the gunwales of his ships. It was the easiest assault we had ever performed since our attack on the Pope's galleys many years before.

Portudo met an heroic death trying to defend his ships and a group of Spanish and Venetian officers. The rest of the Spaniards, including his son, were captured along with the fleet.

Our ships were now overloaded with passengers and if the sea had been rough at that time, they would definitely have sunk.

We headed towards Formedera, where the Moors observing the battle from the shore where we had left them were ready to disperse in case they were chased by the Spaniards.

Aidini methodical and well organized as he had always been separated the gentlefolk from the rest of the captives and boarded them on to his ship for security purposes and to prevent them being slaughtered by the Moors on their way to Algiers. The rest of the passengers were piled up like sacks in the holds of the fleet.

I was watching the captured Italians and the Spanish on Aidini's ship; many were weeping with despair and others were beseeching for mercy.

It was then that my eyes fell on a middle-aged couple. The man was apathetic, probably because of his confusion, whilst his wife, holding on to his arm, was craving his protection. I looked at the woman attentively for something about her face attracted my senses. And yes, it was her...

I approached her gently, but as I did so, she clutched her husband's arm even more and cried out.

'Please, do not let me go! Protect me from this filthy pirate!'

I was upset by her description as I had not expected such a reaction to my kind intentions. However, when she insisted upon ascribing names to me, I abruptly seized her by the arm and took her away from her husband. The wretched man tried to defend her by assaulting me from behind, but a spear stood right in his way, impeding his attempt.

'Stay right where you are, or else I shall push my spear into your miserable body!' the pirate shrieked.

The man recoiled and withdrew into his corner, whilst I was dragging the woman to my cabin by force.

As soon as I had closed the door behind us, she managed to detach herself from my grip and ran into the corner of the cabin, moaning with fear and humiliation.

'Lord, help me! Do not abandon me at this difficult moment!'

At some point, when she had stopped grumbling and beseeching God for help and mercy, she realized that I was watching her without doing any of the grisly actions she had expected from me. My silence and inactivity incited both her curiosity and interest. She turned to me, and stealing looks at my face she murmured:

'Do not torture me anymore. If you want to impose yourself on me, do it now and redeem me from this suffering!'

'I do not have any intention of raping you, lady,' I said, calmly.

'Why not?' she asked, somewhat offended.

'Because I do not wish to do so,' I explained.

My answer infuriated her.

'Why don't you wish to do so...? Am I not good enough for a slimy pirate like you?'

'I said, I am not raping you...'

You are a scoundrel! Do you think that—'

'I am not raping you for you have done it first, my lady. You raped my innocence years ago!'

She was flabbergasted. She scrutinized my face with utter care and asked me, 'Who are you, for God's sake?'

I did not grant her a reply. She got to her feet and came closer to me fearlessly this time.

'Despite your tanned skin you have noble green eyes. Who are you? Are you a bastard?'

'My father's name was Vretos and my mother's Isabelle, and you still have those beautiful blue eyes, Isabelle...'

Her stupefaction was so intense that even if the ship had capsized at that moment she would not taken any notice.

'Leonar!' she cried out. 'Lord, you are Leonar! It can't be true! Leonar!'

'Yes, that's me, Isabelle...'

For a few moments she did not know what to say, then she burst in with her own familiar way.

'Aren't you ashamed of yourself? How could you become a pirate?'

She repeated those words many times and as she was doing so her anger was intensifying. In the end she broke down in tears and thrust herself upon me. She pushed me with such force that she brought me to the ground and then she bestrode me and started hitting me on the face with all her strength.

'Aren't you ashamed of yourself? You... a pirate?'

You made me what I have become!' I yelled at her. If you had not rejected me for someone else...'

'Someone else, who is now my husband, and the father of my four children,' she said, whilst resuming her blows. 'And you... you have turned into a bloodthirsty pirate.'

Fearing nothing, Isabelle went on slapping me.

'Stop... stop!' I screamed, whilst trying to resist her punches and disentangle myself from her hands and legs that had snatched me like the tentacles of an octopus, immobilizing me on the wooden floor of the cabin.

Whilst she was screaming, the guards outside thought that I was raping her and did not intervene to rescue me from her hold men forcing themselves upon captured women was a common thing on our ships anyway. However, when they heard my cries as well, they approached the door to check what was going on in the cabin. When they saw Isabelle on top of me whilst, I was receiving her blows they burst into laughter for it was an odd and funny scene, which pirates were not accustomed to witnessing. Usually they were accustomed to see a pirate upon a lady. A lady upon a pirate was difficult even to imagine such a scene...

They saw me wrestling with a woman and they could not avoid laughing and hurling ironical remarks. I felt ashamed and embarrassed at my inability to liberate myself from the grasp of a woman.

At last, with force I managed to push her off me and dismissed the guards from my cabin, cursing them violently to restore part of my 'blemished' prestige. Then I turned to Isabelle.

'Stop this childish behavior and follow me.'

I pulled her by the arm outside my cabin and after a few moments we appeared in front of her husband who avoided looking at us.

'Do not worry,' I said in fluent Italian. 'I did not insult your honor. Whatever happened, took place a long time ago...'

He turned his face and looked at me with bewilderment, but did not utter a word.

I ordered one of our small, fast ships to converge upon Aidini's galley and transport Isabelle, her husband, myself and four of our strongest men to the shore. Aidini was watching me with eyes full of queries and censure, whilst he was still sorting his prisoners out. I reassured him with a nod when we were moving away from the ship.

Luckily, the wind was fair and did not delay us.

When we reached land, we went ashore and walked on the highroad for a while until we saw a coach coming. Two Spanish noblemen were travelling comfortably in it. We stopped it and I politely asked them to take the couple to the nearest town, but the two men were unwilling to sacrifice their comfort, and started to protest and grumble about our behavior.

As I was upset and disturbed by that time, their complaints and eccentricity aggravated my condition even more.

'Get off' I demanded.

When the two Spaniards refused to obey, my men promptly intervened. They forcefully pulled them out of the carriage and pushed Isabelle and her husband into it.

Before we separated for the last time, Isabelle approached me with eyes full of tears. She kissed me on my cheek and said:

'Leonar, be well. I will pray that you will forgive me some day. And may God forgive you for your sins...'

After many years I was tearful once more. I kissed her forehead and taking a handful of goledn ducats from my pocket, put them in her hand.

'Take these,' I said. 'You may need them on your voyage... If you can spare them, give them as a gift to your children, from Leonar...'

As for the cantankerous Spaniards those noblemen in the carriage we transported them to the fleet where Aidini 'squeezed' them into the hold along with the rest of the captives, since they had not wanted to be 'squeezed' into their carriage!

'I liberated two Venetians, and replaced them with two Spaniards. I do not owe you anything, my friend...' I said to Aidini.

He laughed.

'It is not for me to blame...' Aidini said. 'But you know, I am the one who is obligated to notify Hizr of any discrepancies.'

Aidini was right. We had to register the number of captives on our books along with the merchandise we found on the ships, so that Hizr would know and distribute the wealth evenly amongst his pirates. If any of the captured died on our way to Algiers, we had to cut his ear off, put it in a box and then get rid of the body by throwing it into the sea. The ear in the box indicated, or rather confirmed, the loss of a prisoner...

The computation had to be carried out with probity, so that disputes would not occur. One tenth of the income would go to the country deposits for the needs of the nation so that roads, citadels and other fortification works could be constructed. Another tithe was given to the sultan for the maintenance of his garrison and the rest of the money was split into two parts. The first part was given to the reis of the ship and the other was distributed amongst the members of his crew. Everything was done with utter honesty and precision so that there would not be any dissension amongst the pirates. We always thought that 'good computations made good pirates'.

In the meantime, the separation of the noblemen from the rest was completed on Aidini's galley. We loaded the Moors on to the other ships and set sail for Algiers. The treasures we had gathered were invaluable and so were the slaves, for most of them belonged to the nobility of Spain amongst them was Portudo's son and his men. We always preferred to free people of noble origin and status for handsome rewards instead of selling them in slave markets, for we received much more from their families.

The greatest profit of all, was the sensation the capture of the Spanish fleet would cause throughout the European world. It was an event that unmistakably stained the crowning celebrations of Charles V in Rome.

These events occurred in the autumn of 1529...

*

We returned to Algiers, where Hizr received us with great honors and new military plans. He could not bear to look at the fort of Penion any more jutting out before his eyes at the entrance to the central harbor of his sultanate. It was the 'thorn in the eye' of Algiers, as he had often said, and he had decided to obliterate it. For this purpose, from Turkey he had brought great artillery that could enable us to eradicate the walls of the fort and a huge pelting machine that had the capacity to hurl huge rocks, causing the death and panic of its defenders.

He had already received all these war supplies, and had tested their capacity before our arrival.

Before he started the attack, Hizr sent a message to Don Martin de Vargas, the Spanish governor of the fort, calling him to surrender, so that blood would not be shed, and in return he would be granted his freedom to return to Spain.

De Vargas who was of aristocratic origin did not accept Hizr's offer. He sent us a message in which he stated the following:

I was surprised to receive a message from the man who owns such a powerful military force, the Sultan of Algiers. To advance such a shameful and scandalous offer to someone of equal rank and value is disgraceful. Such proposals can be accepted by individuals that do not respect their honor. However, I have to remind you that you are confronting Spaniards whose breasts can resist many vain and delusive threats.

As soon as we received the answer, Hizr gave orders to his men to besiege the fort, starting with a salvo of cannonballs and rocks against its walls. As he did not wish to expose his men to ineffectual assaults, he resorted to an incessant barrage of blows on the walls of the fort for a whole fortnight.

On the fifteenth day, he ordered a comprehensive attack on the great breach his cannons had opened in the wall. Of the two hundred defenders of the fort, only fifty were still alive, including de Vargas and his daughter who were both captured. Hizr sent his daughter to his harem and de Vargas whom he respected for his military aptitudes was offered a position in our army if he agreed to defect from the Spanish army.

I do not know what happened, for I had withdrawn from the place of hostility earlier than the capture. Later on, I was informed that Hizr executed de Vargas when he, instead of rendering an answer, started insulting his honor. Others told me that after his insults Hizr sent him to the holds of our ships, where he died. I did not know which version of his death was true, and I did not bother to ask Hizr either, for I saw that the Spaniard had upset him immensely with his provocative behavior.

Hizr issued an order that the fort was to be eradicated altogether. He said that he did not wish to look at such a disgraceful Spanish monument, but I believe that deep inside was the fear that the Spanish might recapture the fort in the future, creating the same problems.

Indeed, after the siege the fort was swept away in only a few days. The Spanish slaves worked day and night to pull it down. However, when it had been demolished, a small armada appeared on the horizon. They were looking for their stigma, based at the fort of Penion, but there was no fort anymore and therefore the fleet started to wander around searching for a new stigma.

In a fluster, Hizr issued an order to his piratical galleys to assault the fleet and seize the ships. The command was immediately carried out without much effort on our side. When we captured the ships, we apprehended hundreds of soldiers and their commander, who had been sent over to Algiers to assist de Vargas and his soldiers. That was probably the reason why de Vargas did not want to surrender in the first place.

The artillery and ammunition we purloined was a gift from heaven. The materials from the demolition of the fort were used in the construction of a huge pier in the harbor of Algiers. This pier was called 'the pier of Heyredin' and kept the name for many years after.

If Plutarch had lived then, he would surely have added a new chapter to his book, Parallel Lives, which would refer to Andrea Doria and Heyredin Barbarossa, but Plutarch was not alive then and so I made the effort to write it.

Why Hizr named himself Heyredin is something that I will try to explain right now in this short paragraph.

A few days after the fall of the fort of Penion, we heard from the soldiers who we had arrested in other raids, that Pope Leon IX had given the King of England, Henry VIII, the title of 'Defender of the Faith' for his struggle against Luther. When Hizr found out about it, having always been in a mind to approach the Sultan of Turkey, he thought that he would do the same and change his name as most of the proselytes had done at that time. So, he adopted a new name and called himself Heyredin, which in Arabic means 'Protector of Faith'. He insisted upon acquiring this title and even forbade anyone to call him Hizr again, including me.

And now let's go back to the additional chapter of the book, Parallel Lives. Heyredin Barbarossa and Andrea Doria, two of the greatest admirals of that time, were rivals and sworn enemies, although they had never confronted each other directly. An objective observer might have said that they hated each other, but the truth lies in the fact that they did not wish to endanger their reputation in one naval battle. Both had 'offered' their sword to two powerful men; Hizr to Suleiman and Doria to the Emperor Charles.

Doria had abandoned his birthplace in 1522, when his party in Genoa was repealed after a coup d'état. At first he had offered his services to the French monarch, Francis, but later, when he had realized that Spain was turning into the greatest power in the Mediterranean, he settled in Spain, offering his services to the Emperor Charles V.

Charles appointed Doria chief admiral of the Spanish armada in the Mediterranean, allowing him at the same time to maintain a private fleet of twelve galleys for his personal piratical forays. With his piratical ships manned by Arab and Turkish slaves he made a lot of forays on the coastal cities of the Mediterranean, thus increasing his personal wealth.

In 1513, when Heyredin Barbarossa was still 'under the wing' of his brother Arouz, Doria had attacked and chased him in the streets of Galetta. If Doria could have predicted the future then, he would have pursued him mercilessly in Tunisia to eliminate him altogether.

In the summer of 1531, Doria decided to direct a blow at Heyredin in Shershell, our first citadel, which had been developed into one of the most significant storehouses and centres of war supplies and gunpowder, from the factory Heyredin had created there.

Thus, Doria, taking eight more galleys from the Spanish fleet which raised the number of his ships to twenty, attacked Shershell, liberated eight hundred Christian slaves and seized a lot of spoils. However, his soldiers intoxicated by their great success refused to obey his orders and instead of boarding the ships, started ravaging and preying upon the city. The natives of Shershell, both Moors and Arabs, exasperated by the ruthless marauding expeditions of their Christian enemies, revolted and vehemently attacked their oppressors. They massacred nine hundred Spanish soldiers and seven hundred were captured as slaves.

From his flagship Doria, who was watching the victory turning into a complete disaster, abandoned them and set sail for Spain. In his attempt to mitigate negative impressions about the havoc in Shershell, he appeared before the Emperor Charles as the liberator and deliverer of the Christian slaves in Barbary.

When Heyredin heard about Doria's activities in Shershell, he decided to retaliate. He boarded one of his ships and sailed to the west coast of Italy, where he ensnared two merchant ships that belonged to Naples and were transporting silk from Messina to Spain. In order to avenge the damage and infamy Doria had created by liberating the Christians in Shershell, he captured the crews and passengers who were aboard these ships, and brought them to Algiers where he sold them in the slave markets.

Doria could not tolerate the defamation and disparagement for the misfortune in Shershell, but knowing that the situation was difficult in the western region of the Mediterranean which Heyredin protected he turned his interest to a more secured area, farther east; to the Greek seas

.where the attempts of the Turkish fleet had been unavailing.

In the south of Peloponese he attacked the town of Koroni which safeguarded the Bay of Messini and took possession of it. Then he seized the city of Patras as well as the two forts that controlled the entrance to the Corinthian gulf. He did not meet any substantial resistance from the Turks, because their fleet was unable to carry out expeditions at sea.

The following year, when Loufti pasha had boycotted Koroni's coastline along with our captain, Pirri reis, Doria attacked again and destroyed the Turks. Pirri managed to escape to Constantinople, where he was confronted by the wrath of the sultan...

Doria's new victory in Koroni signalled the 'transference' of hostility and conflict to the Eastern part of the Mediterranean, where the inhabitants of the Aegean and Ionian islands had to endure horrible consequences...

At that time the great vizier in Constantinople was Ibrahim, who had a Venetian mother and was on good terms with the Venetians because of his origin. He was the one who had diverted the sultan's actions as well as the new Turkish war against them. Ibrahim, who was a self-made and intelligent man, had heard about Heyredin Barbarossa and had estimated his value at sea. Therefore, he, urged Sultan Suleiman to send a formal invitation to Heyredin, in which he should request his presence at the High Gate in Constantinople and ask for his help. At first Suleiman was hesitant for he did not wish a pirate who called himself a sultan to visit him in his serai.

But 'necessity makes dignity' as they say, and after the defeat he had endured from Doria, he decided to invite the pirate to Constantinople and receive him with honors and respect.

Heyredin's predictions that someday the High Gate would appeal for his help came true ten years later... But unfortunately this caused a lot of pain to the islands of Greece.

The invitation reached Algiers in 1533, and it was delivered by one of Suleiman's personal ambassadors. The letter was signed by the sultan himself as the representative of Allah on earth and in it he invited the Beilerbey of Algiers to officially visit the High Gate at his earliest convenience. That was a moment of triumph and recognition for Heyredin. Thirty years before, when he had still been a young boy in Mitilini, he could not have dreamt of such an honor; to enter the sultan's palace and to be asked for his help and services. Heyredin had never anticipated anything more honorable.

Personally, I was against this visit to Constantinople and tried to discourage Heyredin's decision, but, although he listened carefully to my admonitions, he was firm in his resolution.

You have to reconsider this meeting,' I said. You must avoid going to Constantinople, at least for the time being.'

'And why for the time being?' he asked.

'Because we must reinforce ourselves on the coasts of North Africa first.'

'I already have the most significant coasts in my possession, Erm...'

'But not all of them,' I insisted.

In my attempt to dissuade him, I referred to the North African countries that we could conquer, starting with Tunisia that was then governed by the tyrant, Hassan, the last of the Arabic dynasty of Hafsidon, who, in order to ascend to the throne, had killed his forty-four brothers and was an ally of Spain.

'We would have the natives on our side for they cannot tolerate the tyrannical despotism of their oppressor,' I pointed out. 'And then we could expand farther to the west, to Morocco. We could occupy it and take hold of its sea, which is coveted by the great Frankish forces. With these conquests we would be respected and feared by everyone... Remember Mehmed the Conqueror?' I continued, since he did not interrupt me. 'He conquered the whole of Asia Minor and no one took any notice. He had to conquer a declining state, such as Constantinople, to be recognized and respected for all posterity. Picture yourself as Governor of North Africa and master of all the seas. Can you imagine what Suleiman would do then?'

Heyredin pondered over my argument for some time and then said, 'A short official visit for commendation purposes will not harm anyone, will it?'

'Suleiman does not give a damn about complimentary calls. He needs your help and this is the only reason he has decided to invite you. If he did not need you he would have completely ignored you. Monarchs are nice to you only when you offer your services, for they are self-seeking rapacious people and that is how they have learned to survive. We have nothing to do with them. We are kings; we are masters and we have everything we need. What is there to ask him for in return for our services? Nothing. They will force us to submit to them and yield to their wishes...

Remember the title the previous sultan had bestowed on you? He called you the Beilerbey of Algiers, not the Sultan of Algiers. Even Suleiman has addressed you the same way in his letter for he considers you his subordinate. We are an independent nation and even the Spaniards are afraid of us.'

Heyredin scratched his beard, indicating that he was considering my words very seriously. This gave me courage to continue.

We are close to sixty,' I said. 'We do not need to visit the serai (the palace) at this age. We do not need to get mixed up in that lair of treachery, machination and conspiracy. Let him implore for our help. Whatever happens, he is not powerful enough to harm us. He is too far away to attempt an attack against us or take his revenge...'

I went on and on until my throat was dry, and Heyredin listened. When I had stopped, sometime of silence followed. We both thought carefully about my arguments. Now even I was convinced that there was no use in going anywhere.

'Do you know something?' he said suddenly. We shall go on this voyage, because it is a dream I have had since I was a boy in Paleokipos. I have always had the ambition to reach the sultan's palace; I have always dreamt of such a visit in the High Gate. And now it is time for me to make it true. It was a childhood dream and I shall not waste the chance. If, at a certain point of our lives, we are given the opportunity to fulfill a childhood dream and do not do it for one reason or another, that would be a crime we commit against ourselves. I understand why you are opposing this trip, but I believe that we should not reject such an occasion. You are saying that we are close to sixty and you are right,, but now the countdown of our lives has started and we must seize every chance that is given to us. What is there to lose, anyway? A few years out of our old age, is the worst case scenario. If it's our makhtoub[1], then let it be so...'

I realized then that Heyredin was determined to go and nothing would affect his determination. Man does not change no matter how old he gets and deep inside he had remained the same barefoot boy in Paleokipos in Lesvos to whom the gates of the palace had opened suddenly to embrace him...

His urgent desire to taste such new experience had no other cause but the root of his humble origin. At the same time his adventurous; fortune hunting nature was egging him on to new challenging experiences. He desired to travel to unknown seas once more and risk everything just as in every new marauding expedition he had taken on.

The following day, we started the preparations for our trip. We cleaned the ships of the fleet that would transport us to Keratio Bay and we transformed the biggest one of them to a flagship according to the standards of the Spanish armada, engraving a long broad golden line along its sides. We loaded about twenty thoroughbred Arabian horses and many more camels, as well as treasures from our looting; gold, precious stones and many slaves of both sexes and all ages, which we aimed to bestow upon the sultan.

A few days before our departure, Heyredin appointed his eunuch and adopted son, Hassan aga the young boy I had mentioned earlier in my

---

[1] Decree of fate

confession, as the viceroy of Algiers. With Hassan, Heyredin left two of his most trustworthy captains.

In the August of 1533, we sailed off to the Aegean Sea.

The Spaniards accused us of plundering the coasts of the Mediterranean on our way to Turkey. It was a lie for we only pillaged four of their ships that were sailing from Sicily to Spain transporting grain. We usurped the merchandise and sent it to Algiers with two of our captains...

Seven

We reached the bay of Keratio to the sound of the trumpets and a salvo of cannons that had been especially lined up along the coast for the occasion. We were all delighted and thrilled by the reception but each one of us harbored different feelings in his heart.

Many pirates regarded this visit as a kind of social restitution or even compensation for the many years of piracy, depredation and buccaneering in the seas of Barbary. Some others considered it a place where with the small fortunes they had made they could start a new peaceful and dignified life. But the most ambitious ones foresaw the beginning of a new era where they would have the chance to seek new pursuits as members of the ruling class of one of the strongest and most powerful nations of that time. Heyredin was one of these people, despite the fact that he was approaching the seventh decade of his life.

Personally, I was looking at Keratio with a piercing pain in my heart as if a knife had been stabbed inside it. I could not help contemplating what the Byzantine Empire had lost because of the strife, discord and religious fanaticism that had resulted in its decline.

Our voyage had been good. On our way, we had made short pauses at several harbors such as Lambethoussa, Zane, Navarine and Methoni before we reached the harbor of Thessaloniki where we had stopped for a few days to relax for we wanted to look rested and fresh when we met with the Padishah. Whilst we were still in the harbor, Heyredin sent an utterly submissive message to Suleiman in which he was actually groveling for permission to sail into the Hellespont to 'kiss the dust of the padishah's shoes'.

Naturally, his permission was immediately granted and our forty galley fleet penetrated the legendary passageway of the Hellespont. Halfway through, however, we were commanded to stop as Heyredin persisted in the accentuation of the golden line upon his flagship to establish the fact that he was not merely a beilerbey but the Sultan of Algiers. When the repainting had been completed, we finally sailed into the Golden Horn of the Byzantine Empire.

Heyredin had .issued orders to the petty officers of his ships to dictate a slow pace to their oarsmen so that our entrance to the bay would be more pompous and reflect splendor and majesty on to the coast where the crowds had been amassed to watch our advent. On the flagship he had also placed flautists both men and women who played soft, mellifluent music that could be heard by everyone on the coast. Heyredin had always been very fond of soft, pleasing music and he invariably had this kind of music played on his ships, even during pillaging and ravaging acts.

As soon as we disembarked at the appointed place in the Golden Horn, our men lined up for the parade; the idea had been conceived by Heyredin whilst he was still in Algiers. Heyredin lead the parade himself wearing a deep purple mantle, adorned with gold and precious and semiprecious stones. Around his waist he had a silk belt that carried his yataghan full of diamonds, and around his head he was wearing a red turban with an Eastern jewel on the top. The mantle had so much gold on it that we could not fold it up on the galley when we had to transport it...

He rode on a thoroughbred Arabian horse, which he had brought along from Algiers especially for the occasion, and was followed by his seventeen reises who were also riding purebred horses. The gifts for the sultan preceded us to his palace. About two hundred ravishing Christian women slaves, who were intended for Suleiman;s harem each holding a golden or silver ornament in her hands, were led to his private quarters. Then the camels followed, burdened with precious stones, silk and velvet material. Farther behind came the lions and other weird looking but admirable animals from Africa accompanied by their tamers, also gifts for the sultan, and many other rare gifts which I do not recall any more...

The sultan had commanded his people that we were to be received with utter enthusiasm and fervor. Along the length of the parade, he had aligned his janissaries. These were Turkish infantrymen in the sultan's guard. During the Turkish occupation in Greece, Turkish soldiers kidnapped young boys from their families, transformed them into tough military men and turned them into ruthless enemies of their own compatriots. Very few janissaries knew about their origin. They were cheering along with the crowds who had gathered to watch and marvel at the 'Lions of the Seas', a title that was attributed to us after our copious triumphs and victories at sea, especially over the Spaniards.

However, whilst I was riding my horse, I did not fail to notice that many people in the crowd did not hesitate to openly demonstrate their detestation and disapproval of the pretentious, yet hypocritical reception that the sultan had reserved for a bunch of 'bloodthirsty pirates'. This expression of hate mixed with envy, we felt ever more intensely when we reached the palace of the sultan, where all the military officers of the Ottoman Empire had gathered.

The parade proceeded through and passed in front of renowned areas of historical significance such as Hippodrome Square with the two Roman obelisks of which all four sides were carved with hieroglyphic inscriptions the Ancient Roman Imperial Palace which, although partially destroyed, was still used to accommodate stately visitors of the sultan and Saint Sofia the magnificent dome of which could only be compared to the nine spheres of paradise,

We ended up in the serai of Sultan Suleiman. Unlike European palaces, it was not guarded by high walls but was surrounded by impressive and extraordinary gardens of rare flowers that attracted and bewildered our senses that had been numbed after so many years of living in the wilderness of Barbary. Those gardens that were embellished by a great number of fountains were maintained as we were informed later by four hundred gardeners supervised by a chief gardener.

In the middle of the gardens that were separated by uneven and varying levels were two rocks called the Rocks of Exemplary Punishment. On the top of each one of them, the heads of betrayers and other officials who did not faithfully carry out the orders of their sultan were placed and exposed to public sight. On the day that we visited the serai, one of these rocks accommodated the head of the chief gardener because, as we were told, he had failed to produce a type of rose with green foliage, which he had earlier promised the sultan he would offer as a gift to Heyredin on his arrival...

Entering the serai was a marvellous and unique experience. The first gate we crossed was named 'Bab I Joumajoun' or 'The Imperial Gate'. It was guarded by one hundred and fifty 'Kapitzis', the armed soldiers who were appointed especially to safeguard the gate day and night with their spears and arrows. The visitors were allowed to enter only if they were accompanied by their interpreters.

Farther down to the right side of the entrance was the imperial infirmary together with the kitchens, courtiers' chambers and other administrative services of the palace. On the left-hand side, the old church of Saint Irene had been transformed into an armory.

Around four thousand spahis and janissaries stood there in line to pay their respects to the honorable guests. The guests were received by the aga of the janissaries, who was also responsible for receiving the gifts of the sultan for security purposes.

The second smaller gate was called 'Orta Kapi', or the 'Middle Gate', and was more exuberantly adorned. The guests always escorted by their interpreters had to dismount their horses and then they were taken through a paved marble passageway encompassed by tall cypresses, to the nine cookhouses of the palace, where about one hundred cooks were zealously working.

At the end of this passageway, next to the 'Kanza', the private treasury of the sultan, there was a pavilion where the Padishah granted an audience to his Viziers and the higher officials of his empire every Monday, Tuesday, Saturday and Sunday. This was called the Dewan, and it was a chamber of huge proportions that was embellished with precious and semiprecious stones and arabesques adorned with gold. The fireplace was decorated with pure silver, and next to it was a fountain made of fine crystal. Even the floor was covered with flakes of gold. In this chamber and its adjacent rooms, formal banquets were held, like the one that was offered to us on the evening of our arrival.

    Since the very first moment that we set foot in the premises of the serai, I had noticed that after Heyredin Barbarossa, most of the attention was mainly given to me, and that the behavior of the officials towards me implied both submission and caution. They observed every movement i made and every word I said. They were certainly well aware of my influence upon Heyredin, for the Turks had intelligence services everywhere, but the one thing that they seemed to have ignored about me was the fact that my origin was Greek. They tried to find out more about it by asking me indirect questions about my family and birthplace, but I avoided giving them any information about myself. However, when they placed us at the tables for the meal that preceded our reception by the sultan, they had me seated beside two commanders of the janissaries and two spahis; 'for my security', as they said...

    The meal was served on big plates, but was comparatively plain. It was composed of lamb cooked in a casserole with a mixture of boiled corn and rice, and the desserts that succeeded the meal were all dipped in honey. At the end, instead of alcohol, they served sherbet, which was water mixed with sugar, fruit juices and aromatic herbs.

I laughed at the reises' expressions when they attempted to force themselves to gulp this undrinkable wash, the same way that I laughed at our table companions, the Venetian, French and Genovese delegates, who had also been invited to dine with us, for they were forbidden to eat with bare hands like the Turkish officials and ourselves. The Venetian ambassador was looking at me tenaciously, hoping that he would drag me into one of those wearisome discussions, but I successfully managed to shun his looks.

When the meal had finished, it was announced that we would be received by the sultan in his royal chambers. Suleiman had not made his appearance so far and I was informed that that was part of the High Gate's protocol.

Heyredin was the first to go into the chambers next to the divan and I followed him with the rest of the reises.

The Turks had tried to prevent me from entering the chamber but after I had protested and deliberated with the officials, they I inally allowed me to enter with the rest of the captains, u ider the supervision and vigilance of two Turkish officers who did not leave my side. They stood next to me all the time with their hands placed on the grips of their swords. I was convinced that they considered me the most dangerous.

Sultan Suleiman was seated on a short stool with his legs stretched forwards. He was dressed in a fine white satin robe and on his shoulders there was a kind of mantle. He did not budge from his place but remained seated, whilst Heyredin approached him accompanied by two commanders of his majesty's guards on either side.

The two commanders gently but resolutely obligated Heyredin to kneel and kiss the tip of the sultan's robe and then withdraw without turning his back to him. Heyredin resumed his prearranged position for the audience and after praising the sultan's virtues with humility and submission he introduced his reises one after the other. Every time one of our names was mentioned, the sultan restricted himself to a faint smile or a nod suggesting regard and recognition.

I thought the audience was already coming to an end, when the sultan, after a short deliberation with his grand vizier Ibrahim, handed Heyredin his yataghan, the flag of the empire and his juridical mace, symbols of absolute authority over all harbors and islands that belonged to the Ottoman Empire. He also announced that he was proclaiming Heyredin 'Kapoudan pasha', Admiral of the Fleet and he was awarding him the title 'Haka Koulou el Bahr' or as it was translated to us, 'Master of all Seas'.

When this ritual was over, the commanders who were accompanying us got on their feet indicating that the audience had come to an end. We all arose. However, the grand vizier Ibrahim placed his hand upon Heyredin's shoulder, urging him to stay whilst the rest of us were led outside. It was quite obvious that the sultan desired to speak to Heyredin alone.

To compensate us for our early departure from the sultan's chambers, the Turkish officers showed us the other parts of the palace. They lead us to the third gate very few guests had the privilege of laying eyes upon it which was called

'Bab el Saadet' or 'Gate of Blissfulness'. This gate was guarded by the Kapi aga, the chamberlain who was the chief of the white eunuchs. Then they took us to 'Enteroum', the private chambers of the sultan where the Turkish monarch spent his hours alone. Next to this area were the quarters of the harem or, as it was called in Turkish, 'Harem I Joumajoun'. This was paradise on earth; full of mystery and enchantment; the paradise which was forbidden to any man except the sultan himself and it was guarded only by eunuchs.

A bit farther away, there was a sort of kiosk or gazebo built on four marble columns from which the sultan embarked on his private ship whenever he wanted to take a voyage at sea or depart for one of his offshore destinations.

The officers explained that the whole country was the sultan's property and that all the inhabitants both free and slaves were submitting to his incontrovertible jurisdiction and authority. We were also informed that the sultan had adopted some legislation principles from Seltzuks' law, which are based on the Koran and which the Turkish oulemads support.

When the guided tour was completed, our escorts led us to the premises where we were to be accommodated. They did not take us to the Byzantine palaces where they put up honorable guests, because that was a privilege only Heyredin was entitled to enjoy. After the exceptional treatment and unanticipated reception by the Ottomans Heyredin was utterly exhilarated.

We met with Heyredin the iext day in the shipyards of Constantinople, where the Turkish captains also worked as naval architects but knew little about ships. They were trying to create replicas of Venetian and Spanish vessels but the result was a disaster. When we saw the ships, we could not conceal our disappointment and the Turks did not fail to notice it.

'These are no ships!' Heyredin remarked to the Turkish beilerbey of the sea, whom he would soon replace according to the sultan's command. Then casting a look around him he went on:

'And these are no shipyards... They look more like stockyards to me, and your captains look more like shepherds...'

The beilerbey tolerated the insult for he was afraid of losing his head. The sultan would not have hesitated to have it cut off, if he had heard anything against the admiral he had personally chosen.

In the shipyards we also met with Pirri reis, who was trying to recover from the disaster and the humiliation he had endured from Doria in the south of Peloponese and was still waiting patiently for the sultan's 'judgment'. Pirri would certainly have lost his head, if Heyredin had not interfered in time, choosing him as one of his collaborators. He was well aware of his aptitude and his unrivalled experience in both sailing and map making and he would not allow such talent to be wasted. Thus, Pirri was spared his life and remained with us for a few more years before he retired to dedicate himself to map making...

Heyredin had stipulated with the sultan his annual compensation that reached fourteen thousand ducats a year, a huge sum that was taken in the form of taxes from the inhabitants of his birthplace, Mitilini, as well as Evia and Rhodes, which had already been occupied by the sultan.

The Saint John's Knights of Rhodes after their expulsion from the island had been drifting around the Mediterranean Sea for a long period of time before they were given Malta, a small and barren island not far away from the shores of Barbary. The Knights were entrenched on their island and managed to withhold, it from the sultan's desires for expansion towards the central and western part of the Mediterranean.

We spent the winter in Constantinople working on the ships in the shipyards of Peran, across from the palace of the sultan. We had sent for two hundred skilful Greek workers from the islands of the Aegean, whom we paid handsomely. The rest of the workers the majority of whom were Albanians and other subjects of the sultan were paid four ducats a day. The sultan issued strict orders that we were to be supplied with construction materials every day, and so it was done. Huge cargoes of lumber were transported to us on a daily basis from every part of the Ottoman Empire.

Heyredin worked with his men day and night in the shipyards. The sultan had ordered seven dozen galleys to be constructed by the end of the winter and we managed to build sixty-one which, along with ours, amounted to eighty-four.

In the spring of 1534, the united fleet of the sultan sailed with splendor off the Golden Bay. The sultan watched the magnificent parade from his gazebo whilst counting his ships to ascertain that his order had been carried out completely.

As we were sailing in the Aegean, close to the Greek islands, we saw that the people in the observation posts on the islands were terrified at the sight of this grand procession of ships. They were watching us from the peaks of the mountains after they had abandoned their posts in the harbors because of fear of the pirates an 1 were wondering, full of fear and trepidation, if this fie t was about to attack them.

They were relieved only when the sentries signalled to one another that the fleet was sailing around the Cape of Matapa, or Tenaros, heading towards the Ionian and Adriatic Seas.

We crossed the passages of Scylla and Charibdi leaving Cape Spartivento behind us. It was at this point that Heyredin displayed unprecedented piratical rage and characteristics that I did not recognize any more. His behavior towards even me had changed completely. I do not know if he was influenced by the Turks who did not trust me or that he had just become pompous and conceited after his stay in Constantinople, but he had stopped consulting me and disregarded my existence altogether. However, he did not dismiss me he kept me for some reason that I still ignore. Perhaps, deep inside he felt insecure and feared his new allies.

Nonetheless, as soon as we sailed around Spartivento, his piratical instinct had been kindled once more. Heyredin with the Turks and the other pirates dashed upon the harbors and the villages of the Calabrian land, eradicating everything that stood in their way. They burnt houses down and captured people, both men and women, to enrich the slave markets of Algiers, and the treasures Heyredin sent to the sultan, along with the beautiful women slaves, were countless.

Thus we reached Foudi, an ancient town which was governed by a family of counts. The town was known to the Western world mainly because of a beautiful woman called Countess Julia Gotzaka who lived there. She was descended from an aristocratic family which was related to Pope Martin V, and was the widow of the nobleman called Vespatsio Kolona.

The beauty of the Countess Julia Gotzaka who was very young to be a widow was praised by the poets and many famous painters of that time. Her fame and beauty had reached every part of Europe and perhaps the High Gate, and accordingly Heyredin decided to kidnap her and send her to the sultan as a cherished gift.

One night, our pirates disembarked near Foudi and ran to her tower to execute Heyredin's orders. However, one of her male servants saw the invasion and ran to his mistress's bedroom to warn her. Halfnaked, she rode on her horse followed by her servant and took refuge in one of the caves.

Thus, our piratical raid was unsuccessful. However, our pirates, to vindicate for their failure, ruthlessly attacked the town of Foudi and burnt it to the ground, capturing every single female in the town. When they returned to the fleet, Heyredin was enraged when he realized that Julia was not with them and that his pirates in order to assuage his anger and restrict its consequences had brought him a 'bunch of elderly women'.

'I sent you to bring me a precious pearl and you brought me a herd of goats!' he roared.

In his fury, he could have slaughtered them all, but instead as a fair punishment he distributed the old women equally among his reises and ordered them to 'take care of them' along with the rest of their women.

When we were through with the Calabrian islands we burnt almost all of them and we set sail for Tripoli, for Heyredin had schemed to overthrow Moulai Hassan, who had killed his twenty-two, or according to others, forty-four brothers, to secure the throne.

We triumphantly entered the harbor of Goletta, the same harbor in which, thirty years before, Arouz and I had met Hizr after capturing the two papal galleys.

It did not take much effort to capture Goletta and Tripoli. With the first salvo of cannons Moulai Hassan assembled his women and children and all the treasures he could transport and moved to the hinterland for safety.

Two days later he endeavored to attack us with new allies he had found. However, after the first blasts, the allies were dispersed and Hassan took refuge in the town of Kairouan in the hinterland of Tunisia. From his hideout he started negotiations with the emperor, Charles V, pleading him to liberate his country from the grip of the pirates. This was something that was attained later on.

In the meantime, Heyredin as was his favorite habit proclaimed himself Sultan of Tunisia. In the winter of 1534 he started fortification works to strengthen the walls in Tunisia and Goletta and at the same time having overestimated his abilities and power sent all the Turkish soldiers back to Constantinople along with gifts from the new conquered land for the sultan. That was a reckless action of course, because he was then left with few forces with which to confront the great invasion that was on its way.

News of the ordeal in Calabria had circulated around Europe and Charles V, motivated by the outcry of his people, decided to avenge them for the gruesome and inhumane actions of the pirates. He prepared a huge fleet that comprised of six hundred ships placed under the command of Andrea Doria. His previous mishap had made him very cautious about his current plan.

We were promptly informed about this invasion and Heyredin, knowing that the worst that could happen to his fleet was to be caught by surprise whilst it Was still anchored, issued an order to all his captains to set sail and take refuge in Algiers and the city of Bon that was situated between Tunisia and Algiers. Thus our fleet was saved.

Emperor Charles and Doria sailed to Goletta's sea and with a salvo of cannons from one of the ships, destroyed the fortification we had built around the city. We soon found out that the flagship of the Knights of Rhodes who had been roving in the Mediterranean after they had been expelled by Suleiman a short while before they had found refuge in Malta r was huge and had eight decks, extensive storing spaces and comfortable accommodation. They had many supplies and enough water to last them for at least six months at sea. This ship was manned by five hundred soldiers and equipped with many cannons of great calibre. The three other ships, although smaller in size, were also well equipped.

After the destruction of the fortification of Goletta we retreated to Tunisia where we tried to hold out against the fleet, but we did not achieve much and everything was destroyed by the forces of Charles and Andrea Doria. Even the sultan's janissaries those few who remained with us fled and dispersed in front of the charging soldiers of Charles. At the same time as this chaos, the slave Christians rebelled in Tunisia, making the situation even worse.

Eventually, Heyredin, Sinan the Jew from Smyrna, Aidini and I managed to run away and take refuge in Bon where our fleet was waiting for us. That was how we were saved. In the middle of this havoc, we were compelled to leave Sinan's son behind for he had been caught by our pursuers.

Following the Western tradition, Charles, instead of pursuing us and annihilating us altogether, chose to seize Goletta and Tunisia and put Moulai Hassan back on his throne, but only after he had declared full submission to the Spanish emperor.

As I have mentioned before, Doria and Heyredin had parallel lives. Now it was Heyredin's turn to try to hedge off the unfavorable and negative impression of the sultan after his failure in Tunisia, the same way that Doria had done with the emperor, Charles. Thus, he waged new wars and shed even more blood.

After our disaster in Tunisia, the captains pressured Heyredin to return to Levante and restrain our operations for some time. They were all afraid that Charles V with Andrea Doria would continue their campaign against us and that, in the end; they would attack Algiers to put an end to our operations and liberate the sea passages in the western part of the Mediterranean. A few even suggested that it would be safer for us to return to Constantinople and submit ourselves to the sultan rather than rove about in the western part of the Mediterranean, which had become very dangerous.

During these deliberations and discussions no one had asked for my opinion; even Heyredin did not bother to consult me as he had done in the past. However, when some of them expressed their opinion that we should return to Constantinople to appeal for the sultan's protection, Heyredin thundered:

'Who do you think I am to ask the protection of the sultan? I am not a coward and I will not budge from where I stand. I will continue my operations in these waters and whoever wants to follow me is welcome the rest of you are free to leave... Is there anyone who does not wish to follow me?'

Now all the reises had lowered their heads. No one dared to contradict or oppose him for it would have been considered treason and the punishment of Kara Hassan had never been erased from their memory.

After a few moments of absolute silence, Heyredin added, 'I am setting sail for Spain!' And without giving an explanation he ordered his crew to prepare his ship for the voyage. In a very short while our fleet was sailing to Spain, followed by the rest of the captains. No one dared to stay behind or direct his bow towards Levante.

The first people who paid the price of our failure were the inhabitants of the Balearic Islands and the population of the villages along the shores of the Mediterranean. They were all taken by surprise, for they believed that Charles and Doria had annihilated us altogether in Barbary and that they could sleep peacefully in their beds. Most of them had even abandoned their observation posts.

Thus we caught them unprepared and new slaves were sent to Algiers to help with the recent fortification works that Hassan the adopted son of Heyredin had initiated to impair a possible attack by Charles.

But the worst damage of all was executed to Doria's ships as they were coming from Tunisia overloaded with liberated European slaves and new Arab slaves that had been captured after the fall of Constantinople. Heyredin commanded that Spanish flags be raised on the masts of all his ships. Consequently, the Spanish galleys approached our vessels without taking any precautions. When they drew alongside our ships, we dashed upon them and captured all of them. We liberated the slaves they had captured, sending them to Algiers to support Hassan's works.

In the end, the victory of Charles and Doria in Tunisia became our victory after the 'prey' we had managed to capture both at sea and on the land of Spain. When Charles heard about his tremendous loss, he ordered Doria to sail back to Spain to check on the pirates' operations. But by that time, we had already raised anchor and were heading for Algiers. With our new cannons, treasures and slaves we reinforced its line of defence so drastically and effectively that Charles and Doria had to reconsider attacking us again... Thus, the Europeans once more postponed their annihilation attempts against us.

We did not stay in Algiers long, for everyone desired to sail back to Levante. On that account, one day in the autumn of 1535 after spending thirty years on the shores of Barbary Heyredin, his captains and I who was now following everyone else were homeward bound for Constantinople, leaving Hassan the eunuch behind us as Viceroy of Algiers... We had conquered Algiers when it was still a small refugee settlement and we had transformed it into a ruling nation, in the centre of the western part of the Mediterranean...

I still have the impression that while Heyredin was making his decision to return to Constantinople after his reises' exhortations he had always had in mind to ask for the sultan's endorsement to launch a new attack on Tunisia. However, things were now different there. Moulai Hassan, who had declared submission to Charles, died shortly after resuming his duties and his successors very soon hastened to declare obedience to Sultan Suleiman. Thus, even if Heyredin had decided to ask for help or support, the sultan would not have shown an interest any more, since he was already in control of the newly created situation.

In the spring of 1536, a very significant event took place in the serai, which reversed the sultan's policy and created new problems for us.

Suleiman was very fond of one of his wives, Roselyn, the first of the harem. She was the daughter of a Russian Orthodox priest and had a great influence on him. Roselyn was a shrewd and cunning woman and never stopped conspiring and manipulating the sultan when he was in her bed. She persuaded him to kill his son and heir Mustafa; so that her son Selim he was nicknamed the 'drunkard' could take the throne. Now, she was scheming against the grand vizier, Ibrahim, so that her brother-in-law, Roustem pasha, could take his place. After a series of conspiracies, Ibrahim was found strangled in his own bed.

Luckily for Heyredin, Roselyn did not have any other relative to appoint as Admiral of the

Fleet, so she spared his life. Also, the fact that Heyredin had not been on good terms with Ibrahim and had not agreed with him on the issues of maintaining peace with Venice and the continuation of its mastership in the Aegean, may have affected her judgement.

Ibrahim, who was an advocate of peace between Turkey and Venice, was born in Dalmatia which occupied the majority of the islands of the Aegean Sea. Every time Suleiman expressed his intention to declare war against Venice, Ibrahim dissuaded him and averted his plans. However, despite their opposition on the issue of peace, Ibrahim admired Heyredin and constantly supported him in the islands.

A few months after the assassination of Ibrahim and as things were still disordered in the palace, some Venetian captains started attacking Turkish galleys they were transporting merchandise to Constantinople from North Africa as they were sailing east of Crete on their way to Constantinople. The situation got even worse when the Venetian governor of Crete, Jirolamo Kanale, attacked Turkish merchant galleys that were being escorted by warships, captured their crews, slaughtered four hundred janissaries and enslaved one thousand of them. Of these men many were thrown into the holds and others were sold in the slave markets of the Aegean.

In the beginning the sultan did not pay much attention to the incident despite Heyredin's exhortations to counterattack and take revenge on the Venetians. The peace agreement that was signed between Venice and Turkey after the second Venetian Turkish war was still prevalent and the sultan was not prepared to start new skirmishes.

However, Andrea Doria as if he wanted to provoke the sultan undertook an expedition against ten Turkish merchant ships that he captured effortlessly and sailed to Messina in Sicily where he sold both the merchandise and the passengers in the local markets. But the Genovese admiral had not had enough. After selling the merchandise and the slaves in Sicily, he set sail for the Ionian Sea where he met part of the Turkish fleet that was under the command of Ali Tselepi, the surrogate commander of the Dardanelles. He attacked his fleet and captured the ships that he sailed through a narrow channel to the safe refuge of the island of Paxi.

This operation finally incensed the sultan and rekindled his wrath which he had been trying to suppress and overpower all this time. Consequently, in May 1537, Suleiman satisfied all Heyredin's requests. He supplied him with men and equipment and sent him to the Adriatic Sea, whilst he with twenty thousand soldiers proceeded to the shores of Albania from where he could cross over to Brindizi in one of Heyredin's ships and undertake an invasion against the coastal cities of Italy.

His plan was simple. The Italian governor of the city, who was a trusted agent of the sultan, would open the gates of the city so that the Turkish troops could invade it unhindered... However, the plan failed before it even started. The treason of the governor of Brindizi was revealed before we reached the shores and Suleiman was forced to withdraw and abandon his plans.

Heyredin resorted to his favorite tactic once more. He began to plunder the coastal cities of Italy despite the fact that Doria was nearby. The Genovese admiral was deaf to the supplications of the Italian governors of the ravaged city and did not budge from Messina where his ships were anchored.

Heyredin would have continued his operations if the sultan had not asked him for help against the island of Corfu, which the Venetians had controlled since 1204, when the Franks had conquered the Byzantine Empire.

Despite the enormous cannons that we unloaded on to the island and the ten thousand soldiers we discharged, the walls and the inhabitants of the city stood firm and Suleiman was forced to abandon the attempt and return to Constantinople.

But Barbarossa did not...

He attacked the defenseless villages of the island, burnt them down and plundered the majority of them, capturing twenty thousand people for the slave markets of Barbary.

He sailed from Corfu to Paxi where he employed the same methods, allegedly as revenge for the inhabitants' enthusiastic and cordial reception of Doria when he had taken refuge there with the captured part of the Turkish fleet. From Paxi he crossed the sea to Parga and after pillaging a number of towns on the mainland, he reached the birthplace of my father, the island of Kythira or Tserigo, as the Franks named it. Nothing could stop his frenzy...

I had long been pushed aside by Barbarossa's men and nobody gave any attention to my advice or counseling. He had gathered a group of Turkish officials around him they were all favored by the sultan who saw in him a step on the ladder of elevation and promotion in their hierarchy. They urged him to resort to barbarous and ruthless operations against innocent people, so that their activities would gain the admiration of the High Gate.

Heyredin had three justifications for his cruel attacks against the Greek islands and every time I tried to approach him and express my objections he would repeat them to me.

He maintained that he was compelled to capture islanders for he needed to man the new ships of his fleet. He even claimed that he did not actually assault the native population but was against the Franks for whom the Greeks did not harbor any respect, and this was partially true. He also purported that in the islands we captured after imposing taxes that the Greeks paid to the Venetians anyhow, we departed leaving the inhabitants unharmed.

In contrast, he said that the Franks who had settled there had garrisons and castles for their noblemen and apart from the onerous taxes they imposed, had also created social discrimination problems after separating the people into privileged, rich landlords and vassals. That was all in addition to the fact that the islanders were constantly being pressured to convert to Catholicism...

To his captains he said that he was supplying them with slaves on account of the fact that the islands were mainly poor and they could carry off treasures from the palaces of the Venetians. Slaves were of a greater value. Finally, to the High Gate he appeared as the patron and defender of its ambitions and aspirations in conquering the Aegean Sea, which emerged as an impenetrable moat to its expansive plans for Europe.

The Turks, although indefatigable soldiers accustomed to the tough and rigid military life, could not array their untamed strength and potency against the intellectual agility of the Greek islanders who were more flexible and pliable to the unpredicted conditions that the sea created...

In a few words, Heyredin beguiled and manipulated both his superiors and subordinates and never left a question unanswered. In my opinion, he was trying everything he could, to counterbalance his failure in Corfu and ameliorate his standing in the eyes of the sultan...

At that time the island of Kythira had three fortresses that were strong enough to withstand an attack. These were the castles of Kapsali, Mylopotamos and Saint Dimitrios. Heyredin and his captains decided to assault the last one despite the adversities that its location might create for such an operation. The castle was built on the tip of a precipitous gorge which made it extremely difficult for us to climb. However, that was our only chance, because the other two castles were even more inaccessible.

Oh the twelfth of September 1537, Heyredin attacked Saint Dimitrios, the medieval city and old capital of Kythira.

We disembarked at Kato Lagadi, which lies on the eastern coast of Kythira across from the Cape of Malea, and after going through a fearful ravine, we reached the fortress. The pirates stormed upon the few defenders of the castle who had not expected such an attack in such a secure area like a tornado and demolished everything in their way.

I remained farther behind. I did not wish to participate in such a gruesome act against the people of my father's birthplace even though he had abandoned it because of my mother. Besides, I was not young enough anymore to attempt such an ascent.

Oddly enough, in contrast Heyredin climbed the wall like a wild cat and with his men he slaughtered the garrison and every man who tried to stand in his way. From Saint Dimitrios and the surrounding villages they captured three thousand men, of whom we kept the strongest for our holds and the rest we sent to the slave markets in Algiers.

Many of those captured returned to Kythira after many years of slavery in Barbary and, refusing to stay in Saint Dimitrios, went farther south to a village called Mitata, where they settled. Those who returned to their country after captivity were nicknamed "sklavos", meant 'slaves', by their fellow villagers.

Saint Dimitrios has remained deserted and forsaken ever since that time for the people of Tsirigo never dared to inhabit it again. They said that they could hear the screams and howls of the victims in the night...

From Kythira we sailed to the Martian Sea leaving the Venetian castle of Monemvassia behind us Heyredin did not dare to attack that castle as well as the green sparsely inhabited island of Hydra, and we finally reached the island of Aigina. There we caught six thousand captives...

From Aigina, Heyredin started a naval invasion against the islands of the Cyclades although it was almost the middle of winter and the storms of the Aegean could have hindered such an operation. But, as I have mentioned before, Heyredin was unpredictable and this characteristic gave him an advantage against his enemies.

The majority of the Cyclades islands were, at that time, the private property of the Venetian citizens. All the masters of the Cyclades were Venetian citizens who had taken possession of the islands during the Franks' domination. Progressively, they stopped being bound to their places of origin and acted according to their best interests especially for the security of their assets.

The three most prominent Frank families the Krispis of Naxos, the Gozadines of Sifnos and the Somaripas of Andros were always willing to repudiate affiliation bonds with Venice so that they would be able to preserve their property.

Our operations in the Cyclades were neither shielded nor guarded. Winter was ferocious and our seventy galleys were vulnerable to bad weather conditions for they were on a sea which had very few hideouts in case of strong storms or high waves.

The first island we attacked was Paros. Its ruler, the Venetian nobleman, Bernard Sagredos, abandoned the island; left his people unprotected and took refuge in his citadel, which was called Kefalos. As he was powerless and did not have any supplies, he was soon compelled to surrender.

After conquering Paros, Heyredin directed his fleet against the island of Naxos, the occupation of which not being as simple as that of Paros. During the siege of the mountainous fort of

Paros, we had had the fortune to take shelter in the spacious harbor of Naoussa. In contrast, Naxos had very narrow seashore that was only suitable for military landing and did not offer us any protection from unfavorable weather conditions. An extensive siege of the fort of Naxos would have proved to be irredeemably dangerous.

As Heyredin was, naturally, in a hurry to conclude the operation before any changes in the weather could take place, he found a more suitable solution. After plundering the capital of the island and keeping the Krispi's palace for himself, he gave the duke who had been barricaded in Apanokastro in the mountains the choice between surrendering with reasonable terms, paying an annual compensation to the sultan, or complete annihilation of the island.

Krispi chose the reasonable solution and surrendered to Heyredin after he had recognised the sultan as the absolute sovereign of the island, and agreed to pay him five thousand ducats for the islands of Naxos, Milos, Syros and Santorini.

Right after the capitulation of the duke, Heyredin with a part of his fleet advanced to the islands of Thermia and Kea that both belonged to neutral Frank rulers.

Kea was already divided between the Premarinis, a Venetian family who resided in Venice most of the time, and the Gizanides family from Bolognia who usually dwelt in Sifnos. Both parts were surrendered to Heyredin without any resistance.

Then Heyredin went to Mykonos, which at that time was an autonomous Greek community, and it had the same fate as the rest of the islands already mentioned.

It was then that we received a message from Sultan Suleiman, and he commanded us to abandon the Aegean islands and return to Constantinople. On our way, however, Heyredin did not hesitate to attack Chios, the neighboring island of his native island, Lesvos. Lesvos had always been under his protection but it had suffered greatly from the Frankish pirates who attacked it every now and then to avenge Heyredin's actions.

But let's remain in Chios for a while and refer to the information we had received from our noble Frankish slaves who had been visiting the island before they were captured.

The island was renowned for its beautiful women and sweet-smelling mastic gum; two 'commodities' that captivated the attention and the interest of both the sultan and his harem.

The inhabitants of Chios were gentle, kind people who enjoyed music and singing. The women, both young and old, had sophisticated manners and unprecedented liberality. Nowhere in the East were there more beautiful, intelligent, and open-minded creatures than in Chios. They were elegantly dressed and spoke so graciously that they looked more like goddesses than mortals.

The ladies of the aristocracy wore dresses made of velvet damask or sheer white silk. Velvet cord adorned their colorful sleeves, whilst their aprons were made of linen and the hems were embellished with golden fringes. They covered their heads with bonnets made of white satin embroidered with gold and pearls and on their foreheads they wore yellow bands with gold cords that they tied at the back of their heads.

The younger girls had the ends of the cords hanging in front of their belts and over them they wore veils decorated with pearls and gold. The married ones wore the same attire only they matched it with white stockings... The only drawback was that they were short and thin and their breasts were not so firm for they bathed very often. However, their only concern was to make themselves beautiful enough to be desired by their men.

As far as the widows were concerned they were obligated to pay taxes to the local authority of the island for as long as they lived unless they remarried.

Heyredin saved the widows from this unfair law for he banned it as soon as he took possession of the island! Forgive me, Lord, but the truth must also be told...

The onslaught on Chios brought us a few thousand slaves men and women as well as children and countless treasures. I must not omit the fact that we also stole the whole harvest of mastic gum one hundred chests that each weighed two quintals that was stored in the warehouses of the island.

We did not leave a garrison in any of these islands, because none of our men wished to remain there. We only imposed annual taxes on the islanders and selected men for our crews.

After Chios, Heyredin, along with one thousand five hundred young men, of which two hundred were below twenty dressed in silk and linen transported chests and boxes filled with gold, silver and embroidered material to the sultan to assuage his anger after our failure in Corfu. I have the impression that we delivered over four thousand gold coins, jewelries and goods to the High Gate, but no one could ever estimate their value.

The sultan was exultant with the abundance and the lavishness of the gifts and treasures and forgot about his anger. Then he ordered the construction of one hundred and fifty galleys in the shipyards of Peran and Nicomedia, which once more operated after a long period of stagnation mainly because of Heyredir's absence.

After a few months, tht construction of the ships had progressed but not to the extent that the sultan had wished. Consequently, Heyredin had to defy the resentfulness and jealousy of the sultanate's old guard who wove webs of treachery around him so that Suleiman would stop trusting him.

As he was cunning and shrewd, Heyredin realized what was developing behind his back and reacted in his own peerless way. On the pretext of having received information that the Venetians were preparing a great fleet, he asked for permission from the sultan to once more depart from Keratio's bay with all the ships that he had built so far, allegedly to confront them in the Aegean. Thus, he managed to disentangle himself from the conspirators' web and at the same time uncover the identity of the schemers.

The sultan had stood in his gazebo overlooking the Bay of Keratio to reckon his ships as they sailed off the Golden Horn under the command of Heyredin. When he had counted them, he found out that there were only eighty-four. He had ordered one hundred and fifty to be constructed so he avenged his anger upon the conspiratorial courtiers, for he believed they had disobeyed his orders and given false instructions to his Admiral... I do not know for sure what has become of them, but I believe the Stones of Punishment might have accommodated their heads... However, in only three weeks, the rest of the ships were built and very soon joined us in the Sporades islands.

The first island that fell into our hands was Skiathos. We disembarked our soldiers in Koukounaries, whilst at the same time our artillery relieved the castle of its harbor. The Venetian garrison was annihilated and many natives were taken to our holds. Our success was vital because, with the seizure of Skiathos, we became the masters of Pagasitikos bay. For this reason, Heyredin left a small garrison there comprised of Turkish janissaries, in case the Venetians endeavored to repossess the island.

Then we headed farther to the south, capturing one island after the other from the hands of the Venetians who had no significant castles for their defense. Thus, we took possession of Serifos, Tinos Andros, Skyros and other smaller islands on which Heyredin imposed an annual tax that he called 'haratsi'.

The inhabitants of a few islands did not even resist. They surrendered without any combat and were immediately placed under the sultan's protection.

Then we turned our forces to the island of Crete, aiming to expel the Venetians who had developed it into a commercial centre and fortified its cities with impermeable castles. However, in Crete there prevailed an absurd situation between the Venetian aristocracy and the Greek vassals, which was typical of all islands that were occupied by the Franks at that time.

In addition to the onerous taxes the Venetians had imposed upon their vassals for the lands they allowed to them to cultivate, they also obligated them to deliver a 'good and plump hen' to their Venetian lords as it was clearly stated on the first day of every month. Progressively, one hen was not sufficient and the lords required more every time. When the number of hens reached four, the bondsmen started to rebel against the law and instead of hens they gave them their... addled eggs!

The Venetians were incensed by the impudent behavior of the Greek bondsmen and sent them all to court with false accusations. The inhabitants of Crete, exasperated by this unfair treatment, sent a petition to the Council in Hania written in Greek in which they stated their complaints and accused the Venetians of being prejudiced.

The members of the council, instead of considering the petition, felt insulted because it was written in Greek. They were preparing to take measures against the vassals when the people of Crete were informed about their intentions. They rebelled and prepared to confront the army of the Venetians, which was made up mainly of Turks, Curds and Saracen mercenaries. A violent encounter would have taken place if Heyredin's fleet had not appeared on the scene.

Fearing Barbarossa, the Franks hurried to bargain with the Cretans to put the 'hen war' problem to an end and at the same time inviting the Greeks to unite with them so that they could confront the enemy. Their offer was accepted by the Cretans and resulted in the complete destruction of Barbarossa's fleet outside the walls of Handaca which proved stronger than our cannons. However, before he reached Handaca, Heyredin with a fleet of two hundred and seventeen ships disembarked thousands of Turkish soldiers at the port of Castelli. Then he went to Rethymnon, where the natives and Venetians managed to divert him and after two months of attempts to no avail, Heyredin was forced to retreat and direct his fleet to Souda. There, he disembarked his soldiers once more who eradicated everything in their way. They pillaged the rich families of the surrounding villages and then attacked the town of Apteron, set fire to it and wrecked everything.

Afterwards Heyredin advanced to Habia where the Venetian governor, Andrea Griti, along with the Cretans, resisted with courage and repelled him. Heyredin, like a raging beast after three consecutive failures, set upon and pillaged the outskirts of the city of Keramia and burnt it down. In the end, despite his efforts he was compelled to retreat.

Being determined to conquer Handaca and retaliate for his losses, he directed his fleet to Cape Fraskia and discharged all his army, but even there, the Venetian commissioner Amoulios, with the support of the Cretans, managed to repel him. Barbarossa attacked and desolated Mirabellon Sitia and the whole area around Lasitthi and burnt down at least twenty-five villages.

Exhausted and humiliated by his failures in Crete despite the fact that he had caught a great many captives for his ships Heyredin returned to Constantinople.

On that trip, I had an adventure which almost cost me my life. It all started after an argument we had in his cabin. He had called me to console him and to suggest excuses or expressions of regret to convey to the sultan, but instead of comforting him I accused him of changing towards me since we had left Algiers.

'You were the King of Algiers and Master of Barbary. We could have reached the Atlantic, if we had occupied Morocco. But you chose to become a pirate again and a servant to the sultan. Suleiman is using you to fulfill his ambitions and has turned you into his vassal who serves him. What was your profit in all this? The title of pirate! They all hate you now and even the Turks do not trust you. You are not safe anymore and you might find yourself strangled in your own bed like grand vizier Ibrahim. And now you are looking for excuses to justify yourself so that your life is spared. Why? We have lost our freedom and independence; we have become the victims, the bait on the sultan's hook.'

At first Heyredin listened without uttering a word. He was thoughtful and looked shattered. His helpless look gave me the courage to continue hurling my accusations at him. But Heyredin did not stand my impertinence any more. He raised his hand and screamed at me.

Out, get out! I do not want to lay eyes on you ever again!'

If I had not been Arouz's best friend I would not have remained alive. He would have cut me into pieces and had them thrown into the sea. However, the old reises came in time and saved me from his hands. Dragoud who was born a

Christian took me on to his ship to let Heyredin calm down.

Whilst I was on Dragoud's ship, we encountered a storm and our ship drifted away on the tide. It was then that a galley of the Saint John's Knights, commanded by Lavalet, attacked us near the Cretan Sea and captured us. Lavalet later became the leader of the Knights in Malta and its capital took his name.

Our crew was captured and we were all driven to the holds of the galleys. Luckily I was not recognized; otherwise the tortures would have been worse than death itself. Lavalet, who had once served in our holds, recognized Dragoud.

'Senor Dragoud,' he exclaimed, overbearingly. This is the law of war... Yes, this is the law of war and we call it fate. One day you are the master and the next you are the slave...'

To my great surprise three days later, one of Heyredin's ships commanded by Aidini reis brought our emancipation ransom.

Lavalet was astonished at Heyredin's immediate response to the amount he had demanded to liberate us and as he had ignored who I was he called me up on deck and asked me who I was.

'A navigator,' I said.

'In my holds there are many navigators. Why is Barbarossa interested in you?

'I do not know, Sire. Perhaps he wishes to have revenge on me...' Why?'

For something I may have committed before I was captured,' I said, with a look filled with sadness.

My expression convinced Lavalet and in the end he consented to deliver me into Heyredin's hands accompanied by Dragoud reis. If Lavalet had known what he was to endure from Dragoud, he would never have liberated him for a few hundred ducats.

I have to mention here for history's sake that Dragoud seized the castle of Tripoli and became its sultan. Then with Piali reis the successor to the leadership of the Turkish fleet he defeated the Spanish armada and destroyed it completely outside Jerba, the first sultanate of Arouz Barbarossa. In the end, he took part in the siege of Malta against Lavalet whom he managed to capture and ruthlessly kill with his own hands.

When I returned to the fleet, Heyredin reproached me for abandoning him and having had to pay money to liberate me.

'Next time you will not leave my side,' he demanded.

I did not reply. I was in no mood for contradicting him after all those hardships I had been through at my advanced age.

Heyredin continued his tactics, pillaging the islands in the name of the sultan, imposing heavy taxes on the natives and capturing men for his ships' holds. However, before we reached the waters of Bosporus we received a message from the High Gate in which we were being warned that the Franks were assembling an immense fleet in the Adriatic Sea aiming to reclaim certain islands in the Aegean and the Ionian Seas.

According to this message, the Venetians had assembled eighty-one fully equipped galleys of different sizes and crews the Pope had sent thirty-six and Spain another thirty. Furthermore, Emperor Charles of Spain and Germany to make sure of his fleet's superiority in number and to secure a favorable result sent Doria other forty-nine galleys to unite with the rest of the ships. It was an immense naval force if we estimate the number of soldiers who were transported on all these vessels.

The sultan, feeling that his fleet was numerically inferior to the fleet of the Franks, commanded that twenty more galleys that were on invasion rounds outside Egypt under the command of Sinan, Murat and Salah reis were united with us. Thus the number of our ships amounted to one hundred and fifty.

Although the rival fleet was still superior to ours, Heyredin gave us the command to change course, sail around the Peloponnese and reach the waters of Corfu where we would encounter the allied fleet.

The confrontation of the two fleets would have taken place as we had expected in the waters of Preveza near Aktio, which was controlling the entrance of the Bay of Amvrakikos, where the armed forces of Cleopatra and Mark Antony encountered those of Octavius in 31BC.

As always, the allied fleet was still reluctant to shape a formation, as a result of the neverending disputes between the Venetians and the Genovese. The information we received from our agents referred to the fact that the Venetian admiral, Vincentzo Kapelo, was furious at the emperor's decision to place Doria in command. The same feelings were shared by Marko Grimani, the commander of the papal galleys. The Spanish had little esteem for the nautical war attitude of the Italians and did not hesitate to expose them at any time.

Yet, we were facing similar problems with the Turkish generals whom the sultan had appointed to our ships.

When we anchored the vessels in the bay of Amvrakikos they all condemned Heyredin's decision to anchor the fleet in that narrow bay. These censures were mainly expressed because of hate and jealousy, for they believed that an Imperial fleet should not have been commanded by a pirate. They also accused him of cowardice and sent messages of complaint that were not very flattering towards his admiral to the sultan on an everyday basis.

Prior to our entering the bay when we were still sailing along the western coast of Peloponese the discord between the Frankish admirals was developing dangerously, for Grimani and Kapelo had strict orders to await Doria's arrival in Corfu. However, Doria did not appear and, because he was tired of waiting, Grimani took a few papal galleys and made forays against the town of Arta and its surrounding villages. It was only when he was informed about our sailing within close range of the Frankish fleet that he returned to Corfu. We were still sailing between Zakynth and Kefalonia but, despite Heyredin's urgent calls to his reises to accelerate the rhythm of rowing so that we could catch up with Grimani, he was faster than us.

Thus, we entered the Bay of Amvrakikos, overcoming all the difficulties of its entrance. Reefs were spread everywhere hindering our way and we employed all our naval dexterity to pass though them. However, we sailed into the harbor without any damage, taking our post in one of the safest parts of the Mediterranean.

As I have already referred to battle between Octavius and Mark Antony in which the former won and determined the fate of the latter I must also mention that we had taken Octavius' post and Doria who had joined the rest of the fleet had assumed Mark Antony's post. History is repeated, they say...

The clash of the two giant fleets took place exactly in front of the gates of Amvrakikos, but here I have to add more detail about battles that changed the tactics that had been used in naval battles since ancient times.

Our battleships had cannons on their prows which had very limited aiming abilities, because they could not turn sideways. Thus, the ships would be lined up facing the enemy and with a distance between them that would allow the oarsmen of each vessel to use their oars. The sails were always lowered so that they would not hinder the warriors and the enemy could not set them on fire with flamethrowers and spread panic amongst the crew.

The front line would have a semicircular formation and the target was to surround the enemy's vessels, so that their space would be restricted and problems in the operation and development of offensive movements would be created. In this case the wings of the semicircle were occupied by the fastest and most flexible ships whilst the strongest ones were placed in the centre. For this kind of formation the exact location of the ships was very important.

However, the front line could also be wedge-shaped and the objective aim was to split the enemy line and therefore, the smaller sections of the enemies' vessels, now under pressure, would lose solidarity. This kind of arrangement of the ships indicated aggressive spirit and was favoured by many commanders who had a few stronger ships and better trained crews than those of the enemy.

In all kinds of formations the strong but slow moving ships were placed in the front line along with the flagship, which was always placed in its centre, so that the admiral would have better control of the situation. The admiral who faced the greater and most immediate danger up on the fore of his flagship than any general did on land had a rudimentary optical communication and usually transmitted his orders employing two fast, small ships that were placed on both sides of his ship and were acting as messengers. The objective of the rival admirals was the destruction of the flagship so that administration would be impeded and confusion would prevail amongst the other ships.

Captains who had more and stronger ships tried to draw the enemy into the open sea, so that they would have enough space to operate, whilst the less powerful enemy preferred that the confrontation took place in restricted waters. The commanders would also make sure that the ships were in the right position, facing towards the sun so that the rays would hinder the enemy and also in a windward position so that the gun smoke would cover their maneuvers.

Once the fleets had approached each other, the artillery soon opened fire. Then, when the ships were within shooting range of each other, the soldiers would hurl their arrows at the enemy. In case their gunners were too close, they threw hooks to catch the enemy vessels and drag them so that the battle inside the ships could take place. When this happened, the soldiers had to face the enemy bodily covered with grease and oils so that they could easily slip from the enemies' hands during these battles.

On 25 September 1538, the allied fleet under Doria's command appeared at the entrance to the Bay of Amvrakikos on the Preveza side where we were already moored and waiting for it. It was then that I realized that our position was more advantageous, for Doria would not dare to penetrate the bay with all those obstacles at the entrance and us, supported by the guards on land and the fortress of Preveza, which controlled the bay.

The Genovese admiral, besides the problems he had to face because of the peculiarity of the waters, was also afraid of the unpredictable weather conditions, the local storms and the vehement southern winds that prevail in the Ionian Sea in the autumn. Nevertheless, despite his fears, he moored outside the narrow passage and waited for our move.

The pressure upon Heyredin by the Turkish officials exceeded all limits as they were urging him to attack. Heyredin, being a good diplomat, submitted to their wishes but his decision resulted in the shedding of a lot of Turkish blood. On 26 September, the second day of the blockade, the Turkish generals sent a squad comprised of one thousand janissaries under the command of Murat reis to a narrow stretch of land opposite Doria's vessels. The cannons of the allied fleet slaughtered them before they could find cover and very few survived.

On the same afternoon, Doria sent a squadron of ships to attack us in the bay. Heyredin sent another squadron of equal number and strength. Eventually the two squadrons retreated without obtaining much. It was obvious that the two admirals had avoided assuming initiative alone because they waited for the other to react first.

On the night of 26 September, 1538, Doria decided to retreat from his position in Preveza and find refuge in the Bay of Vassilikos, south of Lefkada. In the morning, when Heyredin saw that his Genovese rival had abandoned the entrance to the bay, he issued an order to his captains to set sail and follow his tracks. We soon realized that his fleet had dispersed along the length of the island of Lefkada because of the still wind. Some of the ships were in the northern part of Cape Juanna, others were near the island of Sesoula and others in the Cape of Ducat, also called Sappho's Rock.

Doria's flagship had docked in the Bay of Meganissi, which did not offer him protection from the northern winds. The folio wing morning very strong winds started to blow and Doria, fearing that the wind would strengthen, raised anchor and headed towards the south leaving many smaller ships behind him.

Amongst these ships was the galley of Venice which was identical to the one of Saint John's Knights which I have already described. Alessandro Kontalmiero, an experienced and brave Venetian captain, was the commander of that ship which was a masterpiece of that time. The vessel had immense durability for its hull was encased with three coats of metal and it had three rows of cannon on both gunwales. It did not move with oars like the rest of the vessels but depended upon its huge sails and naturally on the strong winds because of its weight.

Our ships assumed the semicircular formation and prepared to attack the slow moving ships of the unified fleet and especially the galley of Venice. The left wing of the semicircle was commanded by Salah reis and its right wing by Dragoud reis. Under the command of Barbarossa, the flagship had taken the central position.

The first ships we encountered we either captured or sank without much effort, but things were not that easy for the galley of Venice.

Kontalmiero, who had been becalmed in the middle of the sea because of still wind, saw our fleet heading towards his vessel and he was terrified. He immediately sent a message to Doria informing him that we were within close range and that he was facing the danger of attack. Doria replied that he would be there to assist him in two hours.

In the meantime Kontalmiero decided to face danger alone. He issued orders to his gunners to wait until the enemy ships had reached their powerful cannons' shooting range and then aim and fire without wasting much of their ammunition. Moreover, he commanded them not to aim directly but fire parallel to the water's surface so that the projectiles would bounce on it like small pebbles thrown into the sea by children and consequently hit their gunwales with great force causing them breaches and serious damage...

The gunners executed the order exactly as it was dictated to them. With the first salvo of their artillery, three or four of our ships sank whilst a few of the others listed on their sides. Panic spread amongst the crews whilst the Venetians maintained the same tactics, sinking a few more of our vessels.

Heyredin ordered his captains not to approach the Venetian galley any more. Instead our crews were to hurl their arrows from a greater distance, aiming to eliminate the members of the rival crew. However, the operation was not very successful. We persevered with our assault, hoping that at some point the gunners of the Venetian fleet would run out of ammunition or that there would be no one left alive to operate the cannons.

Kontalmiero, however, resourceful as he was, had given orders to his crew to take cover from the enemy's arrows. Moreover, he had advised them to shoot only when they were absolutely certain of their target. At the same time, the Venetian captain kept looking towards the south anticipating the appearance of the fleet of Doria. Two hours had already gone by and there was no sign of any Frankish vessel on the horizon.

In the meantime, a heated argument had flared up between Doria and the other two admirals Grimani and Kapelo on the Frank's flagship. The Genovese admiral was fabricating a thousand excuses to postpone his departure and exonerate his dawdling at sea. At first, he claimed that he had had no written instructions to assist any one and that he had had to wait until he had received orders from the emperor himself. Then, he confessed that the weather conditions had not been very favorable and that he had not risked his flagship to help unfortunate Kontalmiero when he saw his ammunition was running out and that the pirates' lethal assault was inescapable.

When the other two admirals realized that reasoning with Doria was useless, they openly accused him of being scared of encountering Barbarossa and deliberately slowing down because he had desired the destruction of the Venetian vessel of Kontalmiero.

In the meantime, Heyredin attacked and captured the crew of every 'stray' ship of the allied fleet that he found on his way.

When the situation reached its zenith, Doria finally decided to move. He lined up his ships and set sail to the north keeping a safe distance from our ships. Heyredin rearranged his ships and started attacking Doria's that had detached themselves from the main body of the parading fleet. He captured a Venetian galley belonging to the naval squadron of the Pope, and sank two or three smaller vessels and caused a lot of damage to many others. Doria, although the head of this 'parade' did not even bother to offer them any help. He just passed them by and left them behind.

At dusk, a northern wind started to blow and Kontalmiero, having raised all his sails, managed to remove his ship from its place and head towards Corfu leaving the rest of the vessels behind.

Doria continued his 'parade' until he reached Corfu where he anchored for the night, while our fleet withdrew behind Cape Juan, on the northern side of the island of Lefkada.

After spending the night in Corfu the allied fleet of Doria was soon dispersed and all the ships returned to their own harbors. Not much was heard about him or his compatriots' reaction to his inexplicable conduct, though.

If we had to choose a hero in this battle, it would definitely be Kontalmiero, for he managed to confront our assaults, singlehanded, for a whole day without serious damage and casualties. However, the tactics he employed changed the naval combating art that had dominated since ancient times. The Venetians proved that with full rigged sailing ships that were properly equipped with powerful artillery, they could actually repel an attack from a distance without having to resort to storming the enemy's vessel and without using physical or body to body struggles.

This awkward as well as dubious behavior of Doria was negatively commented upon by many of his peers. Many thought that, because of the hate he harbored for the Venetians, he actually desired that their 'pride' ship was destroyed. Others said, that he was just scared of Heyredin Barbarossa and the consequences of such a confrontation. No one really knew the real reason or was able to justify his conduct and Doria himself did not give any explanation.

Heyredin naturally maintained that Doria was afraid of him and that when his ship had passed near our flagship, he had even had his stern lantern blown out so that we would not recognize it.

'And why did we not attack him?' I asked, clumsily.

His acrimonious look overwhelmed me, thus I did not insist upon his reply, nonetheless, I was affirmed, once more, that Doria and Heyredin deliberately avoided confronting each other directly. They were sworn enemies but did not wish to risk their reputation in a face to face confrontation. They both knew that in such a case one of the two would be defeated and that the glory they had gained in a lifetime would turn into disparagement from one moment to the next.

Heyredin and his fleet sailed back to Preveza from where he sent messages to the sultan informing him of our momentous victory upon the great unified fleet of the Franks.

At that time Suleiman was in the city of Giambol in Yugoslavia. When he received his admiral's message, he issued an order that the whole city was to be illuminated and ordered his administrators in Constantinople to pray to Allah and thank Him for their victory. In recognition of Heyredin's services, he even increased his annual compensation to a hundred aspra[1].

Suleiman the Magnificent, who was frightened of water and could not cross the Aegean Sea, had become the master of all the seas from the Black Sea to the Atlantic Ocean and the protector of the western coasts of Morocco, because of Heyredin.

The doges of Venice, tired of the sickening behavior of their allies, urged the King of France, Francis I, to achieve a peace treaty with the sultan. Eventually, the former 'Mistress of the Seas' was compelled to concede the towns of Monemvassia and Nafplion which were her last conquests in Peloponese to Turkey and defray three hundred ducats to the sultan as compensation for the invasions against Turkey.

Thus, the Venetian domination in the Aegean was terminated. The only spoils that Venice managed to keep were Tinos, Zakynth and Cyprus, with the commitment of paying an annual tax to the Ottoman Empire.

---

[1] Ottoman monetary unit

When we returned to Constantinople, we were received with all the honors the sultan lavishly bestowed upon us. I was harboring vain hopes that at last, we would settle down on firm land after so many years of struggle at sea.

Indeed, in the beginning everything indicated that my hopes were about to become true. Heyredin, immensely rich now, built a great palace in one of the lands the sultan had endowed to him in Beshictash. The building overlooked Bosporus and it was built very quickly and two thousand slaves were involved in its construction.

Heyredin insisted that I settled near him to keep him company, so I built a comfortable mansion next to his palace where i accommodated the few women who always followed me wherever I went, and fifty slaves I had brought with me from Algiers. However, this peaceful life did not last long for it was fated to be interrupted once more.

The sultan had signed an agreement with Francis, the King of France, against Emperor Charles, who was now claiming his territories back. Suleiman's command to Heyredin was to invade Castlenouovo in Italy, which his generals had not succeeded in occupying months before.

We were soon there. We occupied Castlenouovo and returned to Constantinople, but Suleiman would not leave us in peace. It seemed that Masters were never satisfied. The more we gave them the more they demanded of us, and Heyredin should have known about that fact for he was a Master in his own kingdom of Algiers.

But let us go back to the Spanish emperor, Charles, and his French neighbour, Francis. After the defeat in Preveza, Charles ordered a new fleet greater than the one he had conceded earlier to Doria to be constructed. Thus, in the winter of 1540, the shipyards of Spain and Naples undertook the construction of the fleet that was destined to be sent to annihilate Algiers and its viceroy, Hassan, the eunuch son of Heyredin. Yet, Charles committed the same fatal mistake once more and commanded his fleet to depart in the winter. A mere breeze would have been enough to destroy and disperse his ships along the coasts of Algiers; and that is exactly what happened.

A wild storm wrecked all his ships and the bodies of the soldiers were washed ashore. We were informed that the whole coast of Barbary was covered with dead bodies... The few Spanish soldiers who survived were led to the slave markets where they were all sold at very cheap prices.

It was said that they were purchased for less than an onion...

After this disaster, Charles turned to Europe and against his Frencl neighbour, King Francis. The latter, which had always been on good terms with the High Gate, asked for the sultan's support. Suleiman believed that this was the chance for him to set a firm foot in Europe and that his dream of conquering the continent would soon become true. He had long invested his dreams upon the fact that the European monarchs were always in discord and that, in the name of Christianity; they would enter into an alliance with the devil himself, if it meant the annihilation of their rivals. Thus, he immediately accepted to partner Francis and we were compelled to abandon our peaceful life and return to the galleys under the command of Barbarossa.

Once more, we sailed from Keratio Bay and headed for Cape Maleas as Sicily was our destination. Before sailing around Scylla and Charibdi, Heyredin pillaged Rezzio, a small town in Calabria but there, he was captured by... the arrows of love...

The swarms of soldiers who attacked Rezzio brought many captives back to our ships. Among them was the governor of the town a man called Don Diego Gaetano along with his wife and four daughters.

The experienced eye of the sixty year old pirate fell on the youngest of the four, Donna Maria, who was not yet eighteen. Although he could have taken her as a slave, Heyredin wanted to change his lifestyle this time. He desired something more courteous or romantic, for that was usually how it happened in civilized countries. Therefore, he asked her father for her hand in marriage.

In the beginning, poor Gaetano was reluctant, but when he had reconsidered his position and that of his family, he had to accept. However, Donna Maria was courageous enough to turn the mighty pirate down. She was tall and beautiful with black noble eyes and an overbearing look and I had expected Heyredin to be mad at her airs, grab her by her hair and lead her to his cabin. But this time things were completely different. The untamed beast, with which I had shared the greatest part of my life, was transformed into a docile, kind creature. He fell at the girl's feet and actually implored her to accept him as a husband.

The scene was comical to me and everyone who knew the great and fearless Barbarossa; a tough man like Heyredin at the feet of a young girl was just inconceivable. However, little Donna Maria having been pressured by her family accepted his offer, so that her town and its people would be saved... Soon they were married up on deck following all the appropriate formalities of civilised weddings and when the ceremony was over, Heyredin released her family along with all the citizens of Rezzio, as a wedding gift to his beautiful bride.

Heyredin did everything he could to ingratiate himself with Donna Maria she commanded and he granted all her wishes. All the galleys were put under her orders and then her name was changed to Miriam. The violent and ruthless pirate had become a harmless lamb in her hands and he ran behind her fulfilling all her desires for a mere smile.

Heyredin appeared wearing his formal costumes along with his young and beautiful wife whom he never left alone, and oddly enough Miriam truthfully responded to the old man's love, and stood by his side until the last moments of his life...

After Rezzio we continued our voyage pillaging villages such as Iskia, Sienna, Protsinta, Nissinta, even the islands Lipares and Elba, most of which belonged to Charles. In contrast, we respected the villages and towns that belonged to Francis or the ones that we knew favoured him over Charles.

The people of those | places received us with joy and festivities and their governments held banquets in their palaces to pay their respects to us.

We also offered banquets on our vessels and it was quite amusing to watch tough and uncivilized pirates in elegant clothes stolen of course trying to behave like real gentlemen. All this took place after the command of Heyredin who had submitted to his young wife's orders... Miriam enjoyed privileges that no other person did on our vessels. She could roam about the ship's decks at any time of the day she wished while the other women were kept inside a separate galley that followed ours.

Miriam started to give orders to the crew members and hell to anyone who disregarded her wishes. On our ship her word was a sword. Her old husband was ready to take the life of anybody who objected to or contradicted her...

But Heyredin was not the only one who had changed on our boat. I had also changed and the whole world around me seemed to have been changing completely. I had begun to believe that I had already lived long enough, and that I belonged to another era that was not returning that I was now a pariah in a world that I could no longer understand.

A strange incident that really stunned me contributed to the start of these feelings and sowed the seeds of my present condition.

Sinan reis the Jew from Ismir had implored Heyredin to find his beloved son whom the Genovese had kidnapped when Doria had chased us in Tunisia. We had been saved by a miracle, but Sinan's son could not follow us for he had been captured by Doria's troops. A few months later, Sinan received information that his son was still alive and a slave to a nobleman's family in a town called Grosseto. Heyredin found the location and sent for the governor who, most terrified, discovered our ship and feared that his town was doomed to be pillaged by pirates. To his surprise, he heard us asking him to deliver Sinan's son to us and that he would receive money for his emancipation ransom. As I said, the world had completely changed...

The governor swore that he was ignorant of the existence of the boy but he promised that he would do everything possible to trace him. He returned to his mansion and started searching in his logs, but there was no boy in his service with that name. Fearing Heyredin's anger he extended his search to the surrounding areas.

Two days later, he returned to our galley with a young Capuchin, who had his hands crossed over his navel. We did not pay much attention to his companion and asked the Italian nobleman where Sinan's boy was.

'I am Sinan's son,' the monk replied.

We were all startled and surprised, but when we approached the young man we realized that he was the boy we were looking for.

Your father is looking for you,' I explained. ^We have come to redeem you and take you back with us.'

'I was redeemed a long time ago,' the young Capuchin affirmed with a cold, expressionless face that reminded me of the Catholic monks in my school, back home in Mitilini.

Your father wants you back,' Heyredin said, sternly.

'Please, say to my father that I pray for his soul day and night and beseech the Lord to forgive him for all the crimes he has committed,' the Capuchin continued, retaining the same expression on his face.

We were astonished, but Heyredin insisted in his efforts to make him change his mind.

'Will you give no heed to your father's wishes? Have you no shame!'

'I love my father, therefore I pray for his redemption...'

*What do you mean his redemption?' Heyredin roared, obviously offended by the young man's attitude. But the Capuchin did not reply.

It was then that Miriam interfered.

'Let the friar decide for himself,' she said. 'If he wishes to be a monk and save the soul of his father, why should you forbid him? Please, leave him in peace.'

Heyredin submitted to his wife's wishes at once.

'You are absolutely right, my love. Let him alone decide.'

But the young boy had already made up his mind for he left the ship without saying another word and returned to his abbey.

The world had truly changed and this incident shattered me to the roots of my being. I still believe that this young boy was the first to direct a strong 'slap' right in our faces...

Despite this incident, the expedition was accomplished in defiance of the fact that a Christian nation was waging war against another Christian nation that had the Ottoman Empire on its side. The outcry and upheaval of all the other Christian nations against the King of France was comprehensible, but King Francis, in his impetuous fury to rival the Spanish Emperor, did not pay any attention to the protestations.

On his way to the Bay of Lions, in Marseilles, Heyredin pillaged not only Spanish territories but also French. He eradicated the Calabrian and Provegan coastal towns and did not leave anything standing until he met with the forces of the French king in Marseilles.

When we reached Marseilles, Heyredin was outraged because the French had not assembled all the supplies and ammunition he had requested. Thus, the French to appease him and flatter his ego started to hold dinner parties and banquets in their mansions and praised his wife whom he haughtily introduced to everyone. They all smiled at the pie, but they could not resist exchanging derogatory remarks about them, once they had turned their backs.

Finally, Francis decided to attack Nice. He assembled some of his troops and with Heyredin, he laid siege to it, but, as the French were, not sufficiently qualified for such operations, we decided to take control. We followed our usual tactics and after we had bombarded the walls of Nice and caused great breaches in them, we prepared for the final attack. The Governor of Nice immediately surrendered to try to prevent a slaughter... The massacre, however, was not prevented and Nice was burnt down.

We were accused of gruesome acts whilst invading the city, but the truth of the matter was that we had already departed after the governor's surrender and only the French had remained behind...

We returned to our base in Ville France and soon afterwards sailed to Toulon where we had planned to spend the winter. From Toulon, Salah reis under the command of Heyredin made a lot of frays against the Spanish coasts of Catalonia, which were defenseless for the Spanish, believed that we were still sailing near the French coast.

The protestations against Francis and the anger of the French people who saw the Turkish fleet the holds were manned with Christian slaves moored in their own harbor, became so dangerous, that Francis could, not tolerate it any longer. In the end he was forced to sign a peace treaty with Charles and compensate the Turkish fleet because it had been forced to depart from the French harbor.

We left the French harbor in the spring. On our way to Constantinople, Heyredin pillaged and burnt down all the coastal villages of Southern Italy that belonged to Charles. Thus, he again looted and ravaged the islands of Elba and Protsinta, Naples, the islands of Lipares, the coasts of Sienna as well as the coastal villages of Sicily. The only town that we left unharmed was Rezzio the birthplace of his beloved Miriam for Heyredin would never have dared to provoke her anger by ravaging her home town...

*

It was the summer of 1543, when we reached Keratio Bay. After delivering the treasures from our piratical forays to the sultan, I returned to my mansion built next to Heyredin's palace. The very first moment I set foot in it, I exclaimed with relief:

Thank God! That is the end of it!'

I believe Heyredin did the same, although I am not sure if he appealed to God or Allah. Thus, he finally settled in his admirable palace on the northern part of Bosporus with his loving and devoted wife, Miriam. The rest of his women were confined to their private quarters and Heyredin, although he never came near them, ordered his eunuchs to offer them everything they needed, so that they would not distract his attention from Miriam.

In the first few months after our return, Heyredin became involved in 'peaceful works' as he very wittily called them such as gardening and cultivating his orchards that were adjacent to mine. We would grow our vegetables during the day and then meet in the evenings to exchange advice and experiences on cultivation as if we had been farmers all our lives!

In the afternoons, we would stroll to the shore to watch the sunset and smell the saltiness of the sea. Miriam, who did not follow any of the Moslem customs, would take her husband by the hand, as if he were a small child, and walk him to the seaside. Very often we would comment on the handling of ships and the oversights by the new and inexperienced captains, for they did not follow the wind promptly or were late in raising the sails and so on and so forth...

Just before dusk, and after we had made the weather predictions for the following day, Miriam would take Heyredin's hand and walk him up the path to their palace.

With time, Heyredin grew weaker like the fish that rots when it stays outside the water. His body became frail; his movements sluggish and his feet were swollen to such an extent that he couldn't walk any more. He said that they felt like 'anchors nailing him to the ground'.

I saw his deterioration and so did Miriam, but we did not dare to confront him with the truth for we were afraid of his anger, so we never openly spoke about his condition...

However, the rest of the people could not keep their mouths shut whenever they saw the old and weary man, being literally dragged along by his young wife. He had become the mockery and scorn on the mouths of everyone who laid eyes on him, especially his enemies.

The walks to the shore were progressively restricted to walks in the gardens and on the premises of his palace, but even those walks were very soon abandoned as Heyredin started to have memory problems. He suffered from amnesia and could not remember events that had signaled and marked our lives.

In a short time, he was confined to his bed. A strange and persistent cough pestered his chest and jolted his frail body many times a day. When these bouts became more violent, I had to spend the nights in his quarters, so that Miriam, who was always by his side, could sometimes rest and get some sleep. He would awake in the middle of the night, frightened and screaming out with incomprehensible cries or calling to invisible people or ghosts from his past like his mother Katerina and his brother Arouz.

When he had such dreams, Miriam would run to him to soothe him and alleviate his agitation, but his nightmares became more frequent and every night he would dream of flames surrounding him in his room. Then we had to give him syrup sedative that we were supplied by a salesman in Constantinople.

Many times when he awoke in the mornings he did not recognize me and would start screaming again but at other times he would smile gently, take me in his arms and cry like a little helpless child. During his weeping, he would affirm that I was truly his best friend; his only friend, to whom he trusted his whole life and now that he thought that he was going to meet Arouz he thought that Arouz was alive he would speak to him about the good friend they both had.

His condition was getting worse every day. He was in such torment that Miriam and I were praying to God to redeem him from his anguish. Despite his harsh and persistent cough, his spirit would not be delivered; it rested inside him to torment and agitate him whenever the horrible bouts of coughing started.

Finally, one day I remember it was 4 July, 1546, or according to the Turkish calendar, 6 of Aboul, 953 after the Hetzira after spending a nightmarish night, he woke up with a persistent cough from which he was redeemed, only when he with eyes wide open stopped breathing altogether.

He died in the arms of his beloved Miriam who had embraced him and had taken care of him as if he were her own child. The notorious pirate whom emperors and kings, enemies and friends in Europe and Africa had feared, was alive no more...

The sultan issued an order that he would be buried with all the honors of a king, in his palace garden near the sea, for it had been his last wish he had always wanted to be able to hear the waves. His funeral created a lot of disapproval and many of his enemies condemned the fact that a pirate, who had no shred of Turkish blood, had managed to ascend to the highest echelons of office in the Turkish Empire[1]. Two days after his funeral,

---

[1] However, Heyredin did not rest peacefully in his tomb. Heyredin's tomb is still preserved in Beshictash. In

Miriam came to my house, shattered and terrified, declaring that Heyredin's body had come out of the grave and had been found on the shore in front of his house where we used to walk when he was still well. I was dumbfounded and could believe a word that she said. However, I reassured her that I would take care of the matter and sent her back to her house.

Two days after this incident, Miriam appeared again in the same condition. The body of Heyredin had been found on the shore once more.

I went to the place she had indicated and saw that people had assembled around the body. I was greatly alarmed, but as I did not believe in mysteries and after death stories I assumed that his enemies had taken the body out of its grave and thrown it by the sea for revenge, even after his death.

We buried Heyredin again and put a watchdog to guard his grave although this was considered to be an act of blasphemy by the Turks but the next day the dog was found poisoned and Heyredin's body was lying on the shore again. We almost lost our minds for we did not know what to do. Then, some of the officials came to me and suggested that I should take an Orthodox priest to read a few prayers over his grave.

'We are not sure,' they said, 'but perhaps the priests can keep him in his grave for good. Call a priest, but please do it secretly so that no one knows.'

1909, the new Turks pulled down the buildings between the tomb and the seashore, so that the view to the sea would not be obstructed. His insignias are still kept in the Nautical Museum in Istanbul.

I went to the patriarchate and asked for a priest; they were hesitant at first for they knew that Heyredin had renounced Christianity and had never received Holy Communion. Nevertheless, after my persistent urgings and as they did not wish to make trouble with the dovleti, I mean the government, they sent a priest to his grave where in the presence of Miriam and myself he held a short service.

Some Turks who happened to be passing, saw us, and spread the rumor that we had taken a sorcerer to his grave. However, Heyredin was never removed from his grave again...

Heyredin Barbarossa bequeathed his palace to his beloved wife Miriam, two hundred slaves and ninety thousand ducats to Vizier Roustem thirty thousand of which the vizier owed to Heyredin eight hundred slaves to the sultan and a thousand slaves to his adopted son Hassan, the Viceroy of Algiers.

After Heyredin's death I did not feel safe in my own home anymore and started to spend sleepless nights in front of my bedroom window. During my few hours of interrupted sleep, I even had nightmares similar to those of Heyredin. I saw myself and my childhood friends being scalded by the fires of hell and monstrous fiends were chasing us everywhere we went. I would then awaken frightened and terrified awaiting my doom.

At first, I appointed a double guard in my gardens and outside my doors to watch over me during the nights, but the fires and flames were always before me in my dreams. I grew thinner and wearier; I did not rest; I did not eat and I did not meet or speak to anybody. Even my slaves were worried about my condition. In the end they had to give me sustenance so that I would survive.

One night I again dreamt of the flames of the Apocalypse, that were sneaking towards me like horrible snakes about to swallow me alive. Terrified, I tried to find my friends Arouz and Heyredin Barbarossa to protect me, but suddenly, from within the flames the son of Sinan emerged; the young boy who had become a monk in Italy.

'I was delivered from futility and worldly conceit,' he roared harshly. 'Will you continue to live in vanity?'

I was awake, but this time I was not frightened any more. I looked through my window as if I was looking for Sinan's son in the sky... It was then that I made my decision.

At dawn, I called all of my slaves and announced that I was freeing them from bondage. In the beginning they did not speak but then, when they had realized that their lives were going to change completely, they started to implore me asking if they could stay.

'Where shall we go and what shall we do without you? Do not leave us like that on the streets.'

They cried and wailed because of the calamity that had befallen suddenly on them.

'Don't you understand?' they asked me angrily. You give us food and a place to sleep. If you go, what shall become of us? How can you be so heartless?'

I was dumbfounded by their reaction for I had not realized until then that I was solely responsible for the lives of all those people. And they were right. They were used to being looked after and in return they looked after me. Now things were changing and life looked miserable to them.

I reassured them that I would find an appropriate solution and at night, when everyone was sleeping, I wrote my will in which 1 left all my property to my slaves who could then continue living in my mansion and cultivating my gardens and lands. Whatever I had, they had to share between them.

After that I asked for dinner and to the surprise of my slaves I ate my food avidly. When I had finished my dinner I lay down in my bed and slept peacefully. At midnight, I awoke lighthearted and cheerful. The slave who had been watching over me had fallen asleep so I tiptoed past him and went to the window. The sky was clear and the bright stars were smiling at me.

I returned to my bed, took a small leather bag with a little food in it I had prepared for my trip and left my room through my window. I walked cautiously until I reached the wall that was surrounding my garden and jumped over it. No one took any notice of me and the road was free for me to tread.

I left without looking back.

****

After ten days I reached Atho. On my way, I ate the little food I had taken with me and when it was finished, I started eating fruit and roots from the trees. Many passersby would cross their hearts upon meeting me on the road, and gave me a little of the supplies they had with them for I apparently instigated awe and veneration in them my beard had now grown whiter and longer.

In Atho, they gave me a cell in one of the monasteries but I did not stay long there. I recognized many pirates around me, many of whom I had even known personally. They debauched when they were young and now in old age they sought forgiveness and piety just like me.

Many of them had even become hermits and had found refuge in caves or ravines. Others would go to desert areas every morning and flagellate their bodies to punish themselves for the cruelty they had inflicted; as if their body was to blame and not their head. I did not feel at ease in the company of those people and I did not wish to be recognized by any of them. Eventually, I decided to leave. Looking at all those familiar faces around me, made me feel that I had returned to the galleys of my past.

I took my small leather bag, which was now empty, and walked to the south until my feet were swollen. I reached Neapolis, near Cape Maleas with which I was so familiar. There, I met some fishermen from Tsirigo who offered to take me to Diakofti with them. They were all going to the Bay of Saint Nicholas in Avlemonas.

When we passed by the village of Saint Dimitrios, in the Bay of Lagadas, I could not stop myself weeping. I raised my eyes, but the village we had destroyed could not be seen from down there. I remembered that day and tears fell down my wrinkled face. The innocent fishermen were startled at my reaction and did everything they could to comfort me. In the end they agreed that Diakofti was too remote and deserted to be inhabited by an old man like myself; they decided to take me to their village.

We disembarked at the small harbor that was surrounded by rocks and I caught a glimpse of the chapel of Saint George on the top of the hill. I told them that this was the church where I had chosen to take my monastic vows and the fishermen believed that I had some kind of vision or divine orders to obey. And perhaps that was partly true...

They gave me bread and oil and when their wives came out of their houses to meet and help their husbands with their nets, they were surprised to see me. Most of them probably mistook me for some kind of saint or holy man who had emerged from the waves, like Aphrodite.

I asked them if the slaves who had been captured in Saint Dimitrios had returned to their homes and the fishermen replied that many of them had returned. Now they were staying in a village called Mitata, on the west side of Avlemonas for they did not wish to live in their village where the screams of the slaughtered could still be heard at night...

I shivered and looked towards the west. Mitata was a long way from Avlemonas.

'Father...' said one of the fishermen with respect. 'If you wish to meet any of them you must ask for 'the slaves' for this is how we have nicknamed them since their return...'

I nervously shook my head. No, I did not wish to meet or see any of them. I thanked them for all their kindness and took the narrow path up the hill that led me to the chapel of Saint George my sanctuary.

I have been living here since that day. The wives of the fishermen send their children with food or a fish sometimes and they ask for my blessing. I wonder what kind of blessings a man like me can give these children for I am more sinful than sin itself... However, with this food I get by, for I do not need and do not seek for anything more except my redemption.

Here, I am ending my written confession which I am placing beneath the altar... Whoever finds this manuscript let him pray and supplicate for my anguished soul...

"Merciful Father of heaven and earth, You who are aware of both the unseen and the evident deeds that my heart and mind have committed, please bestow upon me Your pardon and take pity on my tormented soul for the sake of your sinless and immaculate son, Jesus...
Ermolaos Your slave"

I have confessed, in Saint George of Avlemonas in the year of 1548, after the birth of our Savior.

Bibliography

Greek sources

Argyros, S, Piracy, from 1500 BC until i860, Athens, 1963 History of Lesvos, Association of Philologists in Lesvos, Mitilini, 1996

Karavassilis, T, Paleokipos (Pages of legends and traditions), Mitilini, 1987

Koukoules, F, Life and Civilisation in Byzantine, n.p. 1949 Krantoneli, A, History of Piracy in the First Years of the Turkish Occupation, 13901738, vol. A, Estia Publications, 1985.

Paparigopoulos, K, The History of the Greek Nation, n.p. 1896.

Paraskevaidis, P, Travellers in Lesvos, Mitilini, 1996.

Psilakis B, The History of Crete, vol. B, Arkadi publications.

Simopoulos, K, Foreign Travellers in Greece, vol. A, Athens, 1984

Sfyroeras, B. The Greek Crews of the Turkish Fleet, Athens, 1968.

Taxis, S. A Brief History and Topography of Lesvos, Cairo, 1909, reprinted in 1995 by the University of the Aegean, Mitilini, 1995

Tsitsilas P, The History of the Island of Kythira, vol. A, Athens,

The Society of Kytherian Studies, 1993 Varfis, K, VenetianTurkish Wars and RussianTurkish Wars in the Greek Seas (14531821), n.p. Iris Publications, n.d.

Foreign sources

Belachemi, JeanLouis, Nous les Freres Barberousse corsaires et roi d'Algiers, n.p. Fayard, 1984.

Clissold, Stephen, The Barbary Slaves, n.p. Purnel Book Services Ltd, 1977.

Clot, Andre, Soliman le Magnifique, Paris, Fayard, 1983.

Cordingly, David, Life among the Pirates. Thie Romance and the Reality, N.P. Warner Books, 1995.

Philip Allan Co, 1910 de la Graviere, Jurien, Doria et Barberousse, Paris, 1887.

De Haedo, Abbot Diego, Topographia e Historia General d'Argel, n.p. 1612.

Farine, C, Deux Pirates au Sixieme Steele. Histoire des Barbarousses, n.p., n.d.

Fisher, Sir Godfrey, Barbary Legend, n.p. 1957.

Gosse, Philip, The History of Piracy, London, Longmans

Green & Co, 1932 Haji, Khalifeh, The History of the Maritime Wars of the Turks, translated from Turkish by James Michell, London, 1831

Lane Poole, Stanley, The Barbary Corsairs, Dublin, T FisherUnwin, 1890

Lenzini, Jose, Barberousse, Chemin de Proies en Mediterranee, N.P.. Actes Sudes, 1995 Morgan, J, A Complete History of Algiers, n.p. 1731

Morgan, J, The History of the Piratical States of Barbary, Algiers, Tripolis, Tunisia and Morocco, n.p. 1750. Morgan, who lived in Algiers for quite some time as an envoy of the British government, writes about the love of Arouz to Zaphira: 'Arouz's love for Princess Zaphira was a common secret in the State for many years.' This love story, despite its violent character, has maintained its romantic touch. I translated those letters from the authentic manuscripts that Sidi Abed Haraam, a descendant of Selim, entrusted to me for a while, to show his admiration and respect for my person.

Piri reis, Bahriye, Conquering Navigation in the Aegean (1521), n.p. Telethrion publications, n.d.

Rachid, Ekrem, La Vie de Khaeredin Barberousse, n.p. Libraire Gallimard, 1931

Sauger, R (Jesuit monk), History of the Ancient Dukes and Other Potentates of the Aegean, translated by Al Karalis, Syros, Ermoupolis, 1878

Slot, B., The Turkish Conquest of the Cyclades 153738, vol. G, Athens, Kimoliaka, 1978.

Tenenti, Alberto, Piracy and the Decline of Venice, 15801615, London, Longmans Green & Co, 1967

Trousset, Jules, Histoire Illustree des Pirates, n.p. Corsairs, 1994

Viallon, Marie, Venise et la Porte Ottoniane (14531566), Paris, Editions Economica, 1995.

BIOGRAPHY

OF GEORGE LEONARDOS

George Leonardos (in Greek Γιώργος Λεονάρδος) is a Greek author of historical novels. Son of Anastase and Maria, he was born in Alexandria Egypt on 20 February 1937. His father died when he was two years old. He lived with his mother in Alexandria until 1954. He was an avid reader of fiction and history, and as a high school student in Alexandria had his short stories published in "Tahidromos" and "Anatoli", the two Greek daily newspapers of the city. In 1954 he moved to Greece to study Physics at the University of Thessaloniki. After his graduation, he studied journalism and began to work as a journalist.

He worked as a reporter for major Athens newspapers Apogevmatini, Eleftherotypia, Mesimvrini, Eleftheros Typos, Ethnos and as a columnist in the financial paper Kerdos. He was the first correspondent of the Athens News Agency in Belgrade in 1964, and later in New York in 1976, where he was also appointed managing editor of the local Greek newspaper Ethnicos Kirikas (National Herald). He has also worked as a newscaster in the public and private television channels in Greece, ERT and ANTENA accordingly, and has reported on the Vietnam War, the Iran- Iraq War and the Persian Gulf War as well as International Conferences. He is a member of the Editor's Association of Daily Press in Greece and the National Society of Greek Writers. His first novel, Grandma's Red Sofa, was published in 1992.

He was twice awarded by the Greek Society of Christian Studies with the prize of the best historical novel for his novels "Mara, the Christian Sultana" and "The Sleeping Beauty of Mystra". He was also awarded by Botsis Publication Foundation with the honorary prize for his career in journalism and literature.

In 2009 he was awarded with the highest State Award for his historical novel "The Last Palaeologue", which was referring to the capture of Constantinople by the Ottomans, in 1453.

He has also written the novels: "Grandma's Red Sofa", 1992, "The House above the Catacombs", 1993, "Eva", 1994, "The Magnet's Poles" 1995, "Earth's Lovers", 1996, "A Song from the Soul", 1997.

His historical novels are: "Barbarossa the Pirate", 1998, which was also published in England, Italy and Spain, "Mara, the Christian Sultana", 1999, "Mary Magdalena" 2001, "Sleeping Beauty of Mystra" 2003, the trilogy "Michael VIII Palaeologue" 2004, "The Palaeologues", 2006, and "The Last Palaeologue", 2007, which later was expanded with the historical novel "Sophia Palaeologina - From Byzantium to Russia", two books about the Seafarers "Maggelan" and "Thule". "The Alexandria Rhapsody" and the "Last gulp of wine".

Web: www.gleonardos.gr

Printed in Great Britain
by Amazon